THE GUINNESS BOOK OF
CAR
FACTS & FEATS

**A record of everyday motoring
and automotive achievements**

THE GUINNESS BOOK OF
CAR
FACTS & FEATS

A record of everyday motoring and automotive achievements

Edited by Anthony Harding
with contributions by
Anthony Bird   David Hodges
William Boddy   F. Wilson McComb
John Davenport   Cyril Posthumus
Michael Sedgwick

GUINNESS SUPERLATIVES LIMITED
2 CECIL COURT, LONDON ROAD, ENFIELD, MIDDLESEX

© Guinness Superlatives Ltd, 1971
Second Edition revised 1976
Second Impression 1977
Third Edition revised 1980

Published in Great Britain by Guinness Superlatives Ltd
2 Cecil Court, London Road, Enfield, Middlesex
Printed and Bound in Great Britain
by Jarrold and Sons Ltd, Norwich

ISBN 0 85112 207 8

Contents

Acknowledgements

The Editor, the Contributors and the Publishers are greatly indebted to the following for information or for the loan of photographs and drawings, and for their permission to reproduce them in this book:

Charles L. Betts, Jr.
Hugh W. Bishop
Neill Bruce
The late W. J. Brunell
Lieut.-Col. J. R. Buckley
Diana Burnett
Bernard Cahier
A. McGregor Dick
Geoffrey Goddard
Roger Gorringe
Guy Griffiths
Roger Hedlund
A. Hollister
William C. Kinsman
Louis Klemantaski
A. Michael Knapp
Henry N. Manney III
T. C. March
George Monkhouse
George A. Oliver
George Phillips
Marius Prieur
Nigel Snowdon
A. R. and J. A. Twentyman
Andrew Whyte
F. C. Wykes

Antique Automobile
Associated Press Ltd.
Autocar
Automobiles Peugeot et Cie
Automotive History Review
Autosport
BBC Hulton Picture Library
Mrs. M. Warne and the British Drag
	Racing & Hot Rod Association
British Leyland Motor Corporation Ltd.
British Petroleum Co. Ltd.
Castrol Ltd.
Citroën Cars Ltd.
Daimler-Benz A. G.
Ford Motor Company Ltd.
Foster & Skeffington Ltd.
France Reportage
Indianapolis Motor Speedway Corporation
Les Films Art et Science
London Art Tech.
Maranello Concessionaires Ltd.
Midland Automobile Club
Motor
National Automotive History Collection,
	Detroit Public Library
Panther Westwinds Ltd.
Publifoto, Milan
Reliant Motor Co. Ltd.
Rolls-Royce Ltd.
Shell Photographic Service
The Imperial War Museum
The National Motor Museum, Beaulieu
The Science Museum
The William Boddy Collection
Transworld News Service
Ullstein Bilderdienst
Vitachrome Ltd.

Introduction

THIS book is no ordinary narrative history of the development of the motor car. Its contributing authors have set out to tell the story in an amusingly novel and informative way, which will appeal to every car owner and driver, and in particular to those who are disinclined to tackle the more leaden works of motoring history—yet who are inspired by the background of their means of transportation. Nevertheless, the sporting enthusiast and historian, seeking new and out-of-the-way facts, will undoubtedly find much to entertain them.

Some flavour of the draught may be gained by virtue of the book being in the same genre as the celebrated *Guinness Book of Records*, containing as it does a host of "firsts", "lasts", "biggests", "smallests", "fastests" and "slowests", and so on—in a word, superlatives. Thus, here can be found in one book the answers to such sober quests as the first use of tubeless tyres and the origin of the parking meter, as well as the more whimsical, matter-of-fact statement that hot-water bottles were offered as standard heating accessories for motorists in the first decade of this century. Although a large proportion of the book deals with competitive motoring (for this is wherein the glamour lies), this should be read as providing the means by which much progress was made in the development of your everyday automobile. Perhaps it only requires a racing legislating body to stipulate that the cars shall "swallow their own smoke" for real progress to follow in the vexed matter of everyday pollution!

Motor cars have been with us now for nearly a century and, whether or not you approve the contrivances, they *seem* to have come to stay . . . and in ever-increasing numbers. Nevertheless, it may just be, so prolific has the automobile become, that it will ultimately suffocate itself with its own exhaust—as it were—and that the pollution it creates will bring legislation to curb its use, at least in urban areas. Ashes to ashes, dust to dust. . . . More likely perhaps that Mother Nature herself will take a hand, and the dwindling of our treasure-house of oil supplies will force an entire re-thinking of automobile power-unit design—with the emphasis on the motive fuel—be it hydrogen, electricity, the blessed (and free) energy from Old King Sol or *you* name it. . . .

So, before the motor car, as we know it, commits *hara-kiri* and contrives to disappear up its own effluvious exhaust-pipe—or just "runs out of steam"—this would seem to be the appropriate time to take a broad, general and not-too-technical look at the road we motorists have taken to be where we are.

Here, then, are the Facts of Life of the Automobile—how it was conceived, born and reared, how it achieved emancipation and maturity, and how it fared in sport and in society. But there the analogy with life must end—for we should not forget the remarkable records, the inspiring and daring deeds which have been achieved *with* the motor car—and the indefatigable men and women who did the work and took the chances.

Section 1
THE EARLY DAYS, 1769-1919
Compiled by Anthony Bird

The driving compartment of the 1905 three-cylinder Rolls-Royce.

Professional commentators upon the social scene often remark, rather slightingly, upon man's obsession with the motor car. With growing, if belated, anxiety about pollution and congestion, the private car is seen as the villain of the piece and it is conveniently forgotten that pollution is primarily—a word the commentators *will* pronounce prime-airily—caused by there being too many people, rather than that they have too many cars.

There is also, very properly, a great deal of concern about road accidents and once again the sociologists contrive to imply that the root cause lies in the selfish aggressiveness of private car drivers. It is true that the advertising bias which portrays the car as a virility-cum-status symbol, coupled with motor-journalists' emphasis on speed, are responsible for attitudes of mind which lead to some avoidable crashes. If manufacturers allow their ad-men to christen cars "Dart" or "Avenger" they must not be surprised if some empty-headed buyers dart about in vengeful fashion. If you call a car a sting-ray or a barracuda, anthropomorphism in reverse will ensure that those who buy them will assume the characteristics of those unlovely creatures. Nevertheless, the hard fact remains that the accident *rate* is astonishingly low if it is measured in terms of vehicle-miles-per-year.

Those who criticise modern man for letting the motor car dominate his life, ruin his cities and spread a foul asphalt and concrete slime across his countryside overlook two things. Much of the blame which is loosely placed upon motor *cars* in general should be reserved for heavy goods motor vehicles in particular; and whatever its disadvantages the motor car has added a new dimension to man's freedom.

It is true, paradoxically, that the new freedom is in danger of creating a new slavery, but it is the liberating aspect of the motor car which has made man willing to accept it, warts and all.

Social historians say that the motor car was a rich man's plaything in the first two decades of this century, and that it only became a tool of everyday life for everyman relatively recently. This is not really true. For every powerful, expensive, tyre-consuming Mercedes, Panhard-Levassor or Napier there were scores, hundreds even, of little De Dion Boutons, Swifts or Oldsmobiles which brought the cost of personal transportation down below pony-and-trap level. Therefore, with all its imperfections, the early motor car brought unfettered mobility, once the prerogative of the rich, to thousands of people who were well below the level of the "carriage folk". These new horseless-carriage folk may have been only a small proportion of the whole population, but the barrier had been broken.

The process started in the 1890s and has continued at an increasing pace ever since. In *The Image of America*, R. L. Bruckberger wrote that "historians of the twentieth century should see that Ford's revolution is far more important than Lenin's". With this rather portentous statement in mind the interest in motor cars need no longer seem obsessive, and no excuse need be offered for a book such as this in which the salient facts about them are marshalled in condensed but accurate form.

The early motor car is not only fascinating because of its social implications but because it is rich in the sorts of detail and personality which makes a Victorian fire-engine or paddle-steamer a source of wonder to those accustomed to television and computers. The veteran motor car is also often handsome and not infrequently funny. It displays a wealth of ingenuity (sometimes misplaced) in its solutions to new engineering problems and often reflects originality, genius or eccentricity on the part of its designers.

Before motor cars became stereotyped some were bizarre to the point of improbability in their arrangements. There was often good reason for what now seems eccentric, but it added interest to the motoring scene when the owner of a Lanchester could say that his engine had two cylinders, two pistons, two flywheels, two counter-rotating crankshafts and six connecting-rods, only to be slapped down by the owner of a Gobron-Brillié pointing out that *his* engine had two cylinder-blocks, four cylinders, eight pistons, twelve connecting-rods and one six-throw crankshaft.

On a more serious level, no new invention spread its influence so quickly as the motor vehicle. In 1893 the idea of replacing horse buses with mechanical ones would have been dismissed as pure fantasy, but in 1913 the London General Omnibus Company's B-type motor buses covered 55½ million miles and lost only 0·02 per cent of scheduled time from mechanical defects. As late as 1899 few people took the motor car very seriously, but in 1919 its war-time work alone had destroyed for ever its false image as a rather nasty toy for rich eccentrics.

The first full-scale vehicles moved by "artificial" power were:

IN FRANCE: In 1769 the Minister of War authorised the Commandant of Artillery to make a steam truck, for carrying cannon, to the designs of Nicolas-Joseph Cugnot. The first one, the "voiture en petit", was tested early in 1770 and could easily carry four people at 2½ m.p.h., though it had to stop every 15 minutes for the boiler to be refilled by hand. The second, full-sized, truck was designed to carry a 4–5-ton payload and it was finished by May 1771, by which time the Government had lost interest and nothing more was done. Reports of "unofficial" trial runs in the grounds of the Paris Arsenal show that the "fardier à vapeur" ran quite well. It may have run into and damaged a low wall on one of these trials, but the story that Cugnot was "flung into prison" and his vehicle "confiscated" is pure myth. The vehicle belonged to the Government anyway, so there was no need to confiscate it, and it survives to this day in the Conservatoire National des Arts et Métiers in Paris.

IN ENGLAND: Richard Trevithick, the Cornish engineer and pioneer of the non-condensing, high-pressure engine, made a steam road locomotive, little more than one of his high-pressure engines mounted on wheels, which climbed Camborne Beacon with seven or eight men aboard on Christmas Eve 1801. In partnership with Andrew Vivian, Trevithick designed and patented a much better, and more carriage-like, steam carriage. The mechanical parts were made in Cornwall and sent by sea to London where they were assembled and fitted with bodywork in 1803. Trevithick's

"Celebrated London Carriage" proved reliable, controllable and was capable of 10 m.p.h., but no financial support was forthcoming and she was dismantled in 1804; the boiler and engine were used for many years to drive a rolling-mill.

Trevithick's Steam Carriage of 1802.

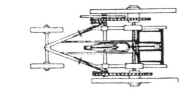

IN AMERICA: Oliver Evans, "America's James Watt", who also developed the high-pressure engine at the same time as Trevithick, was granted a steam-wagon patent by the State of Maryland on 21st May 1787. Eighteen years later, in 1805, he made a self-moving steam conveyance, but in a sense it happened by chance. He was commissioned by the Philadelphia Board of Health to make a dock-cleaning pontoon with steam dredging machinery and stern paddle-wheel. Having made it, Evans had to move it about 1½ miles from his workshop into the river. He constructed a stout wheeled undercarriage underneath the barge and harnessed its 5-h.p. engine to one wheel by a jury-rig of belts and pulleys. After an initial failure, the grandly named "Orukter Amphibolos" (Snorting Swimmer) waddled into the water and was floated off her undercarriage. The "Orukter" is often described as the world's first amphibian motor car, which seems to be going rather far.

IN CZECHOSLOVAKIA: Many steam-carriage plans were drawn, and a few working models made, between the time of Cugnot and Evans, but the next full-scale machine which actually moved under its own power appears to have been a steam "phaeton" made by a M. Bozek of Prague in 1815. Little is known of it except that it is said to have failed because of the "inadequacy of the boiler" . . . these words ring like a Greek chorus through the early history of the steam vehicle.

The first internal-combustion vehicles were:

IN ENGLAND: In 1824 Samuel Brown of Brompton made an ingenious road vehicle driven by an adaptation of his patent "gas-vacuum engine" which burnt coal-gas. On his stationary engines the combustion did not take place in the working cylinders, but the carriage engine was a true internal-combustion machine as the combustion space was combined with the cylinder. Brown's carriage climbed Shooter's Hill, Blackheath, but as two cylinders, 12 in. bore by 24 in. stroke, only gave 4 h.p. the gas-vacuum engine was much more expensive to run than a comparable steam engine and nothing came of it.

IN FRANCE: The first commercially practicable gas engine was patented by Etienne Lenoir in 1860. Though more efficient types were invented soon after, the Lenoir gas engine was still being made in the 1890s as it was simple and reliable. Lenoir's patent describes a method of vaporising liquid fuel, petroleum spirit, so that the engine could be independent of a gas-supply, and in 1862/63 he made a rather crude "motor car" and fitted to it a 1½-h.p. gas engine, with vaporising carburettor, and drove it several times between his works and his home. He admitted the car was heavy and underpowered and he used to take about 1½ hours over the 6-mile journey.

IN AUSTRIA: Siegfried Markus (1831–98) was once a favourite for the title of "inventor of the motor car", based on reports that he had experimented with an atmospheric gas engine in a handcart between 1863 and 1865, and on claims that his surviving motor car was built in 1875. It has now been proven that the vehicle was built by Märky, Bronovsky and Schulz at Adamsthal in 1888/89 though the "1875" fiction first appeared in print when the car was shown at the 1900 Paris *Exposition*.

IN GERMANY: Karl Benz is the man most entitled to be called "inventor" of the motor car as he was the first to sell horseless carriages, made to a set pattern and not "one-off" experiments, to the public. Benz was in business in a small way in Mannheim making stationary gas engines which worked on the two-stroke cycle so as not to clash with the Otto and Langen four-stroke patent. In 1884/85 he succeeded in combining a scaled-down four-stroke gas engine, with electric ignition and a surface carburettor, with a two-seater tricycle. This first effort performed tolerably well and he followed it with improved and more powerful tricars. In 1887 he actually sold one to Emile Roger, a jobbing engineer of Paris. Early in 1888 he granted Roger sole agency rights in France and the modern motor industry had started.

Wilhelm Maybach at the "wheel" of the 1886 Daimler.

Benz's motor-carriage patent is dated 29th January 1886, by which time Gottlieb Daimler had patented his "high-speed" petrol engine, but there was no regular production of Daimler cars until after 1890. An 1888-type Roger-Benz car is preserved in running order in the Science Museum, London.

IN DENMARK: Denmark claims a "first" with the Hammel of 1886, but like Lenoir's effort of 1862 it was only used to carry its designer between home and work and nothing came of it commercially. It was made by Hans Urban Johansen, an employee of Albert Hammel in the latter's engineering works. It has a two-cylinder four-stroke engine with hot tube ignition, a cone clutch and only one forward speed. Maximum speed is about 6 m.p.h., hillclimbing ability almost nil, engine capacity nearly $2\frac{3}{4}$ litres, power developed about $2\frac{3}{4}$ h.p. Although its performance was limited the car was reliable, and it was driven over the course of the London-to-Brighton run in 1954.

IN AMERICA: A Selden car has the date 1877 painted on the side of it, but this refers to the date when Selden made a provisional application for a patent. He kept the application open and did not complete it until 1895. The so-called "1877 Selden" was built in 1905 as part of the legal fight over the Selden patent; the longest run it made under its own power was 1,400 ft. and the engineer responsible for making it run said that it was the hardest job he had ever done. In 1927 a photographer named Walter Lewis swore an affidavit that he had been called by a Mr. Lambert in March 1891 to photograph his three-wheeled "gas-buggy". There is a strong suggestion though that it was really a steam vehicle, and credit for producing America's first petrol car is usually given to the brothers Frank and Charles Duryea. They tried their first experimental car in 1893, and the Duryea Motor Wagon Co. was formed in 1894.

The first motor accident was in 1771 when, according to different accounts, Cugnot's steam truck hit a low wall in the grounds of the Paris Arsenal. Excessive speed should not be blamed, but as the steering was very low-geared it may be that the world's first motorist could not twiddle the steering handles fast enough.

The first fatal motor accident occurred in the 1830s. In 1832 the stoker of one of Walter Hancock's steam omnibuses, *The Enterprise*, was killed by a boiler explosion. As he was proved to have fastened down the safety-valve with wire whilst running the engine and blower to urge the fire, the Coroner brought in a verdict of "Accidental death caused by his own negligence." Two years later one of the Steam Carriage Co. of Scotland's coaches on the Glasgow to Paisley service broke a rear wheel, overturned, burst her boiler and killed five people. The overturn resulted from the deliberate attempt by the Turnpike Trustees to stop the service by heaping loose stones 18 in. deep across the road.

The first mechanical vehicle to cover more than 100 miles without the slightest mechanical trouble was Francis Hill's big steam coach. In 1840 he drove her from London to Hastings and back in the day without a hitch. The distance of 128 miles, without breakdown, was not exceeded for over forty years.

The first end-to-end, Land's End to John o' Groat's, motor trip in Great Britain was made by Henry Sturmey, Editor of the *Autocar*, between 9th and 19th October 1897. The actual running time over 929 miles was 93½ hours, or nearly 10 m.p.h. average speed. The car was a 4½-h.p. Coventry Daimler, and Sturmey described his trip as trouble free. Such chores as putting in new inlet valves, wiring on loose solid tyres, taking links out of worn driving chains, etc., were just part of the game.

The first coast-to-coast crossing of the United States by car was not achieved until 1903 when a Winton car arrived in New York on 26th July, having started from San Francisco on 23rd May. More than 20 days out of the total of 65 were spent making repairs; much of the trouble was caused by the rough going, but the fracture of a connecting-rod which burst through the crankcase was responsible for the longest delay.

The first firm to "offer" automobiles, made to a set pattern, to the public was the Moto-Cycle Co. of Philadelphia who issued a catalogue, probably the world's first, in the Spring of 1886. The firm was set up by a Mr. Northrup to make and sell steam tricycles and other vehicles to the designs of Lucius D. Copeland; but in fact none was sold.

The first firm to "sell" private steam cars, made to a set pattern, to the public was De Dion Bouton et Trépardoux of Paris, who issued a catalogue shortly after the Moto-Cycle Co., but who actually sold light steam tricars and other machines as a result. They began selling petrol tricycles in 1896 and light cars two years later.

The first firm to sell internal-combustion cars to the public was Benz et Cie of Mannheim, gas-engine makers. See page 41 for other details.

F. H. Butler, founder of the Aero Club of Great Britain in 1901, in an early Benz car.

The first full-scale four-wheeled petrol car of wholly British design was the Lanchester, designed by Frederick Lanchester and built, with his brother George's help, at Birmingham, in 1895. It was the first ever to be designed from first principles as a complete mechanical entity rather than as an assemblage of odds and ends. The first production-model Lanchesters appeared in 1900.

1895 Pennington: "By the use of an inclined plane, rising to the height of about two feet only, the Pennington bicycle has been made to jump the extraordinary distance of 65 feet. With a flying start it was 'charged' up the incline at very high speed, alighting on the rear wheel first, and the writer was able to keep his seat without difficulty" (from the original caption of this old woodcut).

The first company formed in Great Britain to produce petrol motor cars was the Daimler Co. It was floated in December 1896 by a financier named Lawson who tried to set up a motor monopoly in Britain by very questionable means. Although the company was supposed to manufacture to the designs of the German Daimler company, whose English manufacturing licence was acquired by Lawson, the first cars they made, in 1897, were copied from the French Panhard-Levassor design. The engines were of Daimler type as Panhard-Levassor were the French licensees of Daimler patents.

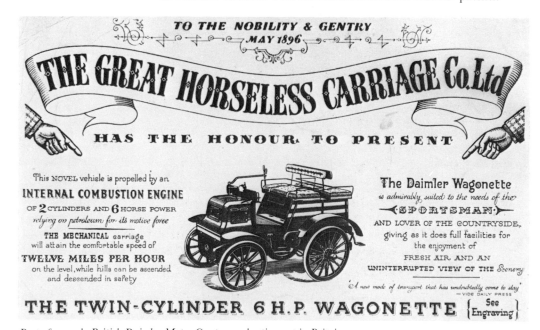

Part of an early British Daimler Motor Company advertisement in Britain

The first company formed in the United States to produce petrol motor cars was the Duryea Motor Wagon Co. of Springfield, Mass., late in 1894. The financial side of the business was looked after by Erwin Markham, but quarrels between Charles and Frank Duryea have obscured who was the principal designer. A Duryea prototype won the *Times-Herald* Race (at an average speed of less than 8 m.p.h.) in November 1895, and regular production did not start until 1896.

Europe's biggest motor company for many years was De Dion Bouton et Cie. Between January 1900 and April 1901 they sold 1,500 "voiturettes" as well as tricycles, quadricycles and hundreds of engines to other manufacturers. Among the many firms who started by making light cars with De Dion engines was Louis Renault who made his first car in 1898.

The 1,500 cars sold by De Dion Bouton up to April 1901 exceeded the combined production of England's three principal motor firms: Wolseley, Lanchester and Daimler.

Victorian ladies atop a De Dion 3½-h.p. car of about 1900.

America's biggest production at the beginning of the century was achieved by Ransom E. Olds who produced 425 of his Merry Oldsmobiles in 1901. Some sources, however, quote the Locomobile Company of Bridgeport, Connecticut, as turning out 1,500 light steam runabouts that year.

France was the world's most prolific producer of motor vehicles until 1906 when she was overtaken by America; nevertheless, she remained the country with the biggest motor export trade until 1913.

The first Grand Prix. The French event of 1906 which was won by Szisz (90-h.p. Renault) at 65 m.p.h. for 769·9 miles over a circuit near Le Mans. (From a painting by F. Gordon Crosby, by courtesy of Autocar.*)*

The 1908 Grand Prix on the Dieppe circuit proved a German triumph. Lautenschlager, on a 120-h.p. Mercedes, won at 68·9 m.p.h. The race proved a tyre massacre and the winner had used his last available spare when he crossed the line. Jenatzy, the famous "Red Devil", driving a Mors, is shown on the left. (From a painting by F. Gordon Crosby, by courtesy of Autocar.*)*

The 200-h.p. eight-cylinder Darracq owned and driven by Sir Algernon Guinness travelling at over 120 m.p.h. on Saltburn Sands in June 1908. Mr. Kenelm Lee Guinness, famous in after years as one of the finest drivers, acted as mechanic to his brother. (From a painting by F. Gordon Crosby, by courtesy of Autocar.*)*

Felice Nazzaro with the Fiat passing Vizcaya's Bugatti in the 1922 Grand Prix at Strasbourg. The winning Fiat averaged 79·2 m.p.h. over the total distance of 500 miles, Vizcaya being second. (From a painting by F. Gordon Crosby, by courtesy of Autocar.*)*

First and only American victory in the French Grand Prix at Le Mans was that of Jimmy Murphy's Duesenberg in 1921 at 78·10 m.p.h. (From a painting by Roy Nockolds.)

Victory in the 1924 French Grand Prix at Lyons went to Giuseppe Campari's P.2 Alfa Romeo depicted here at the Virage de la Mort. (From a painting by Roy Nockolds.)

Robert Benoist (1½-litre Delage) winner of the 1927 R.A.C. Grand Prix at Brooklands at 85·59 m.p.h. (From a painting by Roy Nockolds.)

Count Trossi's 3-litre Maserati temporarily leading a works 3-litre Mercedes-Benz during the 1938 Coppa Ciano Race at Leghorn, eventually won by Hermann Lang's Mercedes. (From a painting by Roy Nockolds.)

An agency advertisement for Oldsmobile cars in Great Britain of April 1905.

A significant part of the rapid growth of the American industry flowed, directly and indirectly, from the introduction of the Model T Ford in October 1908. During 1909, 10,607 units (cars or light commercial vehicles) were sold, and by 1923 the peak was reached at 2,011,125 units. In addition to the parent factories in the U.S.A., there were assembly plants in Canada and England. When production of the Model T stopped in 1927, the grand total had reached 16,536,075 (*not* the 15,007,033 so often quoted, which did not include either British or Canadian deliveries). It was subsequently beaten by the VW Beetle, though not as publicised in 1972. Production of this model had broken 19 million when the parent firm ceased deliveries at the end of 1977, though in 1979 the cars were still being turned out abroad, notably in Brazil.

SOME ROYAL MOTORISTS

The first "royal" motorist was the Prince of Wales, later King Edward VII, who was driven in a Serpollet steam car belonging to Gaston Menier, the chocolate-manufacturer, at Bad Homburg in the summer of 1893. Other drives in other cars followed at intervals, and the Prince of Wales bought his first motor car, an English Daimler, in 1899.

One of the first motor cars to be imported into Russia was a De Dietrich (Amédée Bollée design) which the Tsaritsa Alexandra bought in 1898. By 1901 the Imperial family had several cars and in 1902 Adolphe Kégresse, their motor engineer, made one of them into **the world's first practicable "caterpillar" or tracked vehicle** to meet the Tsar's wish to be able to use a car in snow.

Early long-distance motoring: three chauffeur-driven French ladies set out in their Tony Huber from Notre-Dame, Paris, for the Cathedral of St. Isaac, St. Petersburg (Leningrad) in 1903.

The once-fashionable curvaceous "Roi des Belges", or "tulip phaeton" body-style was named after Leopold II of the Belgians. Perhaps the credit for it should really go to Cleo de Mérode, the King's *amie intime*, who was present when the King 'was discussing with the importer (in her apartment) what kind of body to have on his new 1901 Mercedes. Mlle de Mérode placed two prettily curved, deep-buttoned, small easy chairs side by side and suggested that the seating of the new car should be shaped to correspond. The design was carried out by Rothschild et Cie, the famous Paris firm of coachbuilders.

The young King Alfonso XIII of Spain was an enthusiastic motorist with a taste for fast cars which he drove skilfully. He patronised and encouraged the Hispano-Suiza factory, and one of the most famous pre-1914 sporting cars is known as the Alfonso-Hispano in his honour. It is a production version of the "small" (2,646 c.c.) four-cylinder car, designed by Marc Birkigt, which won the 1910 Coupe de l'Auto race for light cars at an average speed of 55·6 m.p.h. Voiturette racing had been dominated previously by single-cylinder cars, and the four-cylinder Hispano-Suiza set a new trend in light car design.

H.R.H. The Duke of York (later King George V) in a 12-h.p. Panhard in 1900. The driver is the Hon. C. S. Rolls, and his father, Lord Llangattock, is seated behind, in the light bowler-hat. The fourth occupant is Sir Charles Cust, Equerry to the Duke.

The arrival of H.M. King George V at the 1913 Ascot Races in his 1910 Daimler.

The first "conventional" car with front-mounted vertical engine, foot-operated friction clutch and sliding-pinion change-speed gear was produced by Panhard et Levassor in Paris in 1891. The designer, Emile Levassor, said of his gear system (hardly a "gearbox" as the mechanism was not enclosed), "c'est brutal mais ça marche".

The first four-wheeled petrol car to run on pneumatic tyres was a Peugeot, *L'Eclair*, which the Michelin brothers entered for the Paris-Bordeaux-Paris Race in July 1895. They used up their stock of twenty-two spare inner tubes and spent so much time mending punctures and bursts that they gave up after 90 hours. Levassor, who won the race in $48\frac{3}{4}$ hours, said the air-filled tyre would obviously never be of the slightest use for motor cars.

An 1895 Peugeot vis-à-vis *car.*

The first four-cylinder motor-car engine was seen in 1896 when a four-cylinder Panhard et Levassor took first place in the 1,062½ miles Paris-Marseilles-Paris Race at 15·7 m.p.h. average speed. The 80 × 120 mm. engine was rated at only 8 h.p. and had "in-line" cylinders. The Mors firm brought out a V-four engine in the following year.

A Panhard et Levassor, owned by the Earl of Dudley, seen at Elmley Lovett in 1902.

The first eight-cylinder in-line car engine was produced in 1902 by Charron, Girardot and Voigt of Paris. The eight-cylinder CGV car was not very successful; nor were "straight-eight" racing cars made in America soon afterwards by the Winton, Maxwell and Buffum companies as the engines, made by coupling two "fours" together, were long and unwieldy. A straight-eight touring car was also shown at the 1907 Paris Salon by Laurin-Klement (later Skoda).

The first six-cylinder in-line car was produced by Spyker of Amsterdam in 1903. It was a four-wheel-drive racing car and only one or two were made. The credit for successful commercial production of six-cylinder cars goes to Napiers of Acton, England, whose first "six" was on the market early in 1904.

The V-eight cylinder engine was tried by several makers, including Rolls-Royce and Adams, between 1905 and 1909, but nothing came of them and the first V-eight car to be put into series production was the Model CL De Dion Bouton in 1910. The De Dion V-eight engine was copied and improved by Cadillac in 1914/15, and thus led via Lincoln and Ford to the modern V-eights.

The first electric "self-starter" was fitted by a Mr. Dowsing to his Arnold car (Arnolds of East Peckham, Kent, made an English version of the Benz) in 1896, but the first firm to fit electric starting and lighting sets as standard equipment was Cadillac in 1912.

Compressed-air "self-starters" had a certain popularity before electrical ones came into use. The once-famous pioneer American firm of Winton fitted them, as did Delaunay-Belleville in France, Minerva in Belgium, and Wolseley in England.

The controls of early cars varied greatly. The reliable and popular belt-driven Benz cars of the 1890s had seven or eight (according to type) hand controls but only one pedal, while a number of later cars, such as some Mercedes, Delaunay-Bellevilles and Gobron-Brilliés had four pedals to confuse the driver. The gear change on Model T Fords was pedal operated with no hand lever to bother about.

A 1906/7 Delaunay-Belleville photographed at Cessnock Castle, Ayrshire.

SOME CAR NAMES AND THEIR ORIGINS

The name "Mercedes" was originally given in 1901 to a new model 35-h.p. Cannstatt Daimler, after Mercédès Jellinek, daughter of a director of the company. The Austrian branch of the company later used the name of her sister, Maja, in a similar way.

The name "Iris" was chosen for their cars by Legros and Knowles of Willesden, England, in 1905. A little later some bright spark used the name to form a slogan, IT RUNS IN SILENCE, which was more ingenious than truthful.

The name "Rigs That Run" was used by an obscure American (St. Louis) company at the beginning of the century, to distinguish their cars from some of the "rigs" of the time which didn't run very well.

The name "Lion-Peugeot" was taken by an offshoot of the old family firm set up by Robert Peugeot in 1908. Not to be outdone, their racing rivals, Corre, adopted the name Corre-La Licorne, and the old battle between the Lion and the Unicorn was fought again in the Coupe de l'Auto light car races.

The name "Tic-Tac" was given to a short-lived cycle car made by Dumoulin of Paris in 1924, but the "Pic-Pic" was a small model of Piccard-Pictet current from 1920 to 1925. The Geneva firm who made it produced motor cars from 1904 until 1925.

The oddly named "Yaxa" was also Swiss, the name being derived from *y'a qu' ça* which is a corruption of *il n'y a que cela*, or "it's the one and only".

The name "Sex-Auto" was given in all innocence by the Reeves Manuf. Co. of America to their car. It had six wheels which they considered superior to four. They survived for three or four years, but did not last long after they brought out their Octo-Auto in 1911.

Nicknames. Many continental cars once imported into Britain had their awkward-sounding names modified by mechanics and chauffeurs. Thus, the once-popular De Dions became Ding-Dongs, Métallurgique became Metally-jerk, Vinot et Deguingand became Veeno, and then Eno. The Hispano-Suiza was dubbed Banana Squeezer, the Isotta-Fraschini became I-Shot-a-Flash-Sheeny, and the Bégot-Mazurie inevitably turned into a Bag o' Misery.

STEAM CARS

Approximately 4,250 different makes of private car were listed between 1896 and 1939, of which about 180 were driven by steam. Most of these burned paraffin (kerosene), but some early examples used petrol.

Most of the 180-odd steam-car manufacturers were American, nearly all were short-lived, and many produced fewer than a dozen cars.

The most successful early steam car was the Locomobile. The Locomobile Co. bought the patent and manufacturing rights in the Stanley steam car in April 1899 for $250,000. The early popularity of the frail little Locomobiles soon waned, and the twin Stanley brothers bought back the ailing business in May 1901 for only $20,000; their Stanley Motor Carriage Co. of Newton, Mass., carried on until 1924.

The greatest number of Stanley steamers made in one year was 650 in 1912; this was equal to one *day's* production of Model T Fords in 1923.

President Theodore Roosevelt in a 30-h.p. White Model G steam car in about 1908.

Presidential approval was given to the steam car in 1906 by Theodore Roosevelt who often used a White steam car for official functions. This example apparently inspired the New York Police Department to buy a few White steamers for use as prowl cars in 1908. The White Co. of Cleveland, Ohio, stopped making steam cars in 1912.

Steam-car enthusiasts often complained that steamers were eventually barred from competitive events "because they won all the prizes". This is not true. They were barred from some events because of fuel consumption or horse-power formulae, but many others remained open to them. Serpollet steamers even took part—honourably but without winning—in the 1903 Paris-Madrid and other major races.

It is often said that steam-car companies were put out of business by the oil combines; this is also untrue. Steam cars burnt petrol, kerosene or furnace oil, and in greater quantities than internal-combustion cars of comparable power, so the oil companies had no reason to dislike them.

The 1905 White steamer prepared for the Vanderbilt Cup Race.

The World's Land Speed Record was twice taken by steam cars. In 1902 Léon Serpollet (France) raised the record to 75·02 m.p.h., and in January 1906 Fred Marriott, driving a special Stanley, achieved 127·56 m.p.h. at Ormonde Beach, Calif.

In 1907 Stanleys tried to raise the record again but Marriott's car hit a bumpy patch in the sand, the front wheels lifted, the car slewed off course and overturned. The story that it was going at 197 m.p.h. before the disaster is only a myth; F. E. Stanley's own stopwatch calculations put the speed at about 150 m.p.h.—which is creditable enough for 1907. Marriott survived the smash. (See also page 183.)

The best known of the thirteen British steam cars made before 1914 was really Belgian. It was the Turner-Miesse, made by Turners of Wolverhampton under licence from Miesse et Cie of Antwerp. The Belgian factory gave up steam in favour of petrol in 1907, and the English company some five years later, though they, too, had been building petrol cars as well for some time.

Marriott's boat-shaped Stanley Steamer of 1906.

The most famous French steam car was the Serpollet (or Gardner-Serpollet). Léon Serpollet patented the first practicable "flash" boiler, or instantaneous generator, in 1889. His early death in 1907 robbed the steam car of one of its most ingenious designers. The business was taken over by Darracq, but Darracq-Serpollet only made steam buses for a few years and discontinued the private cars.

The most advanced steam cars to enter production before 1930 were designed by Abner Doble. The Doble Steam Motor Corp. functioned in Emeryville, Calif., in the 1920s, but fewer than sixty Doble and Doble-Detroit cars were made between 1910 and 1930. The last type, Model F (of which five or six were sold), was capable of about 95 m.p.h.; it was a magnificent car but it cost more than twice as much as a Rolls-Royce.

ELECTRIC CARS

Electric cars were rivals to petrol and steam in the early days and 565 different makes were listed between 1896 and 1939 but, as with the steamers, most of the companies were very short-lived, and folded up after making fewer than a dozen cars.

The first proper motor-cab fleet in the world was operated by the London Electric Cab Co. between December 1897 and March 1900 when they went bankrupt. Their seventy-seven battery-electric cabs were designed by Walter Bersey. They were too heavy for their solid tyres, too slow (8 m.p.h.) to compete with the hansom cabs, and very much more expensive to run than the promoters had estimated.

New York, Boston and other American cities had electric cabs a little later than London, but the cabs (mostly Electrobats designed by Morris and Salom) were better designed and commercially more successful than those of London.

Thomas A. Edison with his first Baker electric car.

Delightful small electric runabouts for the owner-driver were made in America, but European and English electric cars were usually of the formal brougham or landaulet variety driven from an exposed box-seat by a chauffeur. They were once popular for town work as they were silent, safe and free from smell, but they did not survive because they were expensive to buy (or hire), expensive to run, rather slow and limited to about 25 miles on a battery charge.

Thomas Edison claimed that the new "wonder battery" he was working on at the beginning of the century would solve the problems of weight and limited range, and would put the petrol car out of business. When his new nickel-alkali battery was perfected, however, it did not have enough advantages over the lead/acid variety to make much difference. Now that pollution is such a problem, the "wonder battery" is more urgently needed than ever.

An electric car was the first road vehicle to exceed 60 m.p.h. Jenatzy, Paris, raised the World's Land Speed Record to 65·79 m.p.h. in April 1899. The American maker of electric runabouts, Charles Baker, constructed a sprint machine of advanced aerodynamic shape with which he hoped to exceed 100 m.p.h. at Staten Island in 1902. Spectators strayed on to the course when he was estimated to be doing 80 m.p.h., and as he jammed on the brake a wheel collapsed. It was the last high-speed attempt with an electric car.

The famous electric racing car, La Jamais Contente, *with Camille Jenatzy at the helm. This combination was the first to exceed 100 km./hr. and a mile a minute during a record run at Achères in 1899, in which a speed of 65·79 m.p.h. was recorded.*

MOTOR FUELS

Buying motor fuel was not straightforward for pioneer motorists. Very few oil-and-colour shops stocked "petroleum spirit" (almost a waste product then) and some motorists bought "petroleum oil" (i.e. kerosene) and wondered why their engines would not start. As the petrol engine was often called an "oil engine" in the 1890s the mistake is understandable. The American term "gasoline" was in use before the motor-car era and prevented similar confusion there—but gasoline was not widely available. The firm of Carless, Capel and Leonard registered "petrol" as a trade-name in 1896.

Heavy gauge 2-gallon cans, of the sort still in use, were introduced by Pratt and Co. about 1898, and these provided the principal means of distributing, storing and selling petrol for twenty years. Roadside petrol pumps did not come into general use in Great Britain until the 1920s.

Very low "octane" ratings of pre-1914 petrols enforced the use of low-compression engines. Sir Harry Ricardo analysed the part fuel played in causing "knock" in engines (formerly attributed to pre-ignition), and evolved a scale of "toluene" rating to indicate "anti-knock" properties of different fuels. The modern octane ratings were derived from his work.

The French Government tried to encourage the use of alcohol (mostly from potatoes) as motor fuel, without much success, in about 1903. The British Government had greater success a little later, when the first motor-fuel tax was imposed in 1909, and encouraged the use of benzole—a gas-works by-product—by leaving it untaxed. Benzole gave satisfactory results when mixed with petrol, and motorists would ask for "Two gallons of fifty-fifty, please."

A typical garage in 1912 was Wilkinson's of Uxbridge. Note the speed-limit sign indicating a maximum of 10 m.p.h.

SPEED LIMITS

No particular speed limit was imposed by the British Government on the many steam road coaches which were tried between 1820 and 1840. The first controls were imposed by the Locomotives on Highways Act of 1865. This was the "Red Flag Act" which was intended to regulate the use of heavy agricultural traction engines drawing heavy trains of threshing equipment, etc.

The "Red Flag Act" of 1865 specified that every road locomotive must have "three persons in attendance"—one to stoke, one to steer and one to walk ahead with a red flag to warn oncoming traffic and to help control restive horses. Maximum speeds allowed were 4 m.p.h. in open country and 2 m.p.h. in towns.

Another Locomotives on Highways Act of 1878 slightly modified the earlier legislation, but still did not recognise that what made sense for a 15-ton traction engine, drawing a 20- or 30-ton load, made no sense for the sorts of light "horseless carriages" which inventors would otherwise have been encouraged to develop.

The "Emancipation Act" of 1896 at last "legalised" motoring by recognising a class of "light locomotive" (under 3 tons) which were relieved of the "three persons in attendance" rule and allowed to travel at 12 m.p.h.

The Motor Car Act of 1903 raised the general speed limit to 20 m.p.h., but imposed licensing of drivers and the use of registration marks to identify cars. The motoring gentry objected to being "numbered like convicts and labelled like hackney carriages". The 20 m.p.h. speed limit remained in force until 1930.

Construction and Use Regulations for cars began with the 1896 Act and have been developed ever since. Where it is now illegal to drive with tyres with less than 1 mm. depth of tread pattern, the 1896 Act specified that pneumatic or solid rubber tyres must have *smooth* treads. Two completely independent braking systems became mandatory in 1903, but *four-wheel brakes* are not yet compulsory. Rather curiously, speedometers did not become mandatory until 1927.

Vapour Emission Regulations, so important in view of U.S. legislation, now involve complex analysis of exhaust gases, but they were once very simple. The 1896 Act said flatly that "light locomotives" (as motor cars were officially called) must be so constructed as to "consume their own smoke", and made it illegal to "show visible vapour" except from "some temporary and accidental cause".

Wooden-spoked "artillery" wheels were used on most early cars, with wire-spoked wheels a close second. Wooden wheels survived in use on some American cars until the early thirties (see page 206). Many famous makes of early motor car also had wooden chassis frames—Panhard-Levassors, English Daimlers and Sunbeams are examples. The Brush Runabout Co. of Detroit went one better with their 1908–10 light car and used wood (maple spars) for the axle beams, while the Lanchester brothers made a few experimental light cycle cars which actually had wooden suspension springs.

Wooden body frames were always used in the early days, and many motor-body builders followed carriage-trade practice with wooden (or sometimes patent-leather) mudguards and wooden body panels. As some panels were curved in two planes the processes of shaping and bending in the steam-box were long and costly. Mahogany panels were used for high-grade work. Early cars did not rust, but might succumb to the furniture beetle!

Aluminium was used for crankcases and other mechanical parts in the 1890s and it soon found its way into the coachbuilder's art. The Paris coachbuilders, Rothschild et Cie, introduced aluminium panelling in 1902, and the first production-model Lanchesters (1900–05) had Lanchester-made bodywork, with aluminium mudguards and other parts, integral with a composite steel and aluminium chassis.

The Grégoire two-seater of 1914; note the dicky and the location of the spare wheel.

All-steel bodywork (with no wood framing) was introduced on a small B.S.A. car in 1912, and the 1913 model Hupmobile, made by the Hupp Motor Car Corp. of Detroit, was also steel-bodied. But the real pioneers of the modern system of making pressed-steel bodywork were the Dodge brothers who broke away from their association with Ford and began making Dodge cars in Detroit in 1914.

Many alternatives to the "brutal" sliding-pinion gearbox were tried. Early De Dion Bouton cars had an ingenious constant-mesh gear with individual expanding clutches to engage each speed. Simple two-speed epicyclic gears (also always in mesh and with individual clutches) were popular on many early American cars, including the easy-to-drive Model T Ford. The direct ancestor of the modern "automatic" gearbox was the Lanchester three-speed, compound, epicyclic gear with pre-selector control, patented in 1898.

Other attempts at automatic or semi-automatic transmission are represented by the Barber hydraulically operated, progressively variable, gearbox tried on a Hutton car in 1903, and the Fouillaron belt and expanding pulley system (similar in principle to the modern Daf "Variomatic") of the same period. Numerous American examples include the Entz electro-magnetic system used on Owen-Magnetic and Crown-Magnetic cars. Variable friction-disc transmission was used on numerous light cars, the best-known English example being the G.W.K. (1911–31), and the Lentz hydraulic transmission was fitted to a few Charron cars in 1912.

The first motor cars were both hated and laughed at. One of the first "motor jokes" appeared in *Punch* a few months before the "Emancipation Act" made motoring practicable in England. It showed "The awkward predicament of Mr. Newfangle who, on ascending a steep hill, discovers his motor is exhausted."

While the driver attends to the engine compartment of this 1904 24-h.p. Fiat, his heavily protected passengers recline with ill-disguised resignation.

The Hon. Evelyn Ellis, a pioneer motorist and M.P. who helped push the "Emancipation Act" through Parliament, visited his father in his 1895 Panhard-Levassor. Papa (Lord Howard de Walden) was furious and complained: "If you must bring that infernal thing here, kindly bring a little pan to put under it to catch the filthy oil it drips." "Certainly, father, if you'll bring a big pan for your carriage horses when you visit me."

The Hon. Evelyn Ellis in his Panhard et Levassor.

The public hostility to motorists was reflected by many magistrates who accepted very dubious evidence in "speed-trap" cases and usually imposed the heaviest fines the law allowed. One Surrey Justice of the Peace was so "anti-motor car" that he used to hide behind his garden wall, near the Portsmouth road, and pelt passing motor cars with garden refuse.

The oldest motor club in the world, still the leading authority on international motor sport, is the Automobile Club de France. The A.C.F. was founded in the Spring of 1896 at the instigation of Comte de Dion. H. J. Lawson started the Motor Car Club a few months later as part of his design to monopolise the British motor trade. A breakaway group, disliking his commercial methods, formed the Automobile Club of Great Britain and Ireland in 1897. The Automobile Club was granted the prefix "Royal" by Edward VII in 1907.

Scene at Crawley, Sussex, during the A.A.'s inaugural run from London to Brighton in June 1907.

The Automobile Association was formed in 1905 expressly to provide "Scouts" to warn motorists of hidden "police traps". A legal action in 1906 ruled that the use of A.A. "Scouts" to warn motorists was an illegal interference with the police. The A.A. got round this by instituting their rule: "If an A.A. Scout fails to salute you—stop and ask the reason." This gave the Scout an opportunity to say "Beg pardon, Sir, didn't see you coming—Oh! If I was you, Sir, I'd go a bit steady for a mile or so as the road's very bumpy."

BRAKES

Modern-type brake-linings of woven or bonded asbestos were developed by Herbert Frood of Chapel-en-le-Frith (hence the trade-name "Ferodo"), but they were not in evidence until after 1905. Before that, leather, wood, compressed fibre, or woven camel-hair were used for brake-lining; these gave fair results but were short-lived and easily burnt out. "Metal-on-metal" brakes were used on many cars; these were long-lived and could not burn out, but were often noisy and apt to snatch badly when hot.

The most usual arrangement of brakes before 1914 was for the pedal brake to act on a drum on the transmission shafting, and the hand brake (then often called the "side brake") to act directly on the rear-wheel brake-drums. Most motorists normally "drove on the side brake" and kept the foot brake in reserve for emergencies as it was more powerful but imposed a great strain on the final-drive gears, half-shafts, etc.

Two separate foot brakes, each with its own pedal, were fitted to some heavy, fast cars such as Mercedes, Gobron-Brillié, Delaunay-Belleville, etc. As both acted through the transmission and rear wheels they did not give materially better braking than a single foot brake and they were intended to be used alternately on long hills to avoid overheating.

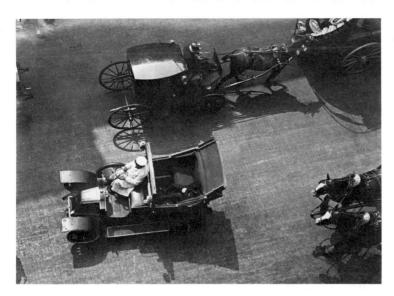

*Old and new in a London
street.*

Water-cooled brakes were also found on some early Mercedes models, *c.* 1902–04. These merely had an arrangement to dribble water from a small tank on to the brake-drum when the pedal was pressed; but the 20/24 and 40-h.p. Hispano-Suizas of 1907–10 had a more elaborate system with hollow cast-aluminium brake-shoes connected to the engine cooling system by flexible pipes.

Brakes on all four wheels did not come into general use until the mid-1920s, but many firms tried four-wheel brakes quite early. They were optionally available on some Mercedes models in 1903—but it is doubtful if anybody actually opted for them. The once-famous Scottish firm of Arrol-Johnston fitted them as standard equipment to their 15·9-h.p. model in 1909. Most "experts" were against the idea, however, and Arrol-Johnston dropped their four-wheel brakes after eighteen months.

By comparison with horsed vehicles most early motor cars were tolerably well braked, but some were notoriously reluctant to stop, particularly in the rain. It was said of the famous Léon Bollée tricar (1896–99) that on a wet day it was necessary to put the brake on before leaving Surrey in order to avoid running into the sea off the Sussex coast.

Dorothy Levitt, well-known pioneer motorist, wrote a little book called "The Woman and the Car" in 1906. She advised the "lady automobilist" to carry a little hand-mirror in the tool-drawer under the driving-seat. This was not only essential to repair the complexion after a drive, but would be found useful, she wrote, to hold aloft from time to time in order to see behind while driving in traffic! Fixed driving-mirrors did not come into general use before 1914.

Or what the best-dressed lady motorists were wearing shortly after the turn of the century.

Windscreens were not fitted to the first cars, but became increasingly popular as cars grew more powerful and went faster. Very curiously the simple mechanical windscreen-wiper, vacuum operated or electrical, did not materialise until the 1920s. On a rainy day our motoring forebears either kept dry and couldn't see where they were going, or conscientiously opened the screen, saw beautifully and got drenched to the skin.

A driver's clothing in 1902.

Before electric lighting and starting sets came into general use (after 1912), most cars had bulb horns—often wonderfully elaborate—but other warning devices were known. Some types (notably early Lanchesters and most electric cars) had "ting-tang" warning bells, while owners of fast cars favoured piercing exhaust whistles and sirens which are now illegal.

London turns out to greet the conqueror of the English Channel. Louis Blériot, accompanied by Winston Churchill, riding in a Napier through the streets after his epic flight of July 1909.

Before suitable small dynamos were evolved, and electric lighting thereby made practicable, cars usually carried oil-burning side- and tail-lamps—although some of the real pioneers had ventured out at night by the light of candle carriage lamps. Headlamps burning acetylene gas came into use about 1898; many of these were large, heavy, elaborate and very expensive. Some of the best were made by Louis Blériot, the first man to fly an aeroplane across the English Channel.

Many motor firms grew out of the cycle business, but a number came from other trades. Panhard et Levassor made woodworking machinery; F. H. Royce and Co. (later to join forces with C. S. Rolls and Co.) made electric dynamos, motors and cranes; Henry Leland, "master of precision" and founder of Cadillac, was in the machine-tool business, Napier made coin-weighing apparatus, Mr. Portwine of A.C. (Autocarrier) was a pork butcher, while the White Co. of Cleveland, Ohio, were famous for sewing-machines before they made steam cars.

Henry Ford is usually credited with "inventing" mass-production, yet the idea originated many years earlier in the Connecticut clock trade and was developed in the American small-arms industry. Henry Leland in America, De Dion Bouton in France and Lanchester in England all based their car production on fully interchangeable machined components, with the minimum of hand-fitting, some years before Ford was in his stride.

Mass production of Model T Fords; dropping the bodies on to the chassis.

Opposed-piston engines, with two pistons in each cylinder working outwards from a central combustion chamber, were used by Arrol-Johnston (Scotland) from 1898 to 1906, and Gobron-Brillié (France) from 1898 to 1914. A four-cylinder, eight-piston, 110-h.p. Gobron-Brillié was officially timed at 103·56 m.p.h. in 1904, and a two-cylinder, four-piston, 18-h.p. Arrol-Johnston won the Tourist Trophy Race in 1905.

The development of the motor car is illustrated by the increase in "volumetric efficiency". In 1896 the slow-running Benz car engines developed about 2 b.h.p. per litre of swept volume; the Panhard-Levassor Daimler type developed 4 b.h.p. per litre, while the new De Dion Bouton high-speed engine achieved 7 b.h.p. per litre. By 1914 the average was about 10 b.h.p. per litre, but special engines for racing cars were producing about 30 b.h.p. per litre.

Because volumetric efficiency was low, very large engines were made, particularly for racing cars. The 1902 "Seventy" Panhard-Levassor racing car had a four-cylinder engine of nearly 14 litres capacity and the car weighed only 1,000 kilos. Even this is dwarfed by a 1906 Métallurgique, originally 10 litres, rebuilt in 1910 with a 21-litre Maybach engine.

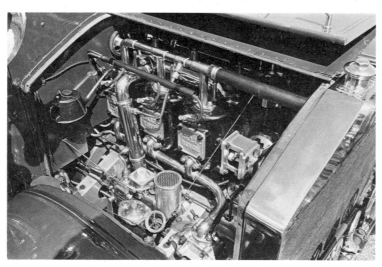

Engine compartment of the 1905 three-cylinder Rolls-Royce as it is preserved to this day.

These huge engines ran slowly by modern standards and the cars were high-geared. The Métallurgique referred to above does about 73 m.p.h. at 1,000 r.p.m. in top gear and has a top speed of about 120 m.p.h. Such giant engines were said to have "pistons like dustbins, moving deliberately up and down like lifts by Nogood-Waytis".

Tyre troubles caused many "breakdowns" and much expense. In 1902 it was reckoned that a light car, carefully driven at not more than 25 m.p.h., might do 2,000 miles on a set of tyres. Heavy, fast cars might do less than a thousand. In 1901 Alfred Harmsworth's tyre bill, for four cars doing less than 3,000 miles each, was about £4,500 at 1976 values. George Lanchester, delivering a car to Rudyard Kipling, suffered twenty-one punctures or bursts on the 200 miles from Birmingham to Rottingdean.

Detachable and interchangeable wheels or rims were not available before 1905. The troublesome tyres had to be repaired or replaced by the roadside with the wheels *in situ*. The first device was the Stepney spare rim which clamped beside the rim of the deflated tyre and allowed the car to be driven slowly home. Then followed the Captain, the Warland and other types of detachable wheel rims, and the famous Rudge centre-lock detachable wheel was marketed in 1908. The modern-type bolt-on wheel was originated by the Sankey Co. in 1910.

The first "motor show" in Great Britain was organised by Sir David Salomons and held in the grounds of his house near Tunbridge Wells. It was part of his campaign, as founder of the Self-Propelled Traffic Association, against the restrictions imposed by the Locomotives on Highways Acts of 1865 and 1878. The date of his show was 15th October 1895, and although there were only five exhibits (six were expected) a good crowd assembled and the newspapers gave brief but encouraging publicity.

Sir David Salomons, famous for his efforts to secure the repeal of the "Red Flag Act", seen here at the tiller of his Peugeot vis-à-vis *during the Tunbridge Wells Show of 15th October 1895.*

The Thousand Miles Trial of 1900 was the most ambitious motoring event staged in Britain during the reign of Queen Victoria. The affair started in London with a static exhibition from 14th to 21st April, and sixty-five vehicles started on the 23rd for Bristol and up the west coast to Edinburgh. The cars returned via the east coast and Midlands, and there were static displays, hill trials and a speed contest in Welbeck Park *en route*. Twenty-three cars finished the course, and although many of the entries were said to be all-British most were disguised importations or native copies of continental designs. Only the Lanchester and Wolseley were of wholly British design.

Two 1913 pictures of charabancs; though both vehicles differ considerably in general, the solid tyres characterised the heavier Edwardian commercial vehicles.

War Needs and Restrictions put a stop to private car production in Great Britain by the end of 1916, except for a small number supplied for war purposes. These included Crossleys which served as light tenders to the Royal Flying Corps, Rolls-Royces used as Staff or King's Messengers' cars, and a number of other makes which were fitted up as ambulances. At the same time a ban was put on civilian car imports from America, which had increased dramatically since the outbreak of war.

Air-raid warning motor car "All Clear", 1917.

Armoured Fighting Vehicles were built on various lorry chassis, notably the American Peerless; these were useful but slow, and consequently vulnerable. The idea of the light, swift, armoured *car* originated with the Royal Naval Air Service. The most successful armoured cars were Lanchesters and Rolls-Royces, with V-eight De Dion Boutons a close third. The Rolls-Royces served with Lawrence in Arabia, and the Lanchesters survived gruelling conditions on the Caucasian front under Commander Locker-Lampson.

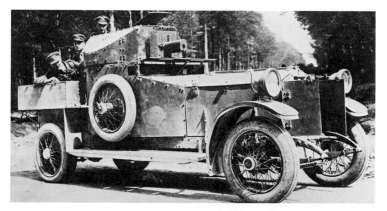

A Rolls-Royce armoured car of the First World War.

Most private car factories were turned over to munitions work, but a few firms produced aero engines. Austin and Wolseley produced Renault engines, Bentley (not yet a car-manufacturer) designed rotaries for the Admiralty. Sunbeam Arabs were made by Sunbeam, Austin and Lanchester—who also made Renaults. Rolls-Royce produced their own famous Eagle, Hawk and Falcon engines, and arrangements were also made to manufacture them in America, but the Armistice intervened before production got under way.

American private car production was not restricted until 1917. In addition to supplying the Allies with cars and lorries on a large scale, many American factories also made aero engines. The most famous was the Lincoln plant which the Lelands (of Cadillac) set up to make the equally famous Liberty engines.

Henry Ford's contribution to the War Effort, apart from his abortive "Peace Ship", lay primarily in the valuable part played by many thousands of Model Ts, in various guises in every theatre. In addition the Ford Co. built tractors for Britain, and planned to defeat the U-boats with a tractor plant in Ireland which was almost ready by late 1918.

A Model T Ford in use as a farm tender in Michigan, U.S.A.

THE PIONEERS

Karl Benz (1844–1929), the son of a railway engine-driver who died when Karl was two, studied engineering at the Karlsruhe Polytechnic. After various jobs he set up business, with successive partners, in a very small way making two-stroke gas engines of his own design in 1880. Although he is entitled to be called the "inventor of the petrol car" (see page 12) he was reluctant to depart from his original design of belt-driven horseless carriage which sold well in the 1890s. Other designers were called in, and after 1902 Benz had little influence on the development of the motor car.

Karl Benz.

Gottlieb Daimler (1834–1900) was born in Schorndorf, the son of a baker. He was apprenticed to a gunsmith, but worked in various engineering firms after learning the gun trade. From 1872 until 1882 he worked for Otto and Langen, gas-engine manufacturers of Deutz, for whom, with the help of Wilhelm Maybach, he designed the first practicable four-stroke internal-combustion engine. He and Maybach set up business as consultant and experimental engineers in Cannstatt in 1882, and in 1883 they produced the first "high-speed" (800 r.p.m. approximately) petrol engine with enclosed crank and hot tube ignition which is recognisably the direct ancestor of the modern car engine. Daimler never worked for Benz, nor Benz for him, as legend has it, and the amalgamation of the Daimler and Benz businesses took place long after his death.

Gottlieb Daimler.

Wilhelm Maybach (1846–1929), Daimler's right-hand man, was more responsible for the detailed

design work of the first Daimler cars than Daimler himself. The Daimler Motoren Gesellschaft was founded in 1890, and limited production of rather primitive but well-made belt-driven cars followed soon after. Maybach was responsible for the two- and four-cylinder Phoenix engines which powered more modern types, after 1896, and were also made under licence by Panhard-Levassor and the English Daimler Co. He also designed the "selective" or "gate" gear-change system and the once-famous "honeycomb" radiator. At the request of Emil Jellinek, a director, he transformed the rather clumsy 24-h.p. Phoenix Daimler into the lighter, lower and swifter Mercedes model a few months after Gottlieb Daimler's death. Maybach set up his own business about 1910 and was famous for aero engines and very elaborate, powerful luxury cars in the 1920s.
Wilhelm Maybach

Selwyn Francis Edge (1868–1940) is best known as a racing driver (he won the 1902 Gordon Bennett

Cup Race among other events), but he also ranks as a motor-manufacturer as he was the moving spirit behind Napier when that firm could claim to be Britain's leading manufacturer. It started in 1898 when "S.F." took his 1897 Panhard-Levassor to Montague Napier's small engineering business in Lambeth to be converted from tiller to wheel steering. Napier then made an improved engine for the car and late in 1899 Edge, who was already dealing in imported cars, set up a selling organisation and contracted to take the whole output of Napier cars. Edge was a fervent advocate of the six-cylinder engine and influenced Napier in making six-cylinder cars from early 1904 onwards. He was also Managing Director of De Dion Bouton, Great Britain, Ltd., and, in the 1920s, of the successful A.C. Co.

Frederick William Lanchester (1868–1946), son of an architect, made Britain's first four-wheeled

petrol car of wholly native design, in 1895, with the help of his brother George. A small company was formed and production was begun late in 1899. Lanchester's designs were always unique and ahead of their time; he was responsible for many innovations which became accepted some years later. These include vibrationless, fully balanced engine, splined shafts, full-pressure lubrication, lightweight pistons, disc brakes, pre-selector semi-automatic gearbox, worm drive, the torsional vibration damper, the harmonic balancer and a lot more. "Doctor Fred" was also a pioneer authority and writer on aerodynamics, and for many years Consultant Engineer to the Daimler Co.

George Herbert Lanchester (1874–1970) was "Doctor Fred's" right-hand man and production engineer in the early days. Many of Frederick Lanchester's innovations involved new manufacturing techniques, with new standards of accuracy, and it was "Mr. George's" business to devise these methods. The strained relations between Frederick and his directors led to his resignation in 1909, and George took his place as Chief Designer. In consultation with Frederick he designed the 1910 38- and 25-h.p. Lanchester models, and was solely responsible for the 1914 Sporting Forty, and post-war O.H.C. Forties, Twenty-Ones and Straight-Eights: he also designed the bodywork. The financial crisis of 1931 led to the Lanchester Co. being taken over by Daimler, and George joined the Daimler design staff. He then worked for Alvis until the Second World War. He continued working as a consulting engineer until his eighty-eighth year.

Herbert Austin (Lord Austin) (1866–1941) worked for the Wolseley Sheep Shearing Machine Co. in Australia. He returned to England in 1895, and when the company thought of toying with the new motor business he designed a tricar, based on the Léon Bollée, in 1896 and followed it with a better one in 1897–98. The prototype four-wheeled Wolseley voiturette appeared late in 1899 and production of horizontal-engined cars started in 1900. In 1905 the company wanted to develop a more modern type of vertical-engined car, which Austin resisted. He set up his own business in Birmingham in 1906 and also started making vertical-engined cars based, at first, on Clément and Gladiator designs. By 1914 the Austin Co. was Britain's largest motor firm; they suffered setbacks after the war, but the famous "Baby" or Austin Seven (production started in 1924) set them on their feet again. The "Baby" was Herbert Austin's personal creation, very largely, and one of the most famous cars of the day.

Henry M. Leland (1843–1932), and his son, Wilfred, are less well known than they deserve in connection with automobile history. Henry, the "master of precision", was a leading figure in the machine-tool and precision-grinding business, firstly with Browne and Sharpe and, from 1890, as head of Leland and Faulconer of Detroit. His firm started making transmission gears and engines for Ransom E. Olds's Merry Oldsmobiles in 1900. In 1901 they offered Olds an improved engine of the same dimensions but more than double the power. This was refused, but the Detroit Automobile Co. was interested and joined forces with the Lelands, being re-formed as the Cadillac Co. Leland laid the foundations of modern volume production of precision-made components, and was also responsible for fitting electric lighting and starting sets, as standard equipment not as an expensive extra, in 1912. The Cadillac V-eight of 1915, derived from a 1910 De Dion Bouton design, is the direct ancestor, via Lincoln and Ford, of all modern American V-eights.

The Hon. Charles Rolls with the 20-h.p. Rolls-Royce, competing in the 1906 Isle of Man Tourist Trophy which he won at 39 m.p.h.

The Hon. Charles Stewart Rolls (1877–1910), third son of Lord Llangattock, was an enthusiastic

motorist before the 1896 "Emancipation Act" was passed. He imported a 3½-h.p. Peugeot in 1896, drove in many of the early continental races, won a special Gold Medal in the Thousand Miles Trial, and in 1903, in association with Claude Johnson, he set up business as a dealer in Panhard-Levassors, Minervas and other imported cars. In 1904 Henry Edmunds persuaded Rolls, rather against his will, to go to Manchester to meet a Mr. Royce who had made a little two-cylinder runabout. Though inclined to dislike small cars Rolls was so impressed that an agreement was soon made that C. S. Rolls and Co. would take all the cars made by F. H. Royce and Co., and would market them as Rolls-Royces. The separate firm of Rolls-Royce Ltd. was formed in 1906, and the famous 40/50 or Silver Ghost model appeared soon after. Rolls's enthusiasm and social connections helped establish the fine new cars in public favour. From 1908 onwards Rolls gave most of his enthusiasm to flying, and he was killed on 12th July 1910 when flying his Wright biplane at the Bournemouth Aviation Week.

Frederick Henry Royce (1863–1933), a self-taught engineer of outstanding skill, started a small

business in Manchester with £70 capital and A. E. Claremont as partner, to make electric lamp holders, filaments, bells, etc. By 1900 F. H. Royce and Co. was famous for electric motors, dynamos, cranes and hoists. In 1903, to the mild derision of his partners, Royce began tinkering and improving a second-hand two-cylinder Decauville. By April 1904 the first of three experimental Royce cars, improved versions of the Decauville, took the road, and the meeting with Rolls and its sequel followed. Royce was a perfectionist, sometimes too much so, and his designs—particularly the Silver Ghost—set new patterns of reliability, refinement and silence. From 1910, when he fell ill, Royce seldom appeared at the factory and directed new designs, and continual refinements of the older ones, from his homes in Sussex or the South of France. This went for the early Rolls-Royce aero engines also. Royce was not an inventive man, but he had the gift, amounting to genius, of taking the best that was going and making it better. He was made a baronet in 1931, but always regarded himself modestly as "Henry Royce, Mechanic".

An early view of the Rolls-Royce factory.

Emile Levassor (1844–1897) was in partnership with René Panhard making woodworking machinery in Paris when, in 1887, they were commissioned by Edouard Sarazin to make Daimler engines for which he held the French manufacturing licence. Sarazin died later in 1887 and his widow, to whom the Daimler licence passed, married Levassor in 1890. The first experimental belt-driven Panhard-Levassor car was tried soon after, and by 1891 Levassor had evolved the classic or conventional design with which his name is associated. This had the Daimler-type engine mounted vertically in front, driving through a pedal-controlled clutch and longitudinal shaft to a sliding-pinion gear system. In addition to his design work, Levassor won fame in 1895 when he drove single-handed (having missed his relief driver) in a 3½-h.p. Panhard-Levassor for 48¾ hours to win the 732-mile Paris-Bordeaux-Paris Race at an average speed of 15 m.p.h. He was thrown from his car during the Paris-Marseilles Race of 1896 and died the following year.

The Bollée family. Amédée Bollée, senior, and his sons Léon and Amédée, junior, played an important part in the early days. Amédée, senior, was connected with a family firm of bell-founders in Le Mans, and between 1873 and 1890 he made a number of very satisfactory steam vehicles. He was impressed with the performances of early petrol cars and encouraged his sons to go ahead with these new ideas. The famous Léon Bollée tricar saw the light of day in December 1895, and was an immediate success. It was temperamental but, for some while, the fastest motor vehicle on sale to the public. Léon then helped to launch one of the most important manufacturers of the early twentieth century by designing a five-speed, four-wheeled petrol car for Alexandre Darracq early in 1899. His brother Amédée similarly designed the first cars to be made by the important De Dietrich industrial combine. Amédée, junior, also produced some remarkable racing *torpilleurs*, or streamlined cars, before the end of the century.

Amédée Bollée père (1844–1917) seated, with Amédée Bollée fils (1867–1926).

The Comte de Dion and Georges Bouton relax in their open landau drawn behind a "steam drag"—the world's first "artic"! An 1895 picture taken in Paris.

Comte Albert de Dion (1856–1946), who became Marquis in 1901, firmly believed in the light horseless carriage when most businessmen would not give it a thought. In 1883 he hired Bouton and Trépardoux to work on his steam-carriage project, and later formed a partnership with them. Many practicable light steam carriages and neat tricars were made, as well as buses and lorries. In 1890 de Dion encouraged Georges Bouton to experiment with petrol engines. Trépardoux would have none of it and left. The first De Dion Bouton petrol tricycle came on the market late in 1895 and was a great success. Small cars followed late in 1898, and by early 1901 over 1,500 had been sold. For some years De Dion Bouton et Cie was the world's largest motor firm, and they supplied engines to scores of other manufacturers. The Comte de Dion was also the prime mover of the Automobile Club de France, and had interests in oil-refining, aluminium-smelting and publishing.

Louis Renault (1877–1944), with his brothers Marcel (see page 116) and Fernand, came into the motor business by chance—as so many others did. In 1898 he took the $1\frac{3}{4}$-h.p. engine off his De Dion Bouton tricycle and used it in a tiny four-wheeled car of his own design. This had a forward-mounted engine, an ingenious gearbox giving direct drive on top gear, jointed propeller-shaft and live axle. Acquaintances asked for similar cars and with a little money borrowed from his father and practical help from his brothers, Louis Renault set up in business at Billancourt and began producing cars with $2\frac{1}{2}$-h.p. De Dion engines. Larger models followed and the firm began making their own engines about 1904. They had many racing successes—including the 1906 Grand Prix—but were chiefly famous for the outstanding reliability and longevity of their ordinary models. The famous Marne taxis, which rushed reinforcements to the Front in 1914, were nearly all Renaults.

Ransom E. Olds (1864–1950) made a steam tricar in 1893–94, but in 1896 he decided the gasoline engine offered a better solution to the problem. Experimental cars followed, but as it was 1901 before Olds was ready to start series production he cannot claim to be America's first motor-manufacturer. For a while, though, he was the largest, and his famous "curved dash" Olds-

mobile—the Merry Oldsmobile of the song—was very successful and widely imitated. It set a pattern for the "gas buggy" type of vehicle which suited heavy going over dirt roads, as it was very high-pitched and had flexible suspension and a simple easy-to-drive two-speed epicyclic gear. The slow-running, horizontal single-cylinder engines, which were somewhat inefficient but very reliable, were made at first by the Dodge brothers, and later by Leland and Faulconer (see Leland, page 43). Boardroom squabbles led Olds to leave the Oldsmobile Co. in 1904, whereupon he set up another company to make Reo cars—the name derived from his own initials.

Lee Chadwick (1875–1958) of Pottstown, Pa., produced very fine cars in very limited numbers at very high prices between 1906 and 1916. He earns a place in automobile history by being the first to make a supercharged car engine—in 1907. Rather curiously, the supercharger was only an expedient to improve the "breathing" of a new six-cylinder engine which disappointed the designer by developing less power than its four-cylinder predecessor of similar swept volume. He then improved the manifolding, and did away with the supercharger—which only came into use on some racing cars another twenty years later.

Frank (1869–1967) and Charles (1861–1938) Duryea. The Duryea Motor Wagon Co. of Peoria, founded in 1894, was America's first company expressly set up to make internal-combustion motor cars. The Duryea brothers' much-altered experimental car of 1892–93 was almost certainly America's first four-wheeled "gas car" to run on the roads, although it may have been ante-dated by a few months by Lambert's tricar. The brothers quarrelled in later life and each claimed to have been the inventor of the Duryea car. It is probable that Frank put forward the first ideas and sketches, and that Charles, who executed them, found that he had to make many alterations as he went along. A Duryea won the 54-mile *Times-Herald* Race (at an average speed of less than 6 m.p.h.) in 1895, and two Duryeas took part in the London-to-Brighton Emancipation Day procession in 1896. Early Duryea cars had many ingenious features, but no great commercial success.

Charles Duryea, above Frank Duryea.

Harry J. Lawson (1852–?), was an English company promoter who saw the potential might of the motor industry when only a handful of motor cars existed. In 1895 he formed the British Motor Syndicate and tried to establish a monopoly by buying every available motor patent and then selling or leasing manufacturing licences to puppet companies bought or set up for the purpose. One of his first creations was the British Daimler Motor Co., in 1896, and his most grandiose was the short-lived Great Horseless Carriage Co. His syndicate also tried to extract a royalty on every imported car. He was a far-sighted man with a touch of genius, but when his schemes did not border on the fraudulent they tended to be farcical. He failed to establish his monopoly and little more was heard of his schemes after 1903.

George B. Selden (1846–1932) was an astute attorney who applied for a patent in 1877 for a carriage

driven by a Brayton-type two-stroke gas engine. It was not really a workable proposition and he delayed the final grant of the patent until 1896 when there was more chance of a commercial opening. In 1899 he sold manufacturing rights to a financial syndicate. This led to the formation of the Association of Licensed Automobile Manufacturers (forerunners of the S.A.E.) who tried to monopolise the industry in the U.S.A., as Lawson had done in Britain, by forcing all manufacturers to join them and pay manufacturing licence fees. Many legal battles ensued, and the Selden patent was finally "busted" on behalf of the Ford Co. in 1911. In 1905, as part of the litigation, a car was made in accordance with the original specification and the misleading date of 1877 was painted on the side of it. With some difficulty and at little speed it covered 1,400 feet under its own power—which scarcely convinced the Court of its practicality.

Henry Ford with his 1896 motor quadricycle. (Photo: Radio Times Hulton Picture Library.)

Henry Ford (1863–1947), like Henry Royce, was not a professional engineer but a natural, empirical mechanic. He was not interested in the car as a luxury for the carriage gentry, but saw that it must be made cheaply but well for ordinary people. He made his first crude, experimental, motor quadricycle in 1896, and followed it with improved versions. In 1899 he resigned his post with the Edison Co. and went as Works Manager to the Detroit Automobile Co., which soon failed. In partnership with Tom Cooper he then made two racing cars for publicity purposes, and with the financial backing they won him he set up the first Ford Co. late in 1901. Horizontal-engined, "gas buggies" of the successful Oldsmobile or Cadillac type were made at first. Four-cylinder, vertical-engined cars, still with two-speed epicyclic gear, followed in 1904–05. With the appearance of Model T in October 1908 (James Couzens was the principal designer) Ford knew that he had what he wanted. His insistence in 1909 on dropping all other models in order to increase production of the T, unchanged, year after year at a constantly reducing price, was a gamble. It succeeded brilliantly, and the Model T won friends and influenced people all over the world to an extent nobody would have thought possible a few years earlier.

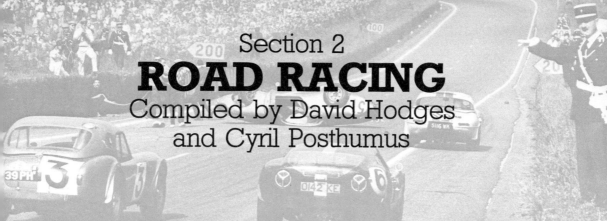

Section 2
ROAD RACING
Compiled by David Hodges
and Cyril Posthumus

Part One, THE RACES

The first road race between mechanically propelled vehicles took place in the U.S.A. in July 1878, seven years before the petrol engine was invented. Run over 201 miles between Green Bay and Madison, in Wisconsin, the contest included long-haul and ploughing tests as well as the race. It attracted six entries, all steam-powered, and two starters, both virtually road locomotives. An Oshkosh built by Dr. J. Carhart and driven by F. Shomer and A. M. Farrand won the race in 33 hours 27 minutes, averaging 6 m.p.h., while a Green Bay built and driven by E. P. Cowles retired 20 miles from the finish after covering part of the journey by railroad. The winner received $5,000 prize-money.

Competition motoring with petrol-engined cars began with the Paris-Rouen Reliability Trial in 1894, and the first motor race was run in June 1895, over the 732 miles, Paris-Bordeaux-Paris. Emile Levassor finished first in 48 hours 48 minutes (15 m.p.h.), driving his Panhard single-handed. Nine of the twenty-two starters completed the full distance.

The first motor sports club, the Automobile Club de France, was formed in 1895 out of the committee which had organised the Paris-Bordeaux-Paris Race.

The first competition between petrol-engined cars in the U.S.A. was the 1895 Chicago *Times-Herald* contest, which consisted of a race and a series of laboratory tests of mechanical efficiency. Only two cars were ready for the first race, a Duryea and a Benz, and only the latter finished the 94-mile course from Chicago to Waukegan, so a rerun was arranged for 26th November. Because of snow the course was shortened to 54 miles, finishing at Evanston; six cars started, and a twin-cylinder Duryea won. The race was also the first ever to be won on pneumatic tyres.

The first motoring competition in Italy was the 1895 Turin-Asti-Turin Trial, won by Simone Federmann, driving a Daimler. The first proper race south of the Alps was the 1900 Brescia-Cremona-Brescia, won by Panhard driver Franchetti.

The first accident in a race led to Prévost's retirement from the 1895 Paris-Bordeaux-Paris; a wheel on his Panhard was broken when he collided with a dog.

The first accident involving personal injury came at the start of the 1896 Paris-Marseilles-Paris Race, when Ferté, driver of a Fisson, ran over a spectator.

The first accidents involving injuries to members of the crews of competing cars occurred during the 1896 Paris-Marseilles-Paris; most serious casualty was one Noblesse, who was thrown out of Villefranche's Panhard.

The first fatal accident in motor racing occurred in the Circuit of Périgueux in 1898, de Montaignac and his mechanic being killed when their Landry et Beyrouc rolled. However, prior to this, Levassor's death was attributed to injuries—at the time apparently slight—received when he crashed in the 1896 Paris-Marseilles-Paris Race.

The first motoring competition to cross international frontiers was the 889-mile Paris-Amsterdam-Paris Race of 1898, which was won by Charron in a Panhard at 26·9 m.p.h. This was also the first race to fall foul of officialdom, when the Paris Prefect of Police ordered that cars be inspected for road-worthiness. To enforce red tape, infantry and cavalry were posted at the official Champigny start; to defeat red tape the start was surreptitiously moved to Villiers in the neighbouring *département*. In case of reprisals, the finishing-point was also moved out of reach of the presumably offended Prefect.

The first mass start was arranged for the 1898 Paris-Bordeaux-Paris Race, in effect a restart after cars had started at intervals and run through a neutralised section. (Cars normally started at intervals in early races, and twenty-four years were to pass before the mass start was introduced into Grand Prix racing.)

The first dead-heat finish occurred in the 1899 Paris-Ostend race between Girardot (Mors) and Levegh (Panhard), who both completed the 201 miles in 6 hours 11 minutes (32·5 m.p.h.)— there was no possibility of a time-keeping error as this was one of the few early races with a mass start (if nine starters can be called a "mass"), and Girardot and Levegh crossed the line at Ostend racecourse wheel-to-wheel.

The first race to include a separate voiturette ("light car") class as such was the 1898 Paris-Marseilles; a weight of 200–400 kg. and two side-by-side seats were the principal stipulations. Winner was Georges Richard, driving a Georges Richard, at 12·7 m.p.h. for 141 miles.

A Winton at Ballyshannon for the 1903 Gordon Bennett Trophy Race. This car was part of the first American racing team to compete in Europe.

The first race in Germany took place in 1898, over 33 miles from Berlin to Potsdam and back. A Humber tricycle won, followed by a Daimler car.

The first race in Belgium, from Brussels to Spa, was run in 1898, the winner being Baron Pierre de Crawhez (Panhard). The first race in Switzerland also took place in 1898 and was won by a Monsieur Jones driving a Delahaye.

The first marque race was arranged for Mors cars in 1898. Levegh won the 79-mile race at 29·3 m.p.h.

A handicap race between walkers, horsemen, cycles, motorcycles and cars was staged from Paris to Trouville (104 miles) in 1899. Horses were allowed 14 hours, and finished first and second; cars, allowed 3 hours, were third and fourth.

The first circuit race, the Course du Catalogue, run over two laps of a 45-mile triangular course at Melun in 1900, was won by Girardot in a Panhard. **The first important circuit race** was the 1902 Circuit des Ardennes (q.v.).

Flag signals were first used by race marshals in 1899, red for "stop", and yellow for "caution". These two still have the same meaning.

The first international race series was for the Gordon Bennett Trophy, between teams representing nations. It was devised in 1899 by *New York Herald* proprietor James Gordon Bennett, it is said after he heard of a challenge issued to Fernand Charron by Alexander Winton, and controlled by the Automobile Club de France. The first race was run in 1900, from Paris to Lyons, and contested by a three-car French team of Panhards, a single Belgian Bolide and a Winton. Two of the Panhards finished, Charron winning at 38·6 m.p.h.

The first national racing colours were allotted to Gordon Bennett Trophy teams in 1900. Some were permanently adopted—yellow for Belgium, blue for France and white for Germany. The American team colour in 1900 was red, later to be adopted by Italy, while blue and white became the American colours. Green, a "lucky" colour on the Continent, was given to Charles Jarrott in 1901 by the Paris-Berlin Race organisers to offset his racing number 13.

Today the requirement that cars in international races be painted in the colours of their entrants, irrespective of the nationality of the driver or country where the car was built, has largely fallen into disuse.

Racing classes were clearly defined for the first time in 1901: *voiturettes*, up to 250 kg. (551 lb.); *voitures légères*, 250–400 kg. (551–882 lb.) and "front-line" cars, over 650 kg. (1,433 lb.).

The first race to carry the title "Grand Prix" was run at Pau in February 1901, and won by Maurice Farman in a Panhard at 46·1 m.p.h. It was, however, a local event without national status or backing.

The first race arranged for promotional purposes was the Circuit du Nord "alcohol race" sponsored by the French Ministry of Agriculture in 1902 to promote the use of this national product as a fuel (it was, of course, a condition that contestants used it). Many, it seems, used it as little as possible, claiming that it made only for a noticeable loss of power. (Outright winner of the 537-mile event was Maurice Farman, who averaged 44·8 m.p.h. in his Panhard.)

*De Knyff (Panhard) before
the start of the Paris–
Vienna Race of 1902.*

**The first motoring competition to be stopped in mid-course by an event quite unconnected
with motoring** was an "endurance contest" organised by the Auto-
mobile Club of America, from New York to Buffalo in 1901; forty-two of
the eighty starters had reached Rochester when news of the assassination
of President McKinley was received, whereupon the contest was
abandoned.

The first international race victory for a British car was gained by Selwyn Francis Edge in the
1902 Gordon Bennett Trophy Race. His Napier triumph is seldom recalled
in perspective, however—the Gordon Bennett Trophy, Paris-Innsbruck,
was run concurrently with the Paris-Vienna Race, in which Marcel Renault
was fastest of all over the 615 miles (average speed, 38·9 m.p.h.) driving a
Renault in the light car class. Edge was eighth in the Paris-Vienna heavy car
class, effectively sixteenth overall.

The first British driver to gain a major international circuit victory was Charles Jarrott,
although Maurice Farman (page 51) was born to British parents. Jarrott
drove a 13·8-litre Panhard to win the six-lap 318-mile Circuit des Ardennes
in 1902, at 54 m.p.h. This was his only significant race victory.

The first race regulations to include an overall weight stipulation were introduced in 1902, when
cars were limited to a maximum of 1000 kg. (2,204 lb.), with a 7 lb.
allowance for a magneto. Contemporary reaction was that in making for
lighter cars, this regulation would make for cars which were easier to handle;
in fact it led to unbalanced cars, with chassis inadequate for ever more
powerful engines.

The first phase of city-to-city racing was decisively ended by accidents in the 1903 Paris-
Madrid, which was halted by the French Government at the end of the
first day's racing, at Bordeaux, because of the numerous major and minor
crashes. Mors driver Gabriel was declared the overall winner, having
covered 342 miles at 65·3 m.p.h. Apart from freak long-distance events,
and the 1907–08 St. Petersburg-Moscow, decades were to pass before
similar point-to-point races were run again—in Central and Southern
America; the last to gain true international status was the short-lived
Mexican Carrera Panamericana (q.v.).

Sir Francis Samuelson in the 1914 Tourist Trophy Sunbeam. He is the only racing driver to have competed before the First World War and after the Second. (Photo: Roger McDonald.)

The 1922 5-litre Delage "La Torpille" was the first racing car to be made by the Delage works after the 1914–18 war, specifically for hillclimbs. It has been restored by Nigel Arnold-Forster who is seen climbing Prescott in 1964. (Photo: Roger McDonald.)

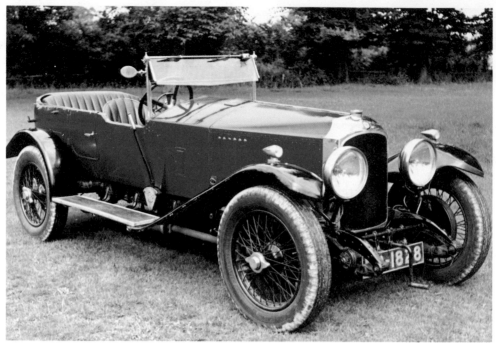

Two classic Vintage sports cars. Above: 1923 30/98 Vauxhall type OE, designed by Laurence Pomeroy, Sr. Below: W. O.'s 1929 4½-litre Bentley. (Photos: Roger McDonald.)

Jenatzy (Mercedes) on the Ballyshannon course for the 1903 Gordon Bennett Trophy Race.

The first international motor race run in the British Isles was the 1903 Gordon Bennett Trophy, and a special Act of Parliament had to be passed to make it possible on public roads. A circuit of two loops was devised on normally empty roads centred on Ballyshannon in Ireland; competitors had to lap the short (40-mile) loop three times, and the longer (52-mile) circuit four times. Winner was Camille Jenatzy, driving a Mercedes at 49·2 m.p.h. British cars occupied the last three places, and the only one to cover the full distance was disqualified!

The first American team to compete in Europe contested the 1903 Gordon Bennett Trophy Race. It was made up of two Wintons and a Peerless, none of which completed the full racing distance.

Racing on public roads has never been permitted on the "mainland" of Britain, but independent legislative bodies in offshore islands—the Isle of Man, Jersey and Ulster—have allowed it on their roads. The first Isle of Man events were the 1904 Gordon Bennett Trophy trials and the 1905 Tourist Trophy.

International motor racing was introduced into the U.S.A. by W. K. Vanderbilt, jnr., who sponsored the first Vanderbilt Cup Race on a 30-mile Long Island circuit on 4th October 1904. The American driver George Heath drove a Panhard to win the 284-mile event at 52·2 m.p.h. by 2½ minutes from Clément's Clément-Bayard.

The first major Italian race, the Florio Cup, was run at Brescia in 1904, and won by Vincenzo Lancia, driving a Fiat at 71·90 m.p.h., while Vincenzo Florio, founder of the event, was third.

The first international governing body of motor sport, the A.I.A.C.R. ("Association Internationale des Automobile Clubs Reconnus") was born out of the committee set up to resolve the first major international wrangle in the history of racing—over the high-handed French proposals to change the Gordon Bennett Trophy rules in their favour in 1904–05.

The A.I.A.C.R. was reconstituted as the Fédération Internationale de l'Automobile in 1946. Since 1922 sporting matters have been delegated, to the Commission Sportive Internationale (C.S.I.) until 1978, and subsequently to its direct successor, the Fédération Internationale du Sport Automobile (F.I.S.A.).

The Targa Florio was first run in 1906 over three laps of the 93-mile Madonie circuit devised by Vincenzo Florio. Ten cars started, and the race was won by Cagno in an Itala at 29·18 m.p.h. The Targa survived into the 1970s as a race, but the trend of racing was against it, and by the end of that decade it had been debased to a rally in the Italian Championship, albeit a high-speed tarmac event.

The first victory for an American car in an international road race was gained by George Robertson, driving the 1906 Locomobile "Old 16" in the 1908 Vanderbilt Cup Race at 64·38 m.p.h.

First definable sports-car competitions (in that they encouraged touring cars with sporting characteristics) are generally agreed to have been the Herkomer and Prince Henry Tours (later Trials) organised in Germany between 1905 and 1911. There were numerous similar events before the First World War, and out of them competitions closely resembling sports-car races began to emerge—for example the 1913 Belgian Grand Prix (a regularity/speed/fuel consumption event, won by Derny's Springuel), and the 1913 Spanish Grand Prix, run in the Guadarrama mountains and won by Salamanca's Rolls-Royce at 54 m.p.h.

The first significant series for "second division" racing cars, known as "light cars", *voitures légères* or *voiturettes*, became established in the year 1906, when the French journal *l'Auto* first sponsored its Coupe des Voiturettes. The first regulations restricted only cylinder bore, not engine capacity, and gave rise to some single-cylinder freaks, but under the revised rules of 1909 the Coupe de l'Auto encouraged the design of really efficient small engines, most notably by Hispano-Suiza and Peugeot.

The first national Grand Prix was the Grand Prix de l'Automobile Club de France, the French Grand Prix. It was born of French frustration with the Gordon Bennett Trophy races, for the French industry felt that as the premier racing country France should not be restricted to one three-car team (and this spelled the end of the Gordon Bennett Trophy series). Team entries from any number of manufacturers were admitted to the first Grand Prix in 1906, and to French Grands Prix run until 1924, when the first "semi-works" entry—a Miller—was accepted.

A Renault Grand Prix car at Le Mans for the first national Grand Prix, the Grand Prix de l'A.C.F. of 1906.

The first Grand Prix was the only one to be run under the 1,000 kg. maximum weight rules (plus a 7-kg. allowance for magneto or dynamo). It took place on a 64·12-mile circuit near Le Mans in June 1906, six laps having to be covered on each of two consecutive days. Eleven of the thirty-two starters finished, headed by Ferenc Szisz on a Renault who covered the 769·3 miles at 62·88 m.p.h.

The first international formula to restrict engine size was devised at the Ostend Conference in the summer of 1907, and came into effect in 1908. This restricted cylinder bore to 155 mm. for four-cylinder engines, and 127 mm. for six-cylinder engines. A capacity limit of 4½ litres was imposed for the Grand Prix in 1914.

The first fatal accident in Grand Prix racing occurred in the 1908 French Grand Prix at Dieppe, when Cissac and his riding mechanic Schaube were killed when their Panhard crashed after a front tyre blew.

The second country to stage a Grand Prix was America, in 1908. The Grand Prize of the Automobile Club of America was run at Savannah, and contested by leading European teams. Louis Wagner in a Fiat won at 65·2 m.p.h. over sixteen laps of the 25·13-mile circuit. No American cars ran the full distance, although Seymour's Simplex was classified as a runner at the end (in eleventh place).

"Pits" entered motor-racing terminology in 1908, when a divided trench with a counter just above ground-level was provided for team crews at the French Grand Prix at Dieppe, and although inappropriate in that structures above ground-level were subsequently used, the term has stuck.

The first major race in Germany, apart from the 1904 Gordon Bennett Trophy Race, which by the regulations of that contest was held in Germany after Jenatzy's Mercedes victory in 1903, was the one and only Kaiserpreis in 1907. Run over four laps of a 73-mile circuit in the Taunus Mountains, this was won at 52·5 m.p.h. by Felice Nazzaro in a Fiat, the supreme driver/car combination of that year.

The only major race in Russia, St. Petersburg-Moscow, was run twice, in 1907 and 1908. The first was won by Arthur Duray in a Lorraine-Dietrich, the second by Victor Héméry in a Grand Prix Benz, at the remarkable speed of 51·4 m.p.h. over 438 miles of "cart-tracks".

Marathon intercontinental "races" were run in 1907 and 1908, the Peking-Paris and the New York-Paris. Five cars started in the first, and four finished, led by a 40-h.p. Itala captained by Prince Scipione Borghese.

Four cars reached the West Coast of America on the first leg of the 20,000-mile 1908 event; to all intents and purposes a German Protos won, but the first prize was in fact awarded on elapsed time (26 days) to an American Thomas Flyer, which had taken a different route.

The first Argentine Grand Prix of the Roads, run in 1910 over 475 miles from Buenos Aires to Cordoba, closely followed the style of the open-road city-to-city races abandoned in Europe earlier in the decade. As the Gran Premio Nacional, it was run in this form over varying courses and distances until 1933, when officialdom stepped in to dilute its character to that of a rally (in that year there had been only one finisher, Roberto Lozano in a Ford Special). It became a full-blooded race again in 1936, reached a pinnacle in the late 'forties with duels between the Galvez brothers and Juan-Manuel Fangio, and then went into a slow decline until *turismo carretera* racing was banned.

The notorious "death curve" at Santa Monica. The Mercer of Pullen loses a front wheel during the 1914 Vanderbilt Cup Race.

Grand Prix racing was temporarily abandoned in Europe after 1908, and the first attempt to revive it came in 1911 at Le Mans, in a race derisively dubbed the "Grand Prix des vieux tacots" ("Old Crocks Grand Prix"). As a Grand Prix this was a pale shadow, but is remembered for bringing the name Bugatti into racing history, as a constructor in his own right.

Much is made of the fact that Friderich drove a 1·3-litre Bugatti into second place behind a 10-litre Fiat, although in fact it lost two laps in the twelve of the race to the Italian car, and there were no other raceworthy cars running at the end—this was by no means a David versus Goliath performance, as it is sometimes recalled.

The first 1-2-3 team victory in a major circuit race was achieved by Sunbeam, in the 1912 Coupe de l'Auto. Moreover, the three cars, driven by Rigal, Resta and Médinger were placed third, fourth and fifth overall in the concurrent Grand Prix de l'Automobile Club of France.

Grand Prix racing reached a peak at Lyons in 1914, in a race to which the sobriquet "The Greatest Grand Prix" has stuck, although later events have at least equal claims to it. The principal role was played by the darling of France, Georges Boillot, who had won the French Grands Prix for Peugeot in 1912 and 1913, and who was seen as defender of French honour against the Mercedes team in 1914. In this race his possibly over-driven Peugeot let him down, and Christian Lautenschlager won the 468-mile race for Mercedes at 65·66 m.p.h. with two team-mates second and third.

The first major race to be run in Europe after the First World War was the Targa Florio, in November 1919.

The start was at 7 a.m., and the first man away was Enzo Ferrari, driving a C.M.N. Winner after a heroic drive was André Boillot in a Peugeot, who spun approaching the finish, crossed the line backwards, and returned to the point of his spin to refinish "correctly"!

The first major American victory in Europe was gained by Jimmy Murphy, driving a Duesenberg, in the 1921 French Grand Prix at Le Mans. Murphy's winning speed was 78·10 m.p.h.

The second of the European "grandes épreuves" to become established as such was the Italian Grand Prix, first run at Brescia in 1921 and won by Jules Goux in a Ballot at 89·94 m.p.h. In 1922 the race moved to Monza, where with three exceptions (Leghorn, 1937; Milan, 1947; Turin, 1948) it has been held up to 1979. The third race, in 1923, was the most notable of the pre-war series: it was the first Grand Prix to be won by a supercharged car—Carlo Salamano's Fiat 805 at 91·06 m.p.h.; Jimmy Murphy's American Miller was third; fourth and fifth were two of the remarkable rear-engined Benz *Tropfenwagenen.*

The first 24-hour road race to be run in Europe was the 1922 Bol d'Or at Saint-Germain, won by André Morel in a 1,100-c.c. Amilcar at 37·54 m.p.h.

The first mass start in Grand Prix racing, and the first rolling start, was for the 1922 French Grand Prix at Strasbourg.

The Le Mans 24-Hour Race was the first international road event run "twice round the clock". Conceived as a test for touring cars, it became a trend-setting sports-car event and in some respects the most publicised and thus the most important of all road races.

    The first Le Mans Grand Prix d'Endurance was run in 1923, and won by Lagache and Léonard in a 3-litre Chenard et Walcker at 57·21 m.p.h.

Until 1924 Grand Prix cars had to carry riding mechanics, but for 1925 the regulations were modified to require that cars provide only room for mechanics in two-seater bodies. At the same time, rear-view mirrors for drivers became compulsory.

The first Belgian Grand Prix for Grand Prix cars was run in 1925 on the Spa circuit in the Ardennes, when Antonio Ascari won with an Alfa Romeo P2 at 74·56 m.p.h. from his team mate Campari. The circuit was last used for a Belgian Grand Prix in

The Duesenberg which won the 1921 French Grand Prix, seen here with Jimmy Murphy and his mechanic, Ernie Olsen.

1970, when Pedro Rodriguez drove a V-12 B.R.M. to victory at 149·94 m.p.h. Modern Grand Prix drivers consider Spa to be dangerously fast, and it has not been used since, save for touring and sports car races. The circuit was revived with a shorter lap in 1979.

Count Conelli was in the process of having an accident as he crossed the line at the end of the 1925 Grand Prix de l'Ouverture at Montlhéry. Trying to beat his Talbot-Darracq team mate Duller, he clipped a wall and spun, and his car rolled over when it had crossed the line; thus Conelli came within an ace of taking second place when upside down.

The first Manufacturers' Championship in Grand Prix racing was instituted in 1925, but was abandoned after three seasons. Winners were Alfa Romeo (1925), Bugatti (1926) and Delage (1927).

The first Moroccan Grand Prix was a touring-car race in 1925, but it was not run as a Grand Prix formula race until 1957, on the Ain-Diab circuit when the winner was Jean Behra driving a Maserati at 112·64 m.p.h. In the following year it was a World Championship event, but was then discontinued.

Smallest field ever to start in a classic Grand Prix was made up of three Bugattis, for the 1926 French Grand Prix at Miramas. One completed the full 100-lap distance, one finished fifteen laps behind, and the third retired.

The first German Grand Prix was run in 1926 on the Avus track at Berlin, and won by Rudolf Caracciola in a Mercedes at 83·95 m.p.h. In 1927 the venue was the then-new Nurburgring, where with two exceptions (1959 and 1970) every German Grand Prix was run until 1976. Since then it has taken place at Hockenheim.

The first British Grand Prix was run on a pseudo-road circuit at Brooklands in 1926. Winners at 71·61 m.p.h. were Louis Wagner and Robert Sénéchal, sharing a Delage—in that year this car so overheated its drivers that changes during a race became customary. Runner-up was Malcolm Campbell in a Bugatti.

The first major race on the famous Rheims circuit was the Grand Prix de la Marne in 1927, won by Philippe Etancelin in a Bugatti, although Bignan driver Clause had won the first, minor, race in this series in 1925, at 62·50 m.p.h. The French Grand Prix was run at Rheims for the first time in 1932, when Tazio Nuvolari won in a Type B Alfa Romeo at 92·32 m.p.h.; fourteen other French Grands Prix have been run on this circuit—more than any other, but after the 1966 race it fell into disuse.

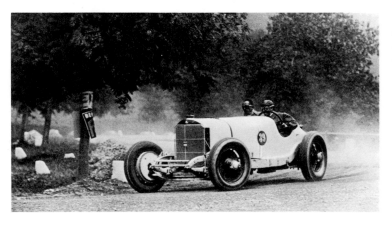

The great Rudi Caracciola at the wheel of an SSK Mercedes-Benz at Semmering in 1928.

Maximum distances for "grandes épreuves" (i.e. national Grands Prix) and later World Championship Grands Prix have been laid down since 1928:

1928–30	600 km. (373 miles)
1931	10 hours
1932	5 hours
1933–39	500 km. (311 miles)
1950–57	300 km. (186 miles)/3 hours
1958–date	300 km. (186 miles)/2 hours

These distance/duration regulations have not always been strictly applied, for example to the Monaco Grand Prix which, until 1968, was always run over 100 laps—regardless of duration. Recent fine-weather Grands Prix on fast circuits have been completed in less than an hour and a half.

The first marque road-race series was arranged by Bugatti, for Bugattis, in the late 'twenties. Some twenty years later Piero Dusio tried to popularise a Cisitalia 1,100-c.c. circus, in which well-known drivers were to draw their cars from a pool immediately before the start of each race; only one event actually took place on these lines, in Cairo. The D.B. Monomill circus, originated by Bonnet in France in the mid 'fifties was a little more successful, but the basic "identical machinery" premise did not really catch on until classes for cars using engines developed from identical production units, as in Formula Ford, were evolved in the late 'sixties.

Ettore Bugatti with a Type 35 Grand Prix car at Lyons in 1924. This was the occasion of the second European Grand Prix, and marked the first race appearance of the 2-litre Type 35. Due to rear tyre trouble Bugattis could only manage seventh and eighth places.

Although born as a touring-car race in 1913, the Spanish Grand Prix was not run as a Formula event until 1927, when it was won by Benoist in a Delage. In effect this sprang from the San Sebastian Grand Prix series, the first of which was run in 1923. Two Spanish Grands Prix were run on the Pedralbes circuit in 1951 and 1954, when the event lapsed until 1967—being revived on the Jarama artificial circuit near Madrid.

The Mille Miglia was a road race in the tradition of the old European city-to-city races, run over a 1,000-mile loop from Brescia to Rome and back. The first race, in 1927, was won by Ferdinando Minoia and Giuseppe Morandi in a 2-litre O.M. at 47·80 m.p.h.; the last, in 1957, fell to Piero Taruffi in a 4·1-litre Ferrari at 94·80 m.p.h. Taruffi thus achieved his greatest ambition at the last opportunity.

The race was discontinued partly because of accidents on a course where it was impossible to arrange adequate safeguards, and in part due to the dislocation of everyday transport when the roads were closed.

The first race to be stopped by a crowd was the 1927 Grand Prix de Provence at Miramas. Bad weather delayed the programme, then Robert Benoist collided with another car at the end of his warming-up lap, and the three Talbot-Darracqs were withdrawn. The crowd was not kept informed and, infuriated by the delays and the depleted field which eventually started, rushed on to the track, stopping the race, and turned on the Talbot *équipe* to emphasise its resentment, vandalising their pit equipment.

In 1970 the first Israeli Grand Prix had to be stopped because the crowd encroached on the track, and the Mexican Grand Prix came near to cancellation for the same reason.

The first Australian Grand Prix was run in 1928 on a loose-surfaced road on Phillip Island, off Victoria, for although there were banked tracks on the mainland (such as Maroubra), road racing was proscribed. The Phillip Island handicap series lasted until 1935, and were contested by a remarkably varied selection of cars, including many pensioned-off Grand Prix machines. Winner of the first race was A. C. R. Waite driving a supercharged Austin 750 at 56·3 m.p.h.

The first Grand Prix accident involving a large number of spectators occurred at Monza in 1928, when Materassi's Talbot crashed into the crowd, killing twenty-three people.

The Monaco Grand Prix was the first "round-the-houses" Grand Prix, being run on a 1·9-mile circuit bounded by walls, passing through a tunnel and alongside a harbour, from 1929—when Bugatti driver Williams won at 49·83 m.p.h.—to 1972. The harbour leg was then extended to eliminate the controversial Gasometer hairpin, giving a lap length of 2·037 miles. The Monaco Grand Prix remains as probably the most prestigious race on the Championship calendar.

The first Czechoslovakian Grand Prix was run on the 18-mile Masaryk circuit at Brno in 1930, when the winning Bugatti was shared by H. von Morgen and Prince zu Leiningen (62·78 m.p.h.). In the following three years Louis Chiron scored a hat-trick of victories in the race, twice driving Bugattis, and in 1933 an Alfa Romeo.

First Monaco Grand Prix victor was W. Williams in 1929 driving a Type 35B Bugatti, seen here at the Virage du Tabac.

The first non-Italian driver to win the Mille Miglia was Rudolf Caracciola of Germany, driving a
7-litre Mercedes-Benz in 1931. Only one other foreigner won the "proper"
Mille Miglia in its thirty-year history—Stirling Moss in 1955 (also driving
a Mercedes-Benz, a 3-litre 300SLR)—although the closed-circuit race in
1940 was won by a German-crewed B.M.W.

The first races of front rank to be run in Africa were the Tripoli Grands Prix, which in the 1930s
were of the status of *grandes épreuves* and were in fact usually regarded as part
of the European season. Fourteen were run, and from 1933 the very fast
Mellaha circuit was used. Here in 1937 Hermann Lang won the first of his
three successive Tripoli victories; his average speed, 132·03 m.p.h., had not
then been approached at Indianapolis, and exceeded only on the Avus
track.
   The last Tripoli Grand Prix was run in 1940, before Italy entered the
Second World War; winner Giuseppe Farina averaged 128·22 m.p.h. in an
Alfa Romeo 158.

The first Grand Prix starting-grid to be determined by lap times in practice, rather than by a
draw, formed up at Monaco in 1933. Achille Varzi took pole position, and
his arch-rival Nuvolari was immediately behind him on the grid. The race
for the lead between these two turned out to be one of the great duels in
Grand Prix history; at the end Varzi gained the last Monaco victory for
Bugatti, while Nuvolari retired on the last lap when an oil-pipe split on his
Alfa Romeo.

*Achille Varzi at the wheel
of an Alfa Romeo in 1934.*

The most notorious instance of rigging in front-line racing arose out of the State lottery run in
conjunction with the Tripoli Grand Prix held in 1933. According to Piero
Taruffi, one of the drivers marginally concerned, Varzi, Nuvolari and
Borzacchini came to a prize-splitting agreement with the ticket-holders who
had "drawn" them, and with other drivers to ensure that the "right" man
won. After this the lottery system was changed, and ticket numbers allotted
to drivers only at the last minute, on the starting-line.

The South African Grand Prix was first run in 1934, the post-war revival came in 1960, and since
1961 it has been run to the current Formula 1. In 1967 the Rhodesian John
Love came close to being the first driver from Southern Africa to win a
Championship Grand Prix—losing the lead when he refuelled seven laps
before the end, eventually finishing second behind Pedro Rodriguez. In
1975 Jody Scheckter became the first South African to win his home round
in the World Championship.

The first airfield road races appear to have been run at Mines Field in California in 1934. Together with a 150-mile race on a 1½-mile circuit incorporating most of the established Legion Ascot oval track in the same year and the 1933 Elgin Race (a one-year revival of the 1910–20 series), this was virtually the only road race of substance in the U.S.A. between the 1920 Elgin event and the 1936–37 races on the Roosevelt "Mickey Mouse" circuit.

The first Swiss Grand Prix was run on the Bremgarten circuit just outside Berne in 1934, and won by Hans Stuck in an Auto Union at 87·21 m.p.h. A Swiss voiturette Grand Prix, held in 1924, was won by K. Lee Guinness (Talbot-Darracq). After the Le Mans disaster of 1955 all racing was banned in Switzerland, but the "Swiss Grand Prix" was revived at the Dijon-Prenois circuit in France in 1975, being won by Swiss driver Clay Regazzoni in a Ferrari.

The first South American races to attract top-level European entrants were run on the Brazilian São Paulo and Gavea (Rio de Janeiro) circuits in the mid 'thirties. Carlo Mario Pintacuda drove his Alfa Romeo to victory at the former circuit in 1936, at the latter in 1937 and 1938; in the 1937 Rio de Janeiro Grand Prix he beat Stuck's Auto Union—a rare achievement in that period of German domination.

The G. Vanderbilt Cup races at Roosevelt Field in 1936–37 brought main-line European teams to the United States for the first time since the early 'twenties, when American and European racing had gone their separate ways. The 1936 race was won by Tazio Nuvolari in an Alfa Romeo at 65·99 m.p.h., the 1937 event was won by Bernd Rosemeyer in an Auto Union at 82·56 m.p.h. Highest-placed American driver in these races was Rex Mays, third with an Alfa Romeo in 1937.

The Donington Grands Prix of 1935–38 effectively marked the return of Grand Prix racing to Britain, particularly the 1937–38 races which were contested by the then-supreme German teams. In both Auto Union defeated Mercedes-Benz, Rosemeyer winning at 82·85 m.p.h. in 1937, and Nuvolari at 80·49 m.p.h. in 1938. The circuit suffered from military use, and abuse, during the Second World War, but during the early 1970s local enthusiast Tom Wheatcroft began rebuilding it, and after a long legal battle obtained permission to reopen it for racing in 1976. By that time his superb racing-car museum at the circuit was well established.

The only pre-war lap record to stand unbroken on a circuit virtually unchanged, through post-war races of equivalent calibre, was set at Berne in the 1936 Swiss Grand Prix by Bernd Rosemeyer in an Auto Union (2 minutes 34.5 seconds, 105·40 m.p.h.). This was improved on in practice by Caracciola in 1937 (107·14 m.p.h.) and Lang in 1939 (106·23 m.p.h.); the fastest lap in the last Swiss Grand Prix, in 1954, was 101·9 m.p.h., achieved by Fangio.

The Crystal Palace circuit in south London was the only British track controlled by a local authority, and until Donington was rebuilt (above) was the only one to be used before and after the Second World War. The original 2-mile course was opened in 1937, and racing was reintroduced on a shorter 1·39-mile layout in 1953. Despite its unforgiving nature and "tightness" the lap record was raised to over 100 m.p.h. (100·89 m.p.h.) by Rindt and Stewart in a 1970 Formula 2 race. The circuit was closed in 1972.

The Mercedes-Benz W125 cars of Manfred von Brauchitsch and Rudi Caracciola during the 1937 Monaco Grand Prix.

The only important Formula race to be run in Eire was the 1938 Cork Grand Prix, won by René Dreyfus in a Delahaye at 92·5 m.p.h.

The one and only Yugoslav Grand Prix was run at Belgrade on 3rd September 1939, six hours after Britain entered the Second World War, and won by Nuvolari in an Auto Union at 81·21 m.p.h.

The longest road race ever staged regularly was the Gran Premio del Norte in South America, held during and after the Second World War, from Buenos Aires to Lima *and back*, over 5,920 miles. Like other ultra-long-distance *turismo carretera* events it was run in stages, over roads which would sometimes seem hardly feasible as special stages in modern rallies. Over the first of these in 1940 Fangio averaged 80·5 m.p.h. for the 850 miles (his overall winning speed in a Chevrolet was 53·6 m.p.h.). Oscar Galvez won the last of these races in 1947.

The last major races in Europe before total war involvement were the 1940 Mille Miglia, run over nine laps of a 100-mile Brescia–Cremona–Brescia circuit and won by Huschke von Hanstein and Walter Baumer in a 2-litre B.M.W. at 103·60 m.p.h., the Targa Florio, run on the Favorita circuit at Palermo and won by Luigi Villoresi in a 1·5-litre Maserati at 88·41 m.p.h. and the Tripoli Grand Prix at Mellaha, won by Farina in an Alfa Romeo 158.

The first post-war race meeting in Europe took place in the Bois de Boulogne, Paris, on 9th September 1945. Winner of the main race was Jean-Pierre Wimille, driving a Bugatti.

The first post-war race in Britain was the 1946 Ulster Trophy, run at Ballyclare and won by Bira, driving an E.R.A., at 78·47 m.p.h. over 50 miles.

The first British circuit to be created on a military airfield after the Second World War was Gransden Lodge, when a race-meeting was organised in June 1946. This circuit was short-lived, but two years later Goodwood and Silverstone were opened; Goodwood was closed in 1966, but Silverstone now has the longest unbroken history of any British circuit.

The Swedish Winter Grand Prix held at Rommehed in 1947 was dominated by E.R.A.s (Parnell, Brooke, Abecassis)—their rival teams' equipment was ice-locked in a ship. When it was rerun a week later on the frozen Lake Vallentuna, Parnell once again won in an E.R.A. at 68·16 m.p.h.

The first race for the 500-c.c. cars which were to become the basis of the first international Formula 3 in 1950 was run at Gransden Lodge in July 1947. Winner was Eric Brandon, driving a Cooper—a foretaste of that marque's coming domination of the class.

The first Formula 2 as such was introduced in 1948, for cars with engines up to 2 litres (unsupercharged) or 500 c.c. (supercharged); it ran until 1953, and during its last two years the World Championship Grand Prix races were run under its rules. A 1½-litre Formula 2 was introduced in 1957, running until 1960, when to all intents and purposes it became the Grand Prix formula. The next Formula 2, for 1,000-c.c. unsupercharged racing cars, came into effect in 1964, and was directly succeeded by the 1,600 c.c. Formula 2 in 1967. In 1972 maximum capacity was raised to 2 litres for production-based engines, and this limit applied when "pure" racing engines were again permitted from 1976.

Seaside beaches have been used for racing as well as record-breaking, although car-against-car competitions on them have never been as important as speed attempts. However, out of the Daytona combined beach and road circuit in 1947 came NASCAR (National Association for Stock Car Racing), now perhaps the most important organisation in this field, and eventually the Daytona International Speedway.

First of the "grandes épreuves" to be revived after the Second World War were the Swiss, Belgian, Italian and French Grands Prix in 1947. The first three were won by Alfa Romeo, at the start of their great period of domination with the 158, and the French event fell to Chiron's Talbot in the absence of the Italian team.

Courses for novice competition drivers were organised annually by the Automobile Club de Suisse for several years from 1948, usually at Monza.

The British Grand Prix, or R.A.C. Grand Prix, was revived in 1948 at Silverstone, over a complex "figure 8" 3·67-mile circuit of runways and perimeter tracks. Winner of the 239-mile race was Luigi Villoresi, driving a Maserati, at 72·28 m.p.h.

After the Second World War road racing was reborn in America on the 6·6-mile Watkins Glen circuit in October 1948. This circuit was devised by Cameron Argetsinger, the infant S.C.C.A. and the local Chamber of Commerce, and was a true road circuit, passing through town streets (and over a level-crossing—the New York Central stopped the trains during racing!). Both races at the opening meeting were won by Frank Griswold in an Alfa Romeo, the 52-mile Grand Prix at 63·7 m.p.h. An accident involving spectators led to the abandoning of the first Watkins Glen circuit; the present artificial road circuit dates from 1956.

Juan-Manuel Fangio at the wheel of the 2½ litre Maserati 250F (No. 2529) during the 1957 French Grand Prix at Rouen. This year was a vintage year for Maserati but was the last in which the factory supported a works team. Fangio had won four Grands Prix during the season.

The longest road race ever held—apart from the early intercontinental events, which were not visible *races*—was the 1948 "La Caracas", from Buenos Aires to Caracas, over almost 6,000 miles. Official winner was Domingo Marimon, driving a Chevrolet. Popular *turismo carretera* driver Oscar Galvez led by 2½ hours at the start of the last stage, but his engine failed some 150 miles from the finish—yet he was classified third, for an enthusiastic follower pushed his Ford, bumper to bumper, to within sight of the end! Competitors then moved on to Lima, for the start of another 3,200-mile race back across the Andes to Buenos Aires and Galvez won this fairly and squarely.

In the first post-war Le Mans 24-Hour Race, in 1949, Ferrari gained the first of nine victories in the event, which included an unbroken six-race sequence in 1960–65. Bentley and Jaguar have each won the "Vingt Quatre Heures" five times. Bentley won four successive Le Mans races (1927–30), as did Alfa Romeo (1931–34) and Ford (1966–69).

The first "road race" car meeting in England was held at Donington Park, some 10 miles from Derby and 125 miles north of London, on 25th March 1933. English law does not permit racing on public roads, but the Donington course is laid out in private parkland. The original lap length was 2¼ miles, subsequently lengthened to 3·13 miles for the Grands Prix of 1937 and 1938. Donington Park was closed on the outbreak of war in 1939, the Army occupying it as a military transport depot until 1956. Tom Wheatcroft of Leicester acquired the site in 1971, spending the next few years and many thousands of pounds in building a museum for historic racing cars and reconstructing the circuit for car and motorcycle racing.

The new lap length is 1·967 miles (3·15 km.), and the first Donington car race meeting for thirty-eight years took place on 27th March 1977. Since then Formula 1, 2, 3 and other racing class events have been run on this well equipped and thoroughly modern circuit.

The longest-established non-Championship Formula 1 race was the Silverstone International Trophy, first run in 1949 (won by Alberto Ascari in a Ferrari at 89·58 m.p.h.) but discontinued as a 'main-line' F.1. race after the 1978 event.

Holland's first car-racing circuit was established at Zandvoort just before the Second World War, and the present artificial circuit was partly built during the war, when the local authorities contrived to arrange that roads built to serve coastal defences might later serve a more useful purpose. The first race meeting on this circuit was organised by the British Racing Drivers' Club in 1948; the principal event, the Zandvoort Grand Prix, was won by Prince Birabongse (Bira), in a Maserati at 73·25 m.p.h.

The first Dutch Grand Prix, sometimes referred to as the "Prijs van Zandvoort", was run in 1949, and won by Luigi Villoresi in a Ferrari at 77·12 m.p.h.

Motorcycle races were run on a grass track at Brands Hatch as long ago as 1928; a hard-surfaced 1-mile car circuit was opened in 1950, and extended to form the present 1·24-mile Club circuit in 1954. An extension to give a lap of 2·69 miles was opened in 1960, to form the Grand Prix circuit. During the years that the B.O.A.C./British Airways-sponsored sports-car race was run, it was the only British venue for World Championship events in Grand Prix and sports-car classes.

The first American cars to race in a European classic after the Second World War were two Cadillacs, a saloon and an open-cockpit special, run in the 1950 Le Mans 24-Hour Race by Briggs Cunningham (they finished tenth and eleventh).

The first international Formula 3, for cars with 500-c.c. unsupercharged engines, was in force from 1950 until 1960. In effect it was superseded by Formula Junior for 1,000-c.c. or 1,100-c.c. unsupercharged cars (minimum weights of 360 kg. (793 lb.), and 400 kg. (882 lb.), respectively applying), with components derived from homologated production cars. This was succeeded by a new 1,000-c.c. Formula 3 in 1964, which gave way to a 1,600-c.c. Formula 3 in 1971. This relies largely on throttling the supply of engine air to restrict engine b.h.p., and thus car performance. With a similar restriction the capacity limit was raised to 2 litres from 1974.

The first Carrera Panamericana was run in 1950 over 2,178 miles and won by Hershel McGriff driving an Oldsmobile at 77·43 m.p.h. The next four events, over a 1,934-mile course, attracted top-line European teams to open-road point-to-point racing for the first time in decades. The 1951 and 1954 races fell to Ferrari, the 1952 and 1953 events to Mercedes-Benz and Lancia respectively. Umberto Maglioli's winning speed in 1954 was 107·93 m.p.h.

The World Championship remained undecided to the final round in 1950 (the Italian GP, when Farina took the title), 1951 (the Spanish GP, when Fangio won), 1956 (Italian GP, Fangio), 1958 (Moroccan GP, Hawthorn), 1959 (U.S. GP, Brabham), 1962 (South African GP, Graham Hill), 1964 (Mexican GP, Surtees), 1967 (Mexican GP, Hulme), 1968 (Mexican GP, Graham Hill), 1974 (U.S. GP, Fittipaldi) and 1976 (Japanese GP, Hunt).

Twenty-two races have been World Championship qualifying events, the Grands Prix of Argentina, Austria, Belgium, Brazil, Britain, Canada, France, Germany, Holland, Italy, Japan, Mexico, Monaco, Morocco, Pescara, Portugal, South Africa, Spain, Sweden, Switzerland and the U.S. GPs East and West. Of these, only the British and Italian races have counted towards the Championship without a break since it was instituted in 1950.

For several years the Indianapolis 500 Miles Race was ranked among the World Championship races, although it was not run to the then-ruling Formula 1 regulations and, of course, was quite outside the character of the road races in the series. The introduction of the United States Grands Prix removed the last possible reason for the perpetuation of this anomaly.

The only major British Formula race to be abandoned because of bad weather was the 1951 International Trophy at Silverstone, when a violent thunderstorm caused it to be cut short at six laps. In the 1975 British Grand Prix at the same circuit most drivers found their cars uncontrollable on "dry" tyres in a sudden downpour, and after a sequence of crashes the race was prematurely ended by officials. The 1978 International Trophy was run in a downpour, bringing a result generally considered a freak, for "Keke" Rosberg won in a Theodore, a car scarcely competitive in normal conditions.

The first New Zealand Grand Prix was a 204-mile *formule libre* race at Ardmore in 1954, won by Stan Jones in a Maybach Special at 72·5 m.p.h.

The first World Championship events to be run in South America were the Argentine Grand Prix first run in 1953 and won by Alberto Ascari, driving a Ferrari, and the Buenos Aires 1,000-km. sports-car race, first run in 1954 and won by the Ferrari shared by Giuseppe Farina and Umberto Maglioli. The Brazilian Grand Prix at Interlagos joined the list in 1973.

In the history of the Monaco Grand Prix only two drivers have retired for the reason anticipated since the race was first run in 1929—crashing into the harbour, Alberto Ascari in 1955 and Paul Hawkins in 1965; neither was seriously injured, and neither needed the help of the frogmen who stand by in boats during every race.

The worst accident in the history of racing occurred towards the end of the third hour of the 1955 Le Mans 24-Hour Race, when a Mercedes-Benz 300SLR driven by Pierre Levegh (Bouillon's racing pseudonym) collided with an Austin-Healey driven by Lance Macklin, without immediate damage to either car. But the Mercedes was deflected off its course, and what might have been an incident became tragedy when it bounced over a "safety" bank and into a crowded public enclosure opposite the end of the pits. Levegh and eighty-three spectators were killed.

The start of the 1955 Monaco Grand Prix; Fangio (Mercedes-Benz), Ascari (Lancia) and Moss (Mercedes-Benz) battle to lead at the first bend. Later in this race Ascari failed to negotiate the chicane and accompanied his car into the waters of the harbour.

Mike Hawthorn (Jaguar) leading Fangio (Mercedes-Benz) at White House Corner during the early stages of the ill-starred Vingt-Quatre Heures du Mans of 1955.

The first Swedish Grand Prix counting as a World Championship round was held at Anderstorp in 1973. It was won by Denny Hulme with a McLaren at 102·65 m.p.h.

The first road race of any account for stock sedans to be run on an American road circuit was a 250-mile NASCAR event at Elkhart Lake in 1956, won by Mercury driver Tim Flock. The now-important NASCAR series did not get under way until 1964, when Dan Gurney drove a Ford to win the Motor Trend 500 Miles at Riverside (the first of Gurney's four consecutive victories in this event). In 1966 the complementary SCCA Trans-Am Championship for saloons up to 5 litres was inaugurated.

The only event which was not a national Grand Prix ever to count as a World Championship qualifying round was the 1957 Pescara Grand Prix, elevated to this status as there were only six other Championship races (apart from the Indianapolis 500 Miles, then ranked in the series). It was won by Stirling Moss in a Vanwall at 95·52 m.p.h., the highest speed ever achieved on the historic Pescara circuit (the Pescara Grand Prix was in direct line of succession from the pre-war Acerbo Cup, first run in 1924 when Enzo Ferrari drove an Alfa Romeo to win).

The 1976 Championship calendar was the first to actually schedule two qualifying rounds in one country, at Long Beach and Watkins Glen in the U.S.A.

The first World Championship win for a rear-engined car came in the 1958 Argentine Grand Prix, won by Stirling Moss in R. R. C. Walker's 1·9-litre Cooper Climax at 83·56 m.p.h.

The first post-war European Grand Prix win for a rear-engined car came in the 1958 Monaco Grand Prix, won by Maurice Trintignant in R. R. C. Walker's Cooper Climax at 67·98 m.p.h.

The first of the post-war U.S. Grands Prix was run as a sports-car event at Riverside in 1958, and in the following year was established as a Formula 1 race at Sebring—the winner, Bruce McLaren in a Cooper Climax at 98·83 m.p.h. In 1960 it was run at Riverside, since then consistently at Watkins Glen, where it is now known as the U.S. Grand Prix East to differentiate from the more recent U.S. Grand Prix West at Long Beach, California.

The only World Championship Grand Prix in which no drivers retired, and none made pit-stops, was the 1961 Dutch Grand Prix—fifteen cars started and fifteen finished, eight on the same lap as the winner, Wolfgang von Trips in a Ferrari.

The first international race in Canada, at the Mosport opening meeting, was the 1961 Players' 200 Miles Race for sports cars, won by Stirling Moss in a Lotus at 86.74 m.p.h.

The first Canadian Grands Prix were sports-car races at Mosport, Ryan winning the first in 1961. The first to be run as a Formula 1 race was at Mosport in 1967, won by Jack Brabham in a Repco-Brabham at 82.65 m.p.h. The Canadian Grand Prix was the first World Championship event to incorporate the name of a commercial sponsor, Players, in its title.

A short-lived Intercontinental Formula was devised for 1961, largely in an attempt to extend the life of the 2.5-litre Grand Prix formula to satisfy British interests, for the British establishment had reacted strongly—and as it turned out misguidedly—against the 1½-litre Grand Prix Formula. The Intercontinental Formula was for single-seaters, with unsupercharged engine of between 2 and 3 litres.

The Tasman series in New Zealand and Australia was originated in 1962, with regulations virtually carried over from the closing years of the 2.5-litre Formula 1, and for some time at least usefully extended the active life of machinery built for Grand Prix racing. It was later run for F5000 cars, but by the mid-seventies had lost virtually all international significance.

The first—and so far only—major sports-car race to be won by a car not at the time of finishing powered by an internal-combustion engine was the 1962 Daytona 3-Hour Race. Just before the end Dan Gurney was leading by several laps in his Lotus 19, when the engine failed; he stopped just short of the line, and as soon as the flag was put out, coaxed his car to finish on the starter.

Hazards of the confined Monaco Grand Prix. A first-lap crash during the 1961 race in which Richie Ginther (B.R.M. No. 8) had a wheel torn off, and the cars of Maurice Trintignant and Innes Ireland were also involved. The B.R.M.'s wheel hurtled off the track, killing a race official.

Formula Vee was the first class for cars built round standard one-make components to gain major international acceptance. Based on Volkswagen components, it came into being in Florida in 1962, by 1965 had spread to Europe, and although later overshadowed by Formula Ford in some countries has had a longer active international life than any other "poor man's racing" class. While Formula Ford continued to flourish through the 1970s, Formula Vee lost favour to Formula Super Vee, which admitted cars powered by Volkswagen water-cooled engines and designed on "proper" racing-car lines (i.e. without insisting on the standard suspension components which had given early Vees rather odd characteristics). In parallel with Formula Super Vee, Formula Ford 2000 became well established by the late 1970s.

The face of post-war European touring-car racing was changed from the moment that Dan Gurney in a Ford Galaxie walked away from the hitherto all-conquering Jaguars in a race at Silverstone in 1962. Following this example, the Willment team raced ex-works Monte Carlo Rally Ford Galaxies on British circuits in 1963, enjoying overwhelming success.

The first Mexican Grand Prix was run at Mexico City in 1962, and won by Jim Clark in a Lotus-Climax at 91·31 m.p.h. This circuit is the highest ever used for Championship Grands Prix, at 7,300 feet above sea-level.

The first international road race in Japan was run on the Suzuka circuit in May 1963, and won by Peter Warr, driving a Lotus 23.

The "dummy grid" system of starting Grands Prix was tried in 1963, and was generally used from 1964. Under this system, cars took up their positions short of the actual starting-points, engines were started and nominally 30 seconds before the start, fields moved forward to their "proper" grid places stretching back from the starting-line. This system in turn was superseded by a pace lap arrangement, whereby after individual warm-up laps the entire field completes a further lap, theoretically in grid order and certainly to re-form in grid order on the grid. As soon as this has assembled, a 10-seconds sign is shown, but in practice inexperienced starters have sometimes released a field before all cars have stopped after the pace lap. At Monza in 1978 this error led to a tragic chain of events.

The first victory for a car powered by an American engine in an F.I.A. Constructors' G.T. Championship event came in the 1963 Bridgehampton Double 500, when Gurney won in a Ford-powered Shelby A.C. Cobra at 91·42 m.p.h.

The first Austrian Grand Prix was run at the Zeltweg Airfield circuit in 1963, and won by Jack Brabham, driving a Brabham-Climax, at 96·34 m.p.h. In the following year it gained Championship status and was won by Lorenzo Bandini driving a Ferrari. However, the circuit was quite inadequate for a race of this status, and the Austrian Grand Prix was dropped from the Championship calendar until 1970, when it was revived at the Osterreichring and won by Jacky Ickx in a Ferrari at 129·27 m.p.h.

In winning the 1963 World Championship Jim Clark scored more than twice as many total points as the runners-up (73 total and 54 scoring points respectively, compared with Ginther's 34 and 29, and Hill's 31 and 29).

French racing fortunes went into a sharp decline after Jean Behra won the 1952 Grand Prix de France at Rheims in a Gordini, and did not recover until the Matra programme got under way in the mid 'sixties. Basically a missile firm, Matra acquired René Bonnet's modest specialist car company in 1964, and built their first Formula 3 cars in 1965, winning at Rheims. Matra Grand Prix cars appeared in 1968, and in the Dutch Grand Prix Jackie Stewart drove one to gain the first French car victory in a *grand épreuve* since the first postwar formula—albeit the Matra MS80 was Ford-powered and run by Ken Tyrrell's British-based team. Matra withdrew from Formula 1 after 1969 in favour of prototype sports-car racing, winning Le Mans three years running in 1972, 1973 and 1974, and taking the Championship title in 1973 and 1974. They then withdrew from competition, but their twelve-cylinder engine was used in the 1976 Ligier, another French Formula 1 car, from 1976 to 1978.

The first American car to win a major International sports-car race was a 5·4-litre Chrysler V-eight-engined Cunningham with which John Fitch and Phil Walters took first place in the 1953 Sebring 12-Hours Race in Florida, U.S.A.

The first Championship Grand Prix to be won by a Japanese car was the 1965 Mexican Grand Prix, won by Richie Ginther in a Honda at 94·26 m.p.h.

The first American team to win an F.I.A. championship was Carroll Shelby's racing Ford-engined A.C. (i.e. Anglo-American) Cobras, in the GT category in 1965.

The first American sports car to win a major European sports-car race was a Chaparral 2D, driven by Phil Hill and Jo Bonnier in the 1966 Nürburgring 1,000 Kilometres at 89·4 m.p.h. This was also the first major race victory for a car with automatic transmission.

The first American car to win the Le Mans 24-Hour Race was a Ford Mark 2, in which Chris Amon and Bruce McLaren covered 3,009·5 miles at 129·91 m.p.h. in 1966. A sister car driven by Ken Miles and Denny Hulme covered virtually the same distance, thus sharing the honour of being the first to cover more than 3,000 miles in this 24-hour classic.

The first races to count as scoring events in the U.S.A.C. National Championship to be run outside North America were on road circuits at Silverstone and Brands Hatch in the Autumn of 1978, being won by A. J. Foyt (Coyote) and Rick Mears (Penske), respectively. At Silverstone, Ongais set an outright lap record at 134·55 m.p.h. which stood until the 1979 British Grand Prix.

The first Canadian-American Challenge Cup series of races for sports-racing cars was run in the Autumn of 1966. In the first five seasons there were thirty-nine CanAm races; McLaren cars won thirty-one of these, Lolas six, and single races fell to a Chaparral and a Porsche. Porsche ended McLaren's CanAm reign in 1972 with open Group 7 derivatives of their flat-12 Type 917. With turbo-supercharged engines of 5, then 5·4 litres, the latter producing over 1,000 h.p., these cars crushed all opposition and led to abandonment of the original concept of a sports-car CanAm series for an uncertain F5000 period. A "sports-car" revival came in 1977, although many contestants used F5000 cars fitted with full-width bodywork.

*Denny Hulme driving a
McLaren M8D car in a
1970 CanAm race.*

First—and so far only—European classic to be won by a Japanese car was the 1967 Italian Grand Prix, won by John Surtees in a Honda at 140·51 m.p.h.

During the 'sixties interest in off-the-road racing steadily grew, particularly out of the dune buggy movement, and the Baja 1,000 became the longest extant point-to-point race. This rough-territory event is run in the arid peninsula of Baja, California over courses of around 800 miles, and is dominated by off-the-road specials, such as Volkswagen-based single-seaters.

The first major single-seater race in Japan was the 1966 Fuji 200, where a U.S.A.C.-type field raced on a "road" circuit—at least, it had right and left turns—of 2·68 miles. Winner was Jackie Stewart, driving a Lola-Ford, at 103·64 m.p.h. A Japanese Grand Prix was the last round in the World Championship in 1976 and 1977, both races being run on the Fuji circuit; respective winners were Mario Andretti and James Hunt.

The British round in the Sports-car Championship was originally the Tourist Trophy, at Dundrod and Goodwood. In 1967 the B.O.A.C. 500 (a 6-hour race despite its title) was introduced as the British round in the Championship, at Brands Hatch, and won by a Chaparral 2F driven by Phil Hill and Mike Spence at 93·08 m.p.h. In 1970 the title was changed to B.O.A.C. 1,000 and to British Airways 1,000 km. in 1974. That event was then abandoned, and in 1976 the Silverstone 6-Hours Race became the British round in the World Championship for Makes, as the series had by then been retitled.

Closest ever finish in the Le Mans 24-Hour Race came in 1969, when a Ford GT40 driven by Jacky Ickx and a Porsche 908 driven by Hans Herrmann changed places on the last lap, the Ford winning by roughly 100 yards.

The first French marque to win the Formula Constructors' Championship was Matra, whose Ford-powered cars, entrusted to Ken Tyrrell's team, took the 1969 Championship. The first Grand Prix victory for a Matra-Ford had been gained by Jackie Stewart in the 1968 Dutch Grand Prix; in that race a Matra powered by a Matra V-twelve was second, the best placing for a "pure" Matra Formula 1 car until Chris Amon won the 1971 non-Championship Argentine Grand Prix. A Matra-powered Ligier won the 1977 Grand Prix of Sweden.

The only race ever to come near to losing World Championship status because of organisational deficiencies is the Mexican Grand Prix, after the authorities had completely failed to control the crowd at the 1970 Race. Only in the following Spring were its organisers' assurances of "good behaviour" accepted and the status of the event reinstated. Anti-climax followed, for in fact the 1971 race was cancelled, and the event has not been run since then.

The highest circuit at which Formula races have been run is at Bogotá, 8,000 feet above sea-level, where two Formula 2 events, Colombia's first European-style races, were run in 1971—the first being won by Siffert, the second by Rollinson.

The first "grande épreuve" to incorporate the name of a sponsor in its title was the British Grand Prix, which in 1971 was sponsored by the International Wool Secretariat, so that "Woolmark" was included in its title.

The fastest lap ever achieved on a true road circuit was set by Henri Pescarolo driving a V12 Matra in the 1973 Spa 1,000-kilometre Race. He lapped the Belgian circuit (8 miles 1,340 yards) at an average speed of 163·085 m.p.h.

"Round the houses" or street circuits were once common, but had become very rare by the 1970s, when the Monaco circuit was almost unique—certainly in terms of prestige. Surprisingly, a new street circuit came into use in 1975, at Long Beach, California. An inaugural race, to qualify the organisers to run a World Championship event, was run for F5000 cars, and won by Brian Redman driving a Lola. In 1976 the first U.S. Grand Prix West, qualifying for the World Championship, was staged on the 2·02-mile circuit, Clay Regazzoni (Ferrari) winning at 85·57 m.p.h. Master-minded by expatriate Britisher Chris Pook, the promotion of this race over public roads in a Californian seaside resort was a considerable feat. The course is bumpy and lacks the glamour and tradition of Monaco, but passing is easier and the Long Beach barrier and safety-fence systems have proved effective.

The regulations to which Grands Prix are run have been laid down by the Commission Sportive Internationale (C.S.I.) since its creation in 1922, and under the International Sporting Code, which first came into force in 1926, the C.S.I. gradually extended its control towards achieving uniform regulations covering all classes. This was not finally achieved until after the Second World War.

A works-entered P4 Ferrari in the 1967 B.O.A.C. 500 at Brands Hatch. Jackie Stewart at the wheel.

In 1966 all competition cars were defined in the groups of the famous "Appendix J" (to the Code):

1. Series production touring cars.
2. Touring cars.
3. Grand touring cars.
4. Sports cars.
5. Special touring cars.
6. Prototype sports cars.
7. Two-seater racing cars (i.e. sports-racing cars).
8. Cars defined under any of the racing formulae (1, 2 and 3).
9. *Formule libre* racing cars.

The distinctions between the saloons of Groups 1 and 2 were in numbers produced and in the degree of modification permitted; for Group 4 sports cars a minimum production of fifty cars was required, whereas a prototype sports car (Group 6) could be a one-off (subsequent revision of groupings meant that these became Groups 5 and 6 respectively). Appendix J also lays down very detailed requirements—"articles" —covering car components. In theory these groups should provide clear-cut definitions; in practice there are not infrequent doubts whether cars meet the regulations—for example, in the numbers built to qualify for homologation—while in application the edges tend to become blurred, hence the variations between Group 1 as applied in most European countries and Britain, which has given rise to "Group 1½" in British saloon-car racing.

Grand Prix regulations—formulae—have been laid down since the first national event to carry the title, the French Grand Prix, was run in 1906. These have not always been acceptable to race organisers or entrants, particularly in the late 'twenties and early 'thirties (for example, in 1930 the Belgian Grand Prix was the only race run to the ruling formula). Sometimes the formula has not worked as the C.S.I. intended, most notoriously perhaps the 750-kg. maximum weight formula which came into force in 1934 and was expected to restrain Grand Prix speeds at a fairly constant level, but utterly failed in this because German constructors applied to Grand Prix car design and construction unprecedented technological resources, producing cars which could hardly have been foreseen when the formula was drawn up.

Since 1938 the principal restriction has always been the most sensible one, on engine capacities; other requirements have in effect been subsidiary to this, for example on race distance or duration, car weights and other aspects such as the type of fuel. Since 1961 increasing attention has been paid to safety aspects, in that year the formula for the first time stipulating that cars should be fitted with roll-over bars and dual braking systems, and that oil could not be taken on during a race (this in an attempt to ensure oil-tight engines and gearboxes, to minimise spillage of oil on tracks). Within their spans, formulae have been altered in detail, for example in the ban on "exotic" fuels in 1958 (when "commercial" petrol became obligatory), and in restricting the number of engine cylinders to twelve after the 3-litre formula introduced in 1966 had run five years.

Although secondary classes were defined between the world wars, the term "Formula" was applied to them only after the Second World War, the first Formula 2 coming into effect in 1948, the first Formula 3 in 1950. Exceptionally, World Championship races were run to Formula 2 regulations in 1952–53, as race organisers felt that there would be insufficient competitive Formula 1 cars to make up good fields.

The principal regulations governing Grands Prix since 1906 have been:

1906: Maximum car weight, 1,000 kg. (2,204 lb.).

1907: Maximum fuel allowance, 231 litres (equivalent to 9·4 m.p.g.).

1908: Minimum weight, 1,100 kg. (2,425 lb.); cylinder bores restricted to 155 mm. (four-cylinder engines) or 127 mm. (six-cylinder engines).

1912: Maximum body width of car, 175 cm. (69 inches).

1913: Weight limits, 800–1,100 kg. (1,763–2,425 lb.), without fuel. Fuel allowance 20 litres per 100 km. (equivalent to 14·12 m.p.g.).

1914: Maximum engine capacity, 4·5 litres; weight 1,100 kg. (2,425 lb.).

1921: Capacity limit, 3 litres; minimum weight, 800 kg. (1,763 lb.).

1922–25: Capacity limit, 2 litres; minimum weight, 650 kg. (1,433 lb.). Riding mechanic not required after 1924.

1926–27: Capacity limit, 1·5 litres; minimum weight, 700 kg. (1,543 lb.).

1928: Weights between 550 and 750 kg.

1929–30: Minimum weight, 900 kg. (1,980 lb.); fuel and oil allowance, 14 kg. per 100 km. (approximating to 14·5 m.p.g.).

1931: Minimum race duration, 10 hours.

1932: Race duration, 5–10 hours, single-seater bodies permitted.

1933: Minimum race distance, 500 km. (312 miles).

1934–37: Maximum weight, 750 kg. (1,653 lb.).

1938–39: Maximum engine capacities, 3 litres (supercharged), and 4·5 litres (unsupercharged). Minimum weight of cars with engines to upper capacity limits, 850 kg. (1,874 lb.).

1948–51: Maximum engine capacities, 1·5 litres (supercharged), and 4·5 litres (unsupercharged).

1952–53 Maximum engine capacities, 500 c.c. (supercharged) and 2 litres (unsupercharged).

1954–60: Maximum engine capacities, 750 c.c. (supercharged), and 2·5 litres (unsupercharged).

1961–65: Maximum engine capacity, 1·5 litres (minimum 1·3 litres); minimum weight, 450 kg. (990 lb).

1966–date: Maximum engine capacity, 3 litres (unsupercharged), and 1·5 litres (supercharged). Minimum weight, 500 kg. (1,102 lb.). During the long life of this Formula, the basic regulations have been changed in respect of weight (minimum increased to 575 kg—1,265 lb.) and various subsidiary rules have been introduced, to ban excessive aerofoil devices (this was aimed at "wings") and later moveable aerofoils (which led to controversy about "skirts" and the Brabham BT46 "fan car") as well as high airboxes, to debar engines with more than twelve cylinders, and to improve car safety by excluding space frames and requiring structural systems aimed at driver protection, fire-fighting systems, and fuel tanks.

Stirling Moss in the winning Vanwall after crossing the finishing line of the 1957 British Grand Prix at Aintree. It was the first Grande Epreuve *victory of a British car and driver combination since 1924.*

Part Two, THE CARS

Pneumatic tyres were used in the very first race (Paris-Bordeaux-Paris, 1895) by André Michelin on his Peugeot *l'Eclair*. Tyre troubles meant that he was the last competitor to reach Bordeaux, and got only as far as Orleans on the return leg before exceeding the 100-hour limit for the race. But by 1897 most racing cars were fitted with pneumatic tyres.

The first car with pneumatic tyres to win a motor race was Charles Duryea's Duryea, first home in the Chicago *Times-Herald*'s race from Chicago to Waukegan, held in November 1895.

The first extensive use of aluminium in racing-car construction came in 1897, when the Panhard-Levassor which won the Paris-Dieppe Race had its gearbox housing, carburettor, crankcase and lubricators made of this useful light metal.

The only road race victory by a steam-powered vehicle came in 1897 when the Comte de Chasseloup-Laubat won the 149-mile Marseilles-Nice-La Turbie event in a De Dion at 19·2 m.p.h.

"Streamlining" came early, although its value at the relatively low racing speeds, and mounted above cumbersome running gear, must have been doubtful. In the 1897 Paris-Trouville Race, Charron drove a Panhard with a "wind-cutting" nose; Bollée *torpilleurs*, raced in 1899, had similar noses—and tails—while a Vallée, which ran in the 1899 Tour de France, was distinguished by a "wedge" nose.

The first racing car to use shock-absorbers was a Mors in 1899, employing what were then called "spring checks" of friction type.

The first racing cars to have independent front suspension were Bollées in 1899. These cars also had underslung frames and rear-mounted air-cooled engines. Decauville "Voiturelles", raced in the same year, also had independent front suspension.

The name "Maserati" first appeared in competition motoring in 1899, when Carlo, eldest of the six brothers, won the motorcycle class in the Criterium Brescia-Orzinovi-Brescia on a Carcano.

The name "Bugatti" also appeared in motoring competitions in the same year, when Ettore Bugatti scored the first of several successes on Prinetti and Stucchi motor tricycles, in the Verona-Brescia-Verona Race (at 26·53 m.p.h.).

The first British car to race in a front-line continental race was a Napier, driven by S. F. Edge in the 1900 Paris-Toulouse-Paris Race (but he retired).

The first American car to compete in a European race was a single-cylinder Winton, which Alexander Winton drove as the American representative in the first Gordon Bennett Trophy Race in 1900. It suffered sundry minor problems, and eventually retired with a broken wheel.

New standards were set by the 1901 "35" Mercedes, which Wilhelm Werner drove to victory in the Nice-Salon-Nice Race. Its pressed-steel frame dated the common wooden and armoured wood chassis, and its positive gate gear-change did much to ease the work of drivers who had to cope with the previously universal vagaries of quadrant arrangements.

The first cars which could be considered competition sports cars (although they were, of course, never so described, and only rough parallels can be drawn) were the 60-h.p. Mercedes which were raced in the 1903 Gordon Bennett Trophy Race. The pure racing Mercedes being prepared for this race were destroyed in a fire at the factory, so these basically touring cars were "race-tuned" as substitutes—and Camille Jenatzy drove one of them to victory.

The only opposed-piston engine to be used in Grand Prix racing was installed in a Gobron-Brillié, raced from 1903 until 1907, in its last two years in the first Grands Prix. Its most notable claim, however, was that it was **the first piston-engined car to exceed 100 m.p.h.**

The first eight-cylinder engines in racing were built by Clément Ader and Alexander Winton in 1903, in France and the United States respectively.

Recognisable predecessors of latter-day air-cooled racing engines first appeared in America, in a 1904 Franklin and a 1906 Vanderbilt Cup Frayer-Miller, which had a large fan to force air across its cylinders—shades of Porsche to come!

The first racing engines to have inclined push-rod operated valves in the cylinder-heads were built by Pipe in 1904 and Fiat in 1905. Successful in mainstream racing, the 16·2-litre Fiat engines developed some 120 b.h.p. at a modest 1,100 r.p.m.

Among novelties entered in the American eliminating trials for the 1905 Vanderbilt Cup were an eight-cylinder air-cooled Franklin, which retired; a six-cylinder Thomas with the driver's seat behind the rear axle, which finished fifth; and the first of Walter Christie's front-wheel-drive cars, which completed only two of the four laps but was nevertheless classified.

Tyre failures were frequent in early races, when the general weakness of pneumatic tyres were aggravated by the condition of the roads, not least because horses—upon which transport still largely relied—shed a lot of nails! Until 1905 tyres had to be replaced *in toto*, which took a driver and riding mechanic about a quarter of an hour, although three-man crews at depots at the 1905 Gordon Bennett Trophy Race managed to reduce the time for a single wheel-change to below 5 minutes.

In 1906 the detachable rim was introduced, so that spares with tyres already inflated carried on cars could be bolted on to wheels, and failed tyres did not have to be slashed off and replacements laboriously fitted. The detachable rim was refined, from eight- to single-stud fixing, by 1908, and last used in Grand Prix racing in 1912, by which time it had been made obsolete by the Rudge-Whitworth detachable wheel.

The handicaps of tyre changing. The pit stop which cost Barney Oldfield victory in the 1914 Vanderbilt Cup Race.

The first twelve-cylinder racing engine was used in a Maxwell, entered for the 1906 Vanderbilt Cup Race. It failed to come to the start.

The largest engine built for a road-racing car in the "Age of Giants" was a four-cylinder unit of 26,400 c.c. in the Dufaux entry for the Gordon Bennett Trophy Race of 1905 (but it did not appear for the race at the Auvergne circuit).

The largest engine ever raced in a Grand Prix was the 19,891 c.c. V-four of Walter Christie's 1907 car (q.v.), and this was run close by the 1906 Panhards (18,279 c.c.) and Lorraine-Dietrichs (18,146 c.c.).

The last effective Grand Prix cars of the "Age of Giants" were the 14,137 c.c. Fiats of 1912, one of which finished second in the French Grand Prix, behind a Peugeot with a 7,600 c.c. engine.

The oldest surviving Grand Prix car, albeit much modified, is a Richard Brasier of 1906 in Switzerland. Two 1907 cars, a Fiat and a Renault, survive; and four 1908 cars, a Benz, an Itala, a Mercedes and a Panhard. The Dufaux-Marchand which Dufaux drove in the 1907 Grand Prix is preserved in Switzerland and is the oldest surviving car to have actually run in a Grand Prix. It was built for the 1904 Gordon Bennett Cup when it proved to be overweight and was withdrawn.

Several Grand Prix "firsts" accrue to Walter Christie—his 1907 entry in the Grand Prix de l'Automobile Club de France was the first to have a transverse engine, the first to have a Vee-engine (a V-four) and the first to have front-wheel-drive. It also had the largest engine ever to be raced in a Grand Prix (19,891 c.c.). It was also the source of much amusement as its racing number was applied—WC1—which some members of the European Establishment obviously thought was most appropriate to such an outlandish device!

The first front-wheel-drive car to win a race was a Christie, which won a 250-mile event at Daytona Beach in 1907.

The first radial engine built for racing was installed in a French Burlat in 1907. It was made up of two groups of four cylinders, unlike the later Trossi (q.v.); like that car, however, the Burlat never appeared in a race, although built solely for that purpose.

The first British Grand Prix cars to race were built by D. M. Weigel in 1907. A pair of his cars, which had straight-eight engines over 7 feet long, were run in the French Grand Prix; both retired before half-distance.

The Rudge-Whitworth detachable wheel brought an end to the purgatory of tyre changes, although not as soon as it might have done, for the A.C.F. refused to admit its use in their 1908 Grand Prix—on the grounds that a wheel should be an integral part of a car, and not detachable (out of which the fiery S. F. Edge blew up a fine old teacup storm). Two years later, however, it was in general use, and in 1913 took on its final "knock-off" form.

The six-cylinder Chadwick, raced in the 1908 Vanderbilt Cup and the American Grand Prix, had forced-induction by means of a centrifugal blower—although superchargers did not come into general use on racing-car engines until the 1920s.

Design work was done on superchargers in Europe before the First World War, but because of race regulations they did not progress to practical use. After the war, Mercedes used Roots superchargers on their Targa Florio cars, and in 1923 Fiat introduced the supercharger to Grand Prix racing, with Wittig vane-type "blowers" on their Type 805.

The great Georges Boillot at the wheel of his winning 150-h.p. Peugeot at Amiens for the 1913 French Grand Prix. Jules Goux was second, also in a Peugeot. These cars were also the first to carry "knock-off" hub caps.

Trend-setting car of the second era of Grand Prix racing was the 1912 Peugeot, in particular its 7·6-litre engine. This had four cylinders *en bloc*, and four valves per cylinder, operated by twin overhead camshafts. As well as being a race-winner, it proved to be a model for most other racing-engine manu-facturers. The parts played in its design and construction by four men, driver-technicians Georges Boillot, Jules Goux and Paul Zuccarelli, and Ernest Henry, are often represented as devious; it is sufficient to say that Henry usually gets too much credit, and Robert Peugeot far too little, for his faith in backing the project.

The last Grand Prix cars to use chain drive were Mercedes in the 1913 Grand Prix de France at Le Mans; the best placed of these "Pilette" cars (dubbed after their entrant, the Company's Belgian agent) finished third after two Delages.

The first Grand Prix cars with four-wheel brakes raced in the 1914 French Grand Prix; they were Delage, Fiat, Peugeot and Piccard-Pictet. Isotta-Fraschini had raced a car with four-wheel brakes in other events in the previous year.

The first Grand Prix winner to construct and race a Grand Prix car bearing his own name was Felice Nazzaro, whose Nazzaro 4·5-litre (sixteen-valve s.o.h.c.) cars appeared in the 1914 French Grand Prix. They were fairly successful in racing, Nazzaro winning the 1913 Targa Florio and 1914 Coppa Florio in them, Meregalli the 1920 Targa Florio, and Nazzaro the 1920 Aosta-Grand St. Bernard Hillclimb before he returned to Fiat.

The oldest piece of machinery to be entered for a front-line race was a 1914 Grand Prix Peugeot in which historic-car collector Lindley Bothwell attempted to qualify for the 1949 Indianapolis 500 Miles.

The first outright race victory for a Bugatti was gained by Ernst Friderich driving a T13 in the 1920 Coupe Internationale des Voiturettes at Le Mans (at 56·70 m.p.h. over 257 miles).

For 1922, Vauxhall built a team of 3-litre Grand Prix cars; a 3-litre limit had indeed been in force for the Grands Prix of 1921, but 1922 was the first year of the supremely successful 2-litre formula! So through an incredible oversight this Vauxhall effort was squandered, and the cars were raced only in the 1922 T.T. and British national events.

The first European Grand Prix cars to use hydraulic brakes were the 1922 Bugatti and the 1922–23 Rolland Pilain, both to the front wheels. The first to use them on all four wheels was Maserati in 1933—twelve years after they had appeared on the 1921 French Grand Prix-winning Duesenberg from America.

"Streamlined" Grand Prix cars did not appear until the 'twenties; apart from the tapered tails on the 1914 Peugeots and Fiats, the Ballots and Bugattis in the 1922 French Grand Prix had "barrel" bodies and tapered tails. In 1923 Bugatti introduced his T30 "tanks" with enclosed wheels, and Gabriel Voisin his aerodynamic monocoque Grand Prix cars, while Benz produced the *Tropfenwagen*.

The streamlined 2-litre, six-cylinder, rear-engined Benz Tropfenwagen *in 1923.*

The first V-twelve engine in Grand Prix racing was designed by Planchon and built in only four months in 1923 by Delage. It first appeared in the French Grand Prix of that year, but was not fully raceworthy until 1924.

The supercharger appeared in Grand Prix racing on the Fiat 805 in 1923, and was widely used until the early 'fifties.

The first race win in Europe for a supercharged racing car was achieved by Cagno's 1½-litre Fiat in the 314-mile Gran Premio Vetturette at Brescia in 1923; his winning speed was 80·33 m.p.h.

The first "monocoque" Grand Prix cars were built by Gabriel Voisin, and raced in the 1923 French Grand Prix. In latter-day terminology these might be described as "semi-monocoque", but at least in principle they anticipated the true *monocoque* in Grand Prix racing by thirty-nine years.

The first "production" Grand Prix car was the Bugatti T35, introduced in 1924, which also established the classic Bugatti shape. Best-placed T35 in its first race was seventh, and these Bugattis seldom challenged for victory so long as other manufacturers' teams were competing. But when these were withdrawn, in the second half of the 'twenties, T35s and derivatives made up the bulk of grids, and many private owners won races in them.

The first Grand Prix Alfa Romeo to race was the P2, designed by Vittorio Jano to succeed the P1, which had been withdrawn after a fatal practice accident. Driven by Antonio Ascari, the P2 won its first "test" race, the 1924 Circuit of Cremona, and its first major race, the 1924 French Grand Prix—driven by Giuseppe Campari.

The first Grand Prix car to have its engine behind the driver and its gearbox and differential attached to the chassis—and thus part of the sprung mass—was the Benz *Tropfenwagen* of 1923.

The two-stroke engine has rarely been considered for Formula racing cars. Fiat experimented with their Type 451 1·5 litre engine in 1925, and the Trossi Monaco Grand Prix radial (q.v.) was a two-stroke; but the only two-strokes to be raced in Formula cars have been tuned production engines, rather than "pure" racing engines (for example, D.K.W. units in pre-war 800 c.c. events and in Formula Junior cars, and the Saab unit in that company's only single-seater, also a Formula Junior car).

The last Fiat Grand Prix car was the 806, which had a 1·5-litre supercharged twelve-cylinder engine—in effect a twin-six. It raced only once, in the 1927 Milan Grand Prix at Monza, giving Pietro Bordino an effortless victory.

Probably only one car was built, and after this race it was broken up on the orders of the Fiat management.

The first single-seater built for road racing in Europe was the V-twelve Itala Type 11 of 1926 (the only example built never actually started in a race).

The first Maserati Grand Prix car was built in 1926, a 1·5-litre straight-eight evolved from the 1925 Grand Prix Diatto, which had been designed by the brothers Alfieri and Ernesto Maserati.

In 1926 Alvis built a front-wheel-drive Grand Prix car, which was not ready for that year's British Grand Prix, and not modified in time for the 1927 race. So it never ran in a Grand Prix.

The oldest piece of mechanism to be used in World Championship racing was a Talbot 1·5-litre supercharged engine of 1926 vintage, considerably modified and fitted into a Platé special, entered for the 1949 Swiss and Italian Grands Prix by Enrico Platé.

The first twin-engined road-racing cars (apart from the apparently un-raced Christie, q.v.) appeared conventional, having two in-line engines side by side in front of their cockpits. Notable examples of this type were the Sedici Cilindri Maserati of 1929, which scored some successes, and the Alfa Romeo Type A of 1931, which also had some success—notably at Pescara in 1931 (but killed a driver, Arcangeli).

In 1935 Ferrari built the Alfa Romeo Bimotore, which had a Type B (P3) engine ahead of its driver and another behind him, both driving through the rear wheels. This was very fast in a straight line, but wore its tyres at a prodigious rate on circuits, so that apart from a second place at Avus it was unsuccessful in racing.

The first true single-seater—*monopòsto*—in Grand Prix racing was the Alfa Romeo Type B, introduced in 1932 as soon as the "two-seater body" regulation was dropped. The Type B (P3) set the Grand Prix standard until much more advanced German cars surprised the racing world in 1934.

The first four-wheel-drive car to be entered for a *grande épreuve* was the Bugatti T53, which in fact appeared only once on a circuit—in practice for the 1932 Monaco Grand Prix. It did not start in this race, and was thereafter relegated to hill-climbs.

British prestige in international single-seater road races during the 1930s was largely upheld by E.R.A.s. These straightforward *voiturettes* were built at Bourne by a company backed by Humphrey Cook, and headed by racing driver Raymond Mays and designer Peter Berthon.

As the 1·5-litre supercharged E.R.A.s also complied with the first post-war Grand Prix formula, several raced in World Championship events and—in their teens—gained odd Championship points! All save one of the seventeen E.R.A.s built by the original company survive, and are still actively raced in historic racing car events.

The French S.E.F.A.C. (Société des Etudes Français d'Automobiles de Course) appeared in Grand Prix entry lists from 1934 until 1948 (as the Dommartin); it seldom actually appeared in races, and its finest racing hour came in the 1938 French Grand Prix—when it completed two full laps before retiring.

The legendary Tazio Nuvolari at the wheel of the 3-litre Auto Union.

Von Brauchitsch (Mercedes) at the 1937 Donington Grand Prix.

The first four-wheel-drive car to compete against Grand Prix cars was a Miller driven by Peter de Paolo in the 1934 Tripoli Grand Prix and Avusrennen *formule libre* races.

The first Grand Prix car with all-round independent suspension to win a race was the Mercedes-Benz W25, driven by Manfred von Brauchitsch in the 1934 Eifelrennen.

The first rear-engined Grand Prix car to win a Formula race was the revolutionary Auto Union Type A ("P wagen") of 1934, driven by Hans Stuck in the German Grand Prix.

The Trossi-Monaco Grand Prix car of 1935 had an eight-cylinder two-stroke radial engine mounted ahead of the front wheels, which were of course the driven wheels. It did not progress beyond early trials, but is preserved in the Turin Automobile Museum.

The de Dion rear axle, conceived in the nineteenth century, was introduced into modern racing by Mercedes-Benz on their 1936 Grand Prix cars, became almost universal throughout the next two decades, and was experimentally revived by Ferrari in 1976.

The most powerful Grand Prix car ever built was the Mercedes-Benz W125. Its supercharged 5·66-litre straight-eight engine produced over 600 b.h.p. (646 b.h.p. was recorded with a record-car sprint version of the engine). Save for the ineffectual B.R.M. V-sixteen, this output was not approached again in a road-racing engine until the late 1960s, in CanAm cars. Raced only in 1937, the W125 won seven of the twelve races in which it started.

The first racing car to have disc brakes was a rear-engined four-wheel-drive Miller built for the Indianapolis 500 Miles in 1938 (these were in effect pressure plates working on one face of a disc).

    The now-familiar disc-and-caliper type was first used on aircraft; the first Formula 1 cars to which they were fitted were B.R.M.s and the Thinwall Special Ferrari in 1952. The first sports car to use them was the C-type Jaguar (first raced with discs in the 1952 Mille Miglia).

The last Grand Prix Bugatti to be built under the aegis of Ettore Bugatti was a *monoplace* on a T59 chassis, run with a 4·7-litre eight-cylinder engine in 1936, and a supercharged 3-litre unit in 1938. Bugatti had clung to the two-seater body line longer than any other constructor—his original T59 of 1933 had been the last Grand Prix car on these lines, and aesthetically one of the most pleasing—and this last *monoplace* was his only true single-seater. It was ineffectual in contemporary racing, but Wimille drove one to victory in the first post-war motor race (the 1945 Grand Prix de la Libération in the Bois de Boulogne, Paris); the parallel sports car with all-enveloping body was, however, very successful (first at Le Mans in 1937 and 1939).

The first car built by Enzo Ferrari as an independent constructor (his Scuderia Ferrari had built some Alfa Romeos when it represented that company in racing) was the Vettura 815 of 1940. Precluded by his agreement with Alfa Romeo from using his own name on cars, the 815s were built by the Auto Avio Costruzioni company he had formed with colleagues from Alfa Romeo. Two 815s started in the 1940 Mille Miglia, and both led the 1·5-litre class before retiring.

The first Ferrari model to appear was the 125 sports-racing car, which made its competition début in May 1947; first major victory for the marque came later in the year, on Turin's Valentino circuit, when the car was driven by Raymond Sommer.

The longest unbroken record of team participation in Grand Prix racing is held by Ferrari, who has contested every Formula since 1948 (Enzo Ferrari has of course been intimately involved with racing for much longer—since the early 1920s). Alfa Romeo built their first Grand Prix car in 1914 (as an ALFA, just predating Nicola Romeo's take-over), and with only short breaks were directly or indirectly (when they were represented in racing by Scuderia Ferrari) involved in Grand Prix racing until 1951, and made a partial return in 1970 with an engine used in a Formula 1 McLaren. There was a much greater involvement from 1976, when Alfa Romeo engines (flat-twelves and later V-twelves) were used in the works Brabham cars, which in 1978 once again carried the name Alfa Romeo into the lists of Grand Prix winners. In that year a new Alfa Romeo Grand Prix car was announced – prematurely, for "political" reasons – in preparation for the team's return to racing in 1979.

Maserati Grand Prix cars were built over a longer continuous period than any others, save for the years of the Second World War, i.e. from 1926 until 1958; however, until 1947, when they relinquished control of the firm to Orsi, the Maserati brothers raced works cars inconsistently. B.R.M. first raced a Grand Prix car in 1950, and have built and raced cars to every

Not even the genius of Fangio could raise the Mark 1 B.R.M. from the mediocrity of small-race wins in 1953.

The beautiful Alfa Romeo Monoposto Type Bs, often known as P3s, won dozens of races between 1932 and 1935 in the hands of such immortals as Tazio Nuvolari, Achille Varzi, Rudolf Caracciola and Louis Chiron. (Photo: Geoffrey Goddard.)

"Father" of the E.R.A. Raymond Mays, with R1A, attends the curtain-fall meeting of the London Crystal Palace circuit in 1972. (Photo: Geoffrey Goddard.)

Al Unser, of Albuquerque, New Mexico, in the turbocharged Ford Johnny Lightning Special, winning the 1970 Indianapolis 500 at an average speed of 155·759 m.p.h. He won again in 1971 and 1978.

Grand Prix in the streets: Mario Andretti's Parnelli VPJ4 ahead of Ronnie Peterson's March 761 at Long Beach, California, 1976. (Photo: Geoffrey Goddard.)

subsequent Formula 1 (the Bourne *équipe* ignored the Formula 2 Grands Prix of 1952–53). As Stanley-B.R.M. the team went into a decline in the mid-1970s, and withdrew from Grand Prix racing after the 1976 Brazilian Grand Prix; its return in 1978 was a low-key effort in the Aurora A.F.X. series. It ceased operations in 1979, and was wound up in the Spring of that year.

Team Lotus built up an impressive record in the twenty-one years after their first Grand Prix entry at Monaco in 1958; by the end of the 1978 season Lotus cars had won seventy-one World Championship Grands Prix.

The first four-wheel-drive Grand Prix car to appear post-war was the twelve-cylinder Porsche-Eberhorst-designed Cisitalia Type 360 which ran briefly in an obscure demonstration in Argentina, where Piero Dusio had taken a single undeveloped car after Cisitalia went bankrupt in 1949. The first four-wheel-drive car to complete a race—in first place—was the Ferguson P99, driven by Stirling Moss in the 1961 Oulton Park Gold Cup (at 88·83 m.p.h.).

The only engine to power more than 100 Grand Prix-winning cars has been the Ford-Cosworth DFV, although with engines of varying formats and sizes Ferrari have also scored more than 100 Grand Prix victories. When Coventry Climax withdrew from racing in 1966 their engines had won more International Formula 1 races than any other manufacturer's—96 between 1958 and 1966 in chassis from six constructors. By the end of 1978 the Cosworth DFV had scored 117 victories in World Championship Grands Prix.

Keith Duckworth with a DFV engine on test—one of the most remarkable pieces of Grand Prix machinery ever built, which by mid-1979 had powered cars to more than 120 world championship victories.

The most powerful engines used in World Championship racing have been the twelve-cylinder normally aspirated 3-litre units and 1·5-litre turbo-charged units built by Ferrari, Alfa Romeo and Renault from the late 1970s, which have produced more than 500 b.h.p. By 1979 even the simple Ford-Cosworth V-eight had a power output approaching this magic figure, having been rated at 400 b.h.p. when it first appeared in 1967.

Previously the complex 1·5-litre supercharged B.R.M. V-sixteen of the early 1950s had been generally regarded as the most powerful Formula 1 engine, 485 b.h.p. at 12,000 r.p.m.—even more "on the bench"—being quoted as its power output, although this figure has subsequently been questioned. The engine and car were extremely complex, and, at the time, beyond the resources of the small Bourne company. The only placings for this original Type 15 B.R.M. in Championship racing were a fifth and seventh (Parnell and Walker) in the 1951 British Grand Prix.

By the time it was developed to raceworthiness, the Grand Prix Formula for which it had been developed had been abandoned.

The first Australian racing machines with international potential were the Maybach Specials built by Charles Dean and Stan Jones around war-surplus Maybach six-cylinder s.o.h.c. military engines. Driven by Jones, father of the current Grand Prix driver Alan Jones, the first of these won the first New Zealand Grand Prix, from Gould's Cooper-Bristol and Wharton's 1·5-litre supercharged B.R.M.

A Cunningham C-4R sports car at Rheims in 1953.

The last "distinguished" Grand Prix car to have a mechanically driven supercharged engine was the Alfa Romeo Type 158/159, raced until 1951 after dominating the circuits during the post-war era (in 1946–48 and 1950–51 these cars gained thirty-one victories in thirty-five starts). The only "blown" car to appear under the regulations for the next Formula 1 was a 750 c.c. D.B., which appeared but once, in the 1955 Pau Grand Prix.

In 1977 Renault returned to Grand Prix racing with a 1·5-litre turbo-supercharged car in which the exhaust gases drove the compressor(s), following their considerable experience with this system in sports-car racing. Success in Formula 1 came less easily, and the Renault team did not score its first Championship points until the end of the 1978 season at Watkins Glen,

U.S.A. They won the first Grand Prix Championship victory for turbo-charging at the 1979 French Grand Prix, seventy-three years after a Renault won the first of this illustrious series of races.

The first post-war American competition cars to be raced in European road races were the Cunningham sports cars. The first (C-2) made its début in the 1951 Le Mans 24-hour Race, in which one of the team ran in second place for some time. Best final placings for Cunningham at Le Mans were third, in 1953 and 1954.

The first post-war Coventry Climax-engined car to race was a Kieft with a 1,097 c.c. F.W.A. engine in the 1954 Le Mans 24-hour Race. It retired with rear axle failure. The Coventry Climax engines went from strength to strength in racing.

The first Cooper Grand Prix car was the T20 Bristol-engined car raced in the Formula 2 Grands Prix of 1952–53; the **first rear-engined Cooper** in Grand Prix racing was the T40 used by Jack Brabham in 1955.

First new German cars with front-line pretensions to appear after the Second World War were the Formula 2 Veritas and A.F.M. The former was a modified sports car; the A.F.M., built by Alex von Falkenhausen in 1950 showed considerable promise, but before it was developed to full raceworthiness von Falkenhausen abandoned it.

Front-wheel-drive has been used only spasmodically, and never successfully, on Grand Prix cars—most recently on the 1955 supercharged D.B.

The first use of an air-brake in road racing was on the Mercedes-Benz 300SLR in the 1955 Le Mans 24-hour Race. It took the form of an hydraulically operated full-width panel behind the cockpit, to back up drum-brakes which were considered less than adequate against the discs used by the rival Jaguar team.

Air-cooled engines have seldom figured in Grand Prix cars, successfully only by Porsche. That success was modest, the German 1½-litre flat-8s winning just one Championship race, the French Grand Prix at Rouen, and the Solitude Grand Prix, both in 1962, driven by Dan Gurney. A D.B. powered by an air-cooled 750 c.c. supercharged twin-cylinder engine ran in the 1955 Pau Grand Prix, and the 3-litre air-cooled Honda RA302 ran in the 1968 French Grand Prix; neither was successful, and the underdeveloped Honda crashed.

The first Grand Prix car to be built by Lancia was the novel D50 to the designs of Vittorio Jano, which raced in late 1954 and 1955. During the latter year the near-bankrupt Lancia Co. was bailed out by Fiat, and the D50s handed to Ferrari—to be gradually modified and raced as Lancia-Ferraris through the next two seasons.

The ingenious and highly promising Lancia D50 seen here during training for the 1955 Italian Grand Prix at Monza.

The first Grand Prix car to use the engine as a stressed (load-bearing) chassis member was the Lancia D50, although thirty years earlier Bugatti engines had played a "stiffening" role. The practice became general in the late 'sixties, particularly in cars using the Cosworth-Ford DFV engine, which was designed with this specifically in mind.

The first Grand Prix car to have inboard (shaft-driven) front brakes was the Mercedes-Benz W196 of 1954. The practice was revived in 1970 on the Lotus 70.

The first Grand Prix engine to have desmodromic (i.e. mechanically, positively operated) valve gear was the $4\frac{1}{2}$-litre four-cylinder unit of the 1914 Delage. The first such engine to succeed came forty years later in the 1954 Mercedes-Benz W196. In the interim, Rolland-Pilain had experimented with desmodromic valves in their 1922 Grand Prix engines, while "semi-desmodromic" operation featured on Salmson racing voiturettes from 1922 to 1928.

The first racing car with a transversely mounted eight-cylinder engine was the Bugatti T251, designed by Colombo and raced only once; this was in the 1956 French Grand Prix in which it was driven by Maurice Trintignant, but retired.

The first Lotus single-seater was the Climax-engined Type 12 Formula 2 car, which made its racing début at the 1957 Goodwood Easter Monday meeting; driven by Cliff Allison, it retired when in third place.

The first British Grand Prix car to win a World Championship race was a Vanwall, driven to victory in the 1957 British Grand Prix at Aintree by Tony Brooks and Stirling Moss at 86·80 m.p.h.

The Formula 1 Constructors' Championship was instituted in 1958. Save that only the highest placed car of a marque in the first six finishers scores, the points system corresponds with that for the Drivers' Championship (q.v.). Winners of the Constructors' Championship have been:

The first six-wheel Grand Prix car to be built was the Tyrrell Project 34/2, here seen during its first tests at Silverstone in March 1976. Ken Tyrrell is seen on the right and designer Derek Gardner on the left. The driver is Patrick Depailler. It first ran in the 1976 Spanish Grand Prix at Jarama and won only one race, in Sweden driven by Jody Scheckter.

1958	Vanwall (Great Britain)	1969	Matra (France)
1959	Cooper (Great Britain)	1970	Lotus (Great Britain)
1960	Cooper (Great Britain)	1971	Tyrrell (Great Britain)
1961	Ferrari (Italy)	1972	Lotus (Great Britain)
1962	B.R.M. (Great Britain)	1973	Lotus (Great Britain)
1963	Lotus (Great Britain)	1974	McLaren (Great Britain)
1964	Ferrari (Italy)	1975	Ferrari (Italy)
1965	Lotus (Great Britain)	1976	Ferrari (Italy)
1966	Brabham (Great Britain)	1977	Ferrari (Italy)
1967	Brabham (Great Britain)	1978	Lotus (Great Britain)
1968	Lotus (Great Britain)	1979	Ferrari (Italy)

During the period of the World Drivers' Championship (1950–78), cars of twenty-one marques have won races: Ferrari 73 victories; Lotus 71; McLaren 24; Tyrrell 21; Brabham 20; B.R.M. 17; Cooper 16; Alfa Romeo 10; Maserati 9; Mercedes-Benz 9; Vanwall 9; Matra 9; March 3; Wolf 3; Honda 2; Porsche 1; Shadow 1; Ligier 1; Hesketh 1; Penske 1; Eagle 1.

The most numerous cars through these years were Ferrari, 773 starting in races, 502 officially finishing, for a finishing percentage of 64·94. Following in numerical order were Lotus, 747 starts, 406 finishes (54·35); Brabham 572 starts, 311 finishes (54·37); Cooper 500 starts, 295 finishes (59·00); McLaren 387 starts, 245 finishes (63·31); Tyrrell, 246 starts, 162 finishes (65·85); Surtees 223 starts, 117 finishes (52·47); Matra 116 starts, 79 finishes (68·10). No other marques recorded more than 100 starts in Grands Prix.

The only car not constructed for road racing to take part in a World Championship Grand Prix was a Kurtis midget driven by Rodger Ward in the 1959 American Grand Prix (its clutch failed after twenty-two laps).

The first rear-engined Formula 1 Lotus was a developed version of the 18 Formula Junior car, and was first raced in 1960.

The first Chaparral sports-racing car, built in 1961, was conventional by the standards of the time—and those of later Chaparrals. It had a front-mounted 5·2-litre Chevrolet engine, driving through a normal manual four-speed gearbox. Driven by Jim Hall it finished second in its first race, at Laguna Seca. The name derives from a ground bird common in the south-western States of the U.S.A.

The last "conventional" front-engined Grand Prix car was Lance Reventlow's Scarab. This first appeared at Monaco in 1960, but neither of the two cars entered qualified to start in the race. Half-way through the European season it became obvious that the cars were outclassed, and the team gave up Grand Prix racing.

The last front-engined car to start in a Grand Prix was the four-wheel-drive Ferguson P99, in the 1961 British Grand Prix at Aintree (driven by Jack Fairman and Stirling Moss, it was disqualified).

The first Brabham car made its début as an M.R.D., driven by Gavin Youl in a Formula Junior race at Goodwood in 1961, in which it gained second place. Thereafter Jack Brabham used his own name, coupling it with that of his partner Ron Tauranac in the model designation, "BT". Jack raced his first Brabham Grand Prix car, the Climax V-eight-engined BT3, for the first time in the 1962 German Grand Prix—but retired after nine laps.

The Scarab Grand Prix car seen during practice for the 1960 Monaco Grand Prix.

*The Hill/Ginther Rover-
B.R.M. gas-turbine car
during the 1963 Le Mans
24-Hour Race.*

The first gas-turbine-engined car to run in a classic road race was a Rover-B.R.M., driven by Graham Hill and Richie Ginther in the 1963 Le Mans 24-hour Race. As a formula equating its power unit with a normal piston engine could not be agreed, it ran a solo time trial in a separate category, covering a distance which would have classified it eighth overall, had it been a "normal" entry. In 1965 it raced at Le Mans "on level terms", Graham Hill and Jackie Stewart placing it tenth overall.

The first Grand Prix car with a transversely mounted twelve-cylinder engine was the 1964 1·5-litre Honda, which first appeared in the 1964 German Grand Prix, and won the last race of the 1·5-litre Formula, the 1965 Mexican Grand Prix. (Two years earlier, Alfieri had designed a V-twelve to be similarly installed in a Maserati; the engine was built, but the car was not.)

Only one World Championship Grand Prix has been won by a car with a sixteen-cylinder engine; this was the 1966 American Grand Prix, won by Jim Clark in a Lotus 43 powered by the B.R.M. H-16 (at 114·94 m.p.h.).

The first full driver safety-harness to be used in Grand Prix racing was fitted to Jackie Stewart's B.R.M. for the 1967 German Grand Prix, although safety-belts, and sometimes harnesses, had long been used in American track racing and saloon-car racing.

*John Surtees at the wheel of
a Honda in the 1967
Monaco Grand Prix.*

The first Formula racing car to have a predominantly wooden chassis was the Formula 2 Protos of 1967. Designed by Frank Costin, it had a stressed-skin hull of laminated plywood; its best race placing was a second at Hockenheim.

The stressed hull of the 1966 Formula 1 McLaren was of Mallite, a "sandwich" material consisting of two thin outer layers of aluminium alloy and a centre layer of balsa wood.

The first race use of high-mounted "wing" aerofoils was on a Chaparral 2F sports-racing car in 1967. In 1968 they came into general use on road-racing single-seaters, but were precipitately restricted by regulations in 1969.

The third leading Grand Prix driver to become a constructor, in his own name, during the 1960s was John Surtees. His first car, the TS5 for Formula A/Formula 5000 racing, was built at the end of 1968. The first Surtees Grand Prix car, the TS7, was built in 1970, and during that year Surtees drove it to victory in the Oulton Park Gold Cup. Grand Prix success proved elusive, however, and at the end of the 1978 season Team Surtees was withdrawn from World Championship racing. It continued at a more modest level in the Aurora AFX series.

The first Grand Prix in which more than one four-wheel-drive car started was the 1969 British Grand Prix at Silverstone, where in fact no fewer than four were raced—a Matra MS84 which Jean-Pierre Beltoise drove into ninth place, a Lotus 63 which John Miles placed tenth, a second Lotus 63 (driven by Jo Bonnier) and a McLaren (driven by Derek Bell) which retired.

Jochen Rindt later placed a Lotus 63 second in the Oulton Park Gold Cup, but the best Championship race placing for a four-wheel-drive car in that year was seventh, achieved by J. Servoz-Gavin driving a Matra MS84 in the American Grand Prix. At the end of the season, four-wheel-drive disappeared from the circuits until in 1971 Lotus brought out their 56B turbine car.

The first McLaren car was built in 1964, a space-frame sports-racing car to succeed the Zerex Special Cooper which Bruce had raced so successfully.

The first road-racing car in which "negative lift" was obtained by means other than aero-dynamic was the 1970 Chaparral 2J, which used an auxiliary engine to exhaust underbody air, with flexible skirts at side and rear to part-seal

Tyrrell 003 in the British Grand Prix of 1971. Stewart, with twenty-seven victories, won more Grands Prix than any other driver

Brabham fan-car, Swedish GP, 1978.

this area. Potential was demonstrated, although never proved for the duration of a CanAm race, and the device was then ruled outside the regulations. In 1978 Brabham introduced a similar "sucker" system on the BT46 Formula 1 car, although this did not employ an auxiliary engine. This version of the BT46 had effective chassis "skirts" to provide a seal, air from beneath the car being drawn over a neatly cowled engine compartment and exhausted to the rear by a large fan. This air also served a cooling purpose—indeed, the Brabham team claimed that this was its primary purpose. Its appearance in the 1978 Swedish Grand Prix, when Lauda drove it to a clear victory, caused an enormous furore; it was subsequently banned from racing on safety grounds as it could not clearly be shown to breach the regulations (the C.S.I. retreated in confusion to redraft these!) and therefore the Swedish Grand Prix result was allowed to stand.

Emerson Fittipaldi's turbine-powered four-wheel-drive Lotus 56B at Oulton Park in May 1971.

The first gas-turbine car to race in a Formula 1 event was the Lotus 56B in 1971. Powered by a Pratt and Whitney turbine, this was originally built for the Indianapolis 500 Miles, was modified to comply with Formula 1 regulations in 1970, and raced for the first time in the Race of Champions at Brands Hatch in 1971. Driven by Emerson Fittipaldi, it retired with suspension failure. It first finished a race in the second part of the two-part Silverstone International Trophy, when Fittipaldi placed it third, and first raced in a Grand Prix in the 1971 Dutch event, when Dave Walker crashed it on the streaming wet circuit.

The first Williams car to win a Grand Prix was the Patrick Head-designed FW07, driven by Clay Regazzoni to victory in the 1979 British Grand Prix at Silverstone at 138·80 m.p.h. His team-mate Alan Jones then proceeded to win the next 3 Grands Prix in succession. In all the Saudia-Williams scored 5 victories in the 1979 season.

The first victory for a Wolf Grand Prix car came in the first race for this new marque, when Jody Scheckter drove a WR1 to win the 1977 Argentine Grand Prix. The team was named after its patron, Walter Wolf, and the cars have carried the Maple Leaf emblem of his adopted country, Canada. In 1978 Scheckter also won the Canadian Grand Prix for Wolf as well as the Monaco Grand Prix— and Scheckter is a Monaco resident. Thereafter the cars' fortunes declined and, late in 1979, when Walter Wolf's initial three-year commitment had been fulfilled, they were merged with the Fittipaldi team.

The first successful "ground effects" car in Grand Prix racing was a Lotus. The conventional approach to racing-car aerodynamics had to be abandoned by designers in the late 1970s as Colin Chapman demonstrated with the Lotus 78 and 79 that it was possible to generate considerable down forces by using the airflow passing under a car, and worked towards dispensing with the "wings", which create down forces only at the cost of speed-inhibiting drag. By 1979, every other constructor had been forced to follow the Chapman line, some such as Ligier achieving success with their ground effects cars remarkably quickly, others floundering as they attempted to copy the Lotus lead—a recurring theme through the 1960s and 1970s!

Basically, the Lotus approach was to combine an extremely narrow monocoque with wide venturi side-pods, which necessitated carrying the fuel between cockpit and engine, this in turn leading to cockpits being

First Arrows Grand Prix car, the A1, was designed and built remarkably quickly early in 1978, and first appeared at Silverstone in very unsuitable conditions! In a High Court action later that year it was shown to have more than coincidental design similarities to a Shadow F1 car— most of the members of the Arrows team had been with Shadow in 1977—and had to be withdrawn from racing in the summer but . . .

. . . by that time a successor was ready for racing, and is seen here, driven by Riccardo Patrese in the 1978 Canadian Grand Prix at Montreal.

positioned further forward (within the overall length) than had been customary. "Skirts" beneath the side-pods sealed the airflow through them, and this was obstructed as little as possible, with great care being taken that those suspension members which could not be mounted inboard interrupted the airflow as little as possible.

In 1979 Brabham and Lotus (with the BT48 and 80 respectively) were the first constructors to build cars intended to run without front wings and only minimal rear wings, although these designs were not successful. By that time motor sport's legislators were considering regulations intended to ban skirts.

The first use of radial tyres in top-flight Formula racing was in 1978, when Michelin introduced this type, and broke the long Goodyear monopoly (built on cross-ply tyres, of course). First victory for a car with Michelin radials was gained by Ferrari driver Carlos Reutemann in the 1978 Brazilian Grand Prix. In the following year, Cheever drove an Osella fitted with Pirelli radials to a début victory in the Formula Two Silverstone International Trophy, to give the Italian company its first major single-seater win since their tyres were used by Maserati in Fangio's last Championship season in 1957.

The Lotus 79 was technically advanced, like so many Chapman designs before it setting a standard for other constructors, and aesthetically was perhaps the most pleasing of all 3-litre Grand Prix cars (Mario Andretti at Monza in 1978).

The Michelin success led to a "tyre war", and to controversy as the French company restricted use of their tyres to two teams, while Goodyear continued to make their tyres available to all other teams, protesting that this was an unfair burden, and consequently reducing the supply of "qualifying" tyres—in effect, rewarding success with their allocation of these. Following Goodyear threats to withdraw, "qualifying tyres" were banned by F.I.S.A. in 1980. ("Qualifying tyres" were a phenomenon of the late 1970s, giving exceptional performance for a very short life, which meant that normally they were used only to secure a good grid position— some proved to have a life of no more than a flying lap, and drivers who attempted to use them in races only suffered the self-imposed handicap of pit-stops for tyre changes.)

McLaren M23, here driven by James Hunt in the 1976 Canadian Grand Prix, was a straightforward Gordon Coppuck design which served the team well in the years immediately before "wing" cars and ground effects became de rigueur.

Speed, of course, is relative, *and a lap of the Monaco Grand Prix circuit at over 80 m.p.h. is at least as impressive as a lap of the Monza circuit at 150 m.p.h.—in many respects a greater feat for the machinery of the car as for the driver. Furthermore, optimum gear ratios are chosen to suit circuits, rather than for outright straight-line speeds, and it is most unlikely that the circuit-racing cars with the highest speed potential could be driven round the Monaco circuit at speeds approaching 85.58 m.p.h., the lap record set by Jackie Stewart in 1971. So sheer maximum speed is to a certain extent meaningless in racing cars. Setting aside these provisos,* **the highest speed attained in a road-racing car** *appears to have been the estimated 235 m.p.h. by a special aerodynamic Porsche 917 along the Mulsanne Straight during trials at Le Mans in 1971, higher speed estimates (based on gearing and engine speed) for similar cars a year earlier probably being in error.*

The spotlight of fame and acclamation normally tends to fall on the apex of the motor sporting pyramid—the cars and the drivers. Yet behind the scenes the following designers and constructors have been responsible for some of the greatest competition cars in the history of motor racing.

Ernest Henry (1885–1950), a Swiss, is generally credited with initiating the school of racing-car design

which ended "the Age of Giants" in the Grands Prix. First of the "Henry line" was the 1912 7·6-litre Peugeot which Boillot drove to win that year's Grand Prix, and Goux the 1913 Indianapolis 500. Henry's part in the design of this car, and the equally significant 5·6-litre Grand Prix and 3-litre Coupe de l'Auto Peugeots of 1913 has never been clearly defined. He was one of the famous "Charlatans" of the Peugeot team, the others being Paolo Zuccarelli, Georges Boillot and Jules Goux, their joint knowledge and experience producing brilliantly successful racing designs. The principal characteristics of a so-called "Henry" engine were its long stroke and the twin overhead camshafts, operating four inclined overhead valves in each cylinder.

After the First World War Henry designed Europe's first serious straight-eight racing car, the Ballot, initially as a 5-litre, and in 1920–21 in 3-litre form. He also designed a 2-litre four-cylinder Ballot which was more successful in sports-car form than in racing. Ballot was a singularly unlucky marque in racing, losing several deserved victories between 1919 and 1922. Although Henry quickly faded from the racing scene thereafter his design influence lived on.

Ettore Bugatti (1882–1947) played a shadowy role in the motor industry before he produced his first

Bugatti in 1910. This was a light racing car, round which a sound foundation for the mass of Bugatti lore was laid when Ernst Friderich placed one second in the 1911 Grand Prix de France. Bugatti's first traditional contribution to racing was the principle of the eight-cylinder engine—"principle" because the eight was by no means new in racing, and its first really effective application was not executed by Bugatti; his First World War aircraft engine of double straight-eight configuration is credited with inspiring the layout.

Thereafter Bugatti was an originator only in detail, rather an autocratic perfectionist for craftsmanship and precision, who became increasingly reactionary in his designs.

His first notably successful racing model was the T13 Brescia *voiturette*, but his first Grand Prix cars in 1922 and 1923 drew attention more by their idiosyncratic bodies than by their sound eight-cylinder power unit. This was the basis of Bugatti's classic T35, a most elegant classic Grand Prix car, which made its racing début in 1924. Although this was not outstandingly successful so long as other front-line works teams—such as Alfa Romeo and Delage—contested the Grands Prix, together with its numerous derivatives it was vital to Grand Prix racing through the late 1920s, when there were no other teams in contention. These cars were available to private owners, and Bugatti was thus the first constructor to build Grand Prix cars for sale.

In the new age of science and technology applied to racing cars in the 1930s, Bugatti's Grand Prix cars were obsolete in conception, although sports variants were still successful at the highest level in that department of racing to the end of the decade—which was Bugatti's last as an effective force.

Vittorio Jano (1891–1965) was responsible for the great Alfa Romeo Grand Prix and sports cars of the inter-war years, and for the one and only, and highly original Lancia Grand Prix car in the mid 'fifties. After the First World War Jano was a member of the brilliant Fiat design team, and in 1923 was induced to join Alfa Romeo by Enzo Ferrari, initially to design the P2 Grand Prix car, which became dominant in the races of 1924–25. This was followed by a series of sports cars, notably the 8C-2300, which was also a highly successful Grand Prix car (from its first Grand Prix victory in 1931 it was dubbed the "Monza" Alfa).

This was in effect succeeded by the Type B, popularly P3, the classic *monoposto* Grand Prix car, and the finest flowering of the classic line. Jano's later Grand Prix Alfas of the 1930s were almost stop-gaps in the face of the new breed of German cars, and as such only modestly successful; in 1938 Jano left Alfa Romeo.

Moving to Lancia, he was in charge of production model development, but as Lancia interest turned to out-and-out racing cars in the early 1950s, designed two more outstanding competition cars, the D24 sports-racing car and the D50 Grand Prix car. This had many novel features, for example the engine playing a load-carrying role in the ultra-light space frame and outrigged fuel-tanks between the wheels. By the time the D50 was developed to raceworthiness, the Lancia Company was in liquidation, and with Fiat aid the cars were handed over to Ferrari, to be developed to conform to Ferrari practice. The Fiat-Ferrari-Alfa Romeo-Fiat-Ferrari cycle thus completed left out Jano, who retired.

Enzo Ferrari (b. 1898) is not a designer; he was no more than a fairly good racing driver, but he has been one of the most outstanding constructors, and a central personality in motor sport, for nearly fifty years. For the last twenty of them he has been the patrician figure of the sport.

His association with Alfa Romeo began in 1920, and his first significant contribution was to persuade Jano (q.v. above) to leave Fiat, to design a series of outstanding Alfa Romeos. Effectively, Ferrari took over responsibility for Alfa racing activities in the 1930s; Scuderia Ferrari was established in 1929, and four years later he came to an agreement to race the front-line Alfas through a momentous period. He broke with Alfa Romeo in 1939, produced his own first car in 1940, and after the Second World War set up as a constructor in his own name.

Ironically, his first great rival was Alfa Romeo, whose Grand Prix cars (158/159s which he had in part conceived in 1937) he at last defeated on equal terms in 1951. By that time his Ferraris had already achieved great success—the first of nine Ferrari victories at Le Mans was gained in 1949—and as Alfa Romeo withdrew and Maserati faded, Ferrari became indisputably the foremost Italian racing marque.

Ferrari—the man and his company are almost synonymous—became so important to the prestige of Italian automotive engineering that he was materially supported by Fiat from the mid 'fifties; after a Ford take-over attempt had failed nearly a decade later, Fiat took a majority shareholding in Ferrari (when one of the conditions was that Enzo Ferrari remain in office).

Since he established Auto Costruzione Ferrari in 1946, Enzo Ferrari has survived many personal crises, the death of his son Dino, the matriarchal inclinations of his wife, the tragic deaths of many Ferrari drivers, the spasmodic and sometimes vicious attacks of the volatile Italian Press, as well as the changing fortunes of racing, to maintain an active racing programme at the highest levels for over thirty years.

Gioacchino Colombo (b. 1903) is chiefly recalled for a great car: the Alfa Romeo 158; an engine significant as much for what it represented as for what it actually was: the first Ferrari V-twelve; and for a car which in many respects was years ahead of its time—yet made only one unsuccessful racing appearance: the Bugatti T251.

From the mid 'twenties, Colombo worked under Jano at Alfa Romeo, and in 1937 was seconded to Ferrari at Modena to design a 1·5-litre racing car, the 158. This straightforward machine proved to be an excellent *voiturette* and, after Colombo had left Alfa, a superb Grand Prix car, the last great supercharged machine in the history of Grand Prix racing.

Colombo joined Ferrari after the war, and was responsible for the first Ferrari, the 125, in sports and racing versions, and for the 60-degree Ferrari V-twelve, which in various forms served on in Ferrari sports cars for many years. Succeeded at Ferrari by Aurelio Lampredi, Colombo moved the short distance to Maserati, where with Massimino he was responsible for the 2-litre A6G series, of which the A6GCS was of incidental interest as the last car with a live rear axle to win a *grand épreuve* (the 1953 Italian Grand Prix), and was a direct forerunner of the classic 250F.

When Bugatti essayed a Grand Prix return under the 2·5-litre formula, Colombo designed for the company a most original car. This T251 had a space frame, de Dion axles front and rear, and an eight-cylinder engine mounted transversely behind the driver. Unfortunately, Bugatti lacked the resources to even develop this to raceworthiness; had it been, the great revolution in Grand Prix car design might have been sparked off by Italian genius rather than by Cooper common sense.

John Cooper and standing Charles Cooper.

Charles (1896–1964) and John Cooper (b. 1923), father and son, brought about a revolution by evolution, through a series of extraordinarily simple cars, and when the movement which they had started turned to complexity and sophistication their Cooper Car Company was left behind, and as a racing force just faded away. Quite simply, the Coopers proved through racing success that the correct place for the engine of a racing car is behind the driver—while earlier essays in this configuration had by no means been unsuccessful, they had simply not been overwhelmingly convincing.

The post-war Cooper line sprang from a special for the infant 500-c.c. class, which consisted of two Fiat Topolino half-chassis joined end-to-end, with a J.A.P. motorcycle engine mounted at the rear, because practicability dictated it be placed there. From this car evolved a line of Coopers which completely dominated Formula 3 racing, sports-racing cars, then 1·5-litre Formula 2 cars, and in parallel the first Brabham-inspired Grand Prix Cooper. From the Formula 2 Coventry Climax-engined car was derived the most successful Grand Prix Cooper, the 2·5-litre Type 51, which won the World Championships of 1959 and 1960. The modest success of a Type 54 derivative of this car at Indianapolis in 1961 was then the starting-point of a revolution in American track-car design.

However, in large part because Charles Cooper stubbornly refused to recognise that an evolutionary process cannot be halted, Coopers lost ground to other constructors who had followed their lead, and in Grand Prix racing enjoyed only another brief spasm of success, in the opening period of the 3-litre Formula. In 1969 the line of Cooper racing cars came to an end.

Colin Chapman (b. 1928) is the latter-day *enfant terrible* of the motor industry, a brilliant technical innovator and a very smart business operator—two qualities seldom found in one man, yet essential and complementary in the changing world of motor racing of the last two decades.

Chapman's first Lotus was an Austin-based trials special built in 1948, and in 1950 he gained the first Lotus race victory with the Lotus 2. The 6 established Lotus as a manufacturing company, and established the early Chapman formula for success, for to offset the modest power output of proprietary engines, Chapman developed extremely light and efficient chassis and suspension systems, coupled in succeeding sports-racing cars with highly efficient bodies. This work led to his first involvement with Grand Prix cars, as designer of the space frame of the 1956 Vanwall and the revised suspension of the 1957 B.R.M.

Chapman's own first single-seater, the Lotus 12 Formula 2 car, appeared in 1956, and this was followed by the slim, petite, 16 Grand Prix car in 1958—this looked "right", but on the circuits belied the old adage, in large part through its over-complication. Chapman turned to simplicity in his first rear-engined single-seater, the 18, which was successful in Formula Junior and Grand Prix roles. In 1962 he startled the racing world with his frameless *monocoque* 25, in which frontal area was reduced to the minimum by seating the driver in a semi-prone position; this car gave Chapman a clear class lead, and was to be almost universally followed.

Lotus was by this time established as a manufacturer of road-going cars, and Chapman was also involved in collaboration with the Ford Motor Company, which on one side of the Atlantic was to lead in 1965 to the first Indianapolis victory for a European car since 1940, and in 1967 to Ford's entry into Grand Prix racing—which in turn was to lead to a twelve-year run of extraordinary success, for Ford if not always for Lotus.

Despite his many business commitments, Chapman remained intimately involved with his racing teams, and continued to provide the inspiration, although no longer the actual detailed designs, for a succession of advanced cars, such as the four-wheel-drive turbine-powered Lotus 56. Sometimes self-defeating through over-ingenuity in technical and business matters, Colin Chapman stood head and shoulders above his contemporaries. In cars such as the Lotus 49 and 72, he enjoyed a close and understanding relationship with designers who could translate his ideas into outstandingly successful cars. Lotus racing fortunes went into a decline when the team was forced to continue using the 72 when it was becoming obsolescent, and its immediate successors failed. The 77 of 1976 was widely regarded as another failure (it won only one Grand Prix), but it was progressively used to prove ideas and components for the 78. In 1977 this started the racing world on a new design trend towards "ground effects" cars (q.v.), and its refined 1978 successor, the 79, gave Mario Andretti the "unfair advantage" which gained Drivers' and Constructors' Championships. With Andretti, Chapman developed a relationship matched only by his partnership and close understanding with Jim Clark.

Through the 1960s and 1970s, Chapman generally stood head and shoulders above his contemporaries; beyond that, he has been the outstanding innovative racing-car designer in the history of motor sport.

Record-holder Jackie Stewart with twenty-seven World Championship victories.

Part Three, THE DRIVERS

The first lady racing driver appears to have been a Madame Laumaillé, who drove a De Dion tricycle in the 1898 Marseilles-Nice two-day event. She was actually fastest in the class on the first day, and eventually finished fourth in the class (her husband was sixth!).

Only three drivers who raced in the first Grand Prix in 1906 raced in the French event after the First World War: Felice Nazzaro, who won in 1907 and 1922; Victor Héméry, who raced in the 1907–12 events and in 1922–23; and Louis Wagner, who drove in ten French GPs, for the last time at Montlhéry in 1927 (in his career he drove GP cars for nine teams).

The only man ever to drive his first race in the premier event of the year, and win it, was Christian Lautenschlager (Mercedes), in the 1908 French GP.

The only driver to race before the First World War and after the Second was Sir Francis Samuelson, who competed with cycle-cars in 1913 and their rough equivalents, 500-c.c. Formula 3 cars, in the late forties (and drove a 1914 Sunbeam in historic events much later than that).

The first British driver to win a Grand Prix was Henry Segrave, driving a British Sunbeam, so that the result was a double British first, in the 1923 French GP at Tours (75·30 m.p.h. for 496·5 miles). Two other British drivers were to take the flag first in major GPs before the Second World War (Williams and Seaman), but not until 1957 did another British car win a GP of comparable status (the Vanwall shared by Brooks and Moss in the British GP).

The first American to compete in a European motor race was George Heath, who handled a Panhard in the 1898 Paris-Amsterdam-Paris, finishing thirteenth. He also became the first American to win a major race—two, in fact, the Circuit of Ardennes in Belgium and the Vanderbilt Cup in the U.S.A., both in 1904, and both times with a Panhard.

Giuseppe Campari was the last of the top-line drivers who started racing before the First World War to remain active in Grands Prix. Tragically, this colourful Italian driver died in the race which he had announced would be his last, the 1933 Monza GP. Oil dropped on the South Curve in the first heat was not properly cleared; on the first lap of the second heat both Campari and Borzacchini crashed and were killed at this point; incredibly, the oil remained as the third heat started, and during this Czaykowski also crashed, and died, at the South Curve.

The first British driver to win a front-line post-war Grand Prix was Peter Whitehead, who in 1949 drove his 1·5-litre supercharged Ferrari to victory in the 220-mile Czechoslovakian GP.

The present World Championship of Drivers was instituted in 1950. Basically, placings are decided on a points score, cumulating as the season progresses, although only points scored in a specified number of events have counted (therefore in the unlikely event of a driver scoring in every Championship race, he drops his lowest scores). Until 1960 the Indianapolis 500 Miles was a World Championship race, but since then only Grands Prix have been scoring events, save in one exceptional season the one premier race in each country.

In the early years of the Championship a point was awarded for the fastest race lap, and points gained in shared drives were divided among the drivers concerned. Points are awarded to the first six drivers in a race: 1st, 9 points; 2nd, 6; 3rd, 4; 4th, 3; 5th, 2; 6th, 1 (until 1960, a victory scored only 8 points). A controversial rule introduced for the 1979 season meant that while the points scale remained unchanged, the season was divided into two 8-race halves, and a driver could count only his best four scores in each half. In addition, drivers who raced only occasionally were ineligible—even if such a driver should finish a race in a points-scoring position, he would not be awarded those points.

The first "World Champion": Giuseppe Farina driving a Type 158 Alfa Romeo during practice for the 1950 European (British) Grand Prix at Silverstone. In winning this race Farina completed the 202 miles at an average speed of 90·95 m.p.h.

World Champion Drivers:

1950 Giuseppe Farina (I.), Alfa Romeo
1951 Juan-Manuel Fangio (R.A.), Alfa Romeo
1952 Alberto Ascari (I.), Ferrari
1953 Alberto Ascari (I.), Ferrari
1954 Juan-Manuel Fangio (R.A.), Maserati and
   Mercedes-Benz
1955 Juan-Manuel Fangio (R.A.), Mercedes-Benz
1956 Juan-Manuel Fangio (R.A.), Ferrari
1957 Juan-Manuel Fangio (R.A.), Maserati
1958 J. M. (Mike) Hawthorn (G.B.), Ferrari
1959 Jack Brabham (AUS.), Cooper
1960 Jack Brabham (AUS.), Cooper
1961 Phil Hill (U.S.A.), Ferrari
1962 Graham Hill (G.B.), B.R.M.
1963 Jim Clark (G.B.), Lotus
1964 John Surtees (G.B.), Ferrari

1965 Jim Clark (G.B.), Lotus
1966 Jack Brabham (AUS.), Brabham
1967 Denis Hulme (N.Z.), Brabham
1968 Graham Hill (G.B.), Lotus
1969 Jackie Stewart (G.B.), Matra
1970 Jochen Rindt (A.), Lotus
1971 Jackie Stewart (G.B.), Tyrrell
1972 Emerson Fittipaldi (BR.), Lotus
1973 Jackie Stewart (G.B.), Tyrrell
1974 Emerson Fittipaldi (BR.), McLaren
1975 Niki Lauda (A.), Ferrari
1976 James Hunt (G.B.), McLaren Ford
1977 Niki Lauda (A.), Ferrari
1978 Mario Andretti (U.S.A.), Lotus
1979 Jody Scheckter (Z.A.), Ferrari

Graham Hill's Embassy-Hill in the 1975 Monaco Grand Prix, a race he won a unique five times.

The last driver to attempt to drive single-handed through the Le Mans 24-hour Race was Pierre Levegh in 1952. He was leading with $1\frac{1}{4}$ hours to go when the engine of his Talbot failed. Other notable solo performances in the race were in 1932, when Raymond Sommer was at the wheel of the winning Alfa Romeo for 21 hours, in 1950, when Louis Rosier drove the winning Talbot for over 20 hours, and in 1952, when Briggs Cunningham drove his Cunningham for 20 hours, into fourth place.

The longest run of consecutive World Championship race victories was achieved by Alberto Ascari in 1952–53. He won the last six in 1952 (Belgian, French, British, German, Dutch and Italian GPs) and the first three in 1953 (Argentine, Dutch and Belgian GPs).

The first permanent racing drivers' school—as distinct from occasional courses—was established by Jim Russell at Snetterton in 1957.

The youngest driver ever to win a Championship Grand Prix was Bruce McLaren, twenty-two when he took the flag at the end of the 1959 American GP at Sebring in a Cooper-Climax. Youngest driver to win the World Championship was Emerson Fittipaldi, twenty-five years old when he gained the title in 1972.

In the last Grand Prix of his first Championship season, the American event at Sebring in 1959, Jack Brabham gained 3 points by pushing his Cooper-Climax across the line after he had run out of fuel with a few hundred yards to go (Brabham won the Championship from Tony Brooks, who was third in that Sebring race, by 31 points to 27).

There are doubtless many obscure claimants to have been "the youngest racing driver", but among latter-day top-line drivers the Mexican brothers Pedro and Ricardo Rodriguez both raced cars when they were fifteen, and Bruce McLaren drove competitively at the same age. Pedro Rodriguez, a Mexican motorcycle champion when he was fourteen, was third in his first race (in a Jaguar XK120) and first raced in a European classic (the Le Mans 24-hour Race) when eighteen in 1958; in the following year he shared an Osca at Le Mans with Ricardo (they retired). Bruce McLaren was fastest in class in his first competitive event, a New Zealand hillclimb (driving a 750-c.c. Ulster Austin). Fellow New Zealander Chris Amon raced a converted midget when he was sixteen, a Maserati 250F when he was seventeen, and was a member of a European Formula 1 team when he was nineteen (he first raced a Parnell Lola-Climax in the 1963 Belgian GP).

Ronnie Peterson, the greatest Swedish driver, who started in 123 GPs and won 10. Died following Monza accident in 1978.

Jacques Lafitte, first French driver to win a World Championship race in a French car (Swedish GP, 1977).

Jean-Pierre Jabouille, first driver to win a World Championship race in a turbocharged car (French GP, 1979).

Only one World Championship has been won on the last lap of the last race, in 1964, when Hill, Clark and Surtees all started in the Mexican GP with a mathematical chance of taking the title. A fourth driver, Lorenzo Bandini, played a vital role in deciding the outcome: Hill retired early, after a collision with Bandini; an oil-pipe burst on Clark's Lotus, and his engine seized when he was in the lead on the last lap; Surtees, who had to finish at least second to gain enough points to take the Championship, was allowed through into second place on the last lap by his Ferrari team mate—Lorenzo Bandini (Dan Gurney, who won the race, was almost a disinterested participant, for he finished only sixth in the Championship).

The first driver to win a "grande épreuve" in a car bearing his own name was Jack Brabham, in the 1966 French GP at Rheims (at 136·90 m.p.h.). Second man to achieve this was Bruce McLaren, in the 1968 Belgian GP at Spa (at 147·14 m.p.h.).

The first "professional association" of Grand Prix drivers was U.P.P.I., succeeded in 1961 by the Grand Prix Drivers' Association. An attempt to widen the membership by opening it to all international licence holders was unsuccessful, and after conflict with the Formula 1 Constructors' Association in the mid 1970s, the G.P.D.A. was merged with the F.O.C.A. in 1976. It was then re-formed independently late in 1979.

The only driver ever to win the World Championship driving his own cars was Jack Brabham, who gained the title with his Repco-Brabham in 1966.

The largest number of World Championship victories was gained by Jackie Stewart (27 wins from 99 starts), followed by Jim Clark (25 from 72), Juan-Manuel Fangio (24 from 51), Niki Lauda (17 from 113). Stirling Moss won 16, Jack Brabham and Graham Hill 14 each. Among drivers still active as this edition was being prepared, by the end of 1979 Emerson Fittipaldi 14 from 129 starts. The only other drivers to have won 10 or more Championship races were Alberto Ascari (13), Mario Andretti (12), Jody Scheckter, Ronnie Peterson and James Hunt (10 each). In the 303 World Championship Grands Prix run between 1950 and the end of 1978, 53 drivers gained at least one victory.

Shared drivers, and wins, were admissible in Championship events to the end of 1957, this situation arising when a driver took over a team-mate's car during a race, and points were awarded accordingly. This partly distorts the totals given above; Fangio scored two "half-victories" but nevertheless is

Brabham's "biplane": Jack himself cornering the 1968 Repco-Brabham BT26. "Wings", or aerofoils, of this type were shortly to be banned.

generally credited with 24 victories instead of 22 plus two halves, while Moss also shared a victory, with Brooks in the 1957 British GP, and thus won $15\frac{1}{2}$ races (a nonsense in all save the mathematics of points addition!). Half points have also been awarded more recently, when races have ended prematurely because of outside factors such as weather.

As far as Championship points are concerned, Stewart scored a total of 360, quite clearly more than any other driver. Niki Lauda scored $292\frac{1}{2}$, Graham Hill 289, Fangio 277, Clark 274, Brabham 261 and Hulme 248.

Graham Hill drove in more Grands Prix than any other driver, starting in 176 World Championship events between 1958 and 1975. Jack Brabham started in 126 Grands Prix, Peterson in 123. At the end of the 1978 season, nine other drivers had started in more than 100 Grands Prix: Fittipaldi (115), Regazzoni (113), Hulme (112), Surtees (111), Ickx (108), Bonnier (102), Lauda (101), McLaren (100) and Reutemann (100).

The first race in which two brothers drove in a front-line Formula 1 team was the 1971 Argentine GP, when Brazilians Emerson and Wilson Fittipaldi both started in Gold Leaf Team Lotus cars (a 72 and a 49C respectively; neither finished).

The driver who raced for most marques in Grands Prix was Chris Amon—also rated by many as the most unfortunate driver! He drove 11 makes of Formula 1 car—Lola, Lotus, Cooper, Ferrari, March, Matra, Tecno, Tyrrell, Amon, B.R.M. and Ensign. Other widely experienced drivers were Trintignant (10 marques), Mass and Ickx (9), Surtees and Bonnier (8).

The greatest number of victories scored by a driver in a single season of the European Formula 2 Championship was gained by Bruno Giacomelli, who won 8 of the 12 rounds in 1978, driving a works March-B.M.W.

The greatest number of fastest laps in World Championship races was set by Jim Clark, who recorded them in 28 races; Fangio was fastest in 22, Moss in 18, Lauda in 17; and Stewart in 15.

The first lady driver to score in the World Championship was Lella Lombardi, whose sixth place in the 1975 Spanish GP gained her half a point—a half instead of the customary whole point as the race was stopped prematurely after an accident, and the first six drivers were awarded half the normal score (i.e. $4\frac{1}{2}$, 3, 2, $1\frac{1}{2}$, 1 and $\frac{1}{2}$).

The first World Champion to be awarded the title posthumously was Jochen Rindt, who was killed in an Italian GP practice accident in 1970. By that stage of the season, however, he had scored 45 points, and in the remaining races no other driver equalled this total.

SOME GREAT RACING DRIVERS

ARGENTINA

Juan-Manuel Fangio (Arg.). (b. 1911). A strong candidate for world's greatest driver honours, the phenomenal Fangio from Balcarce, Argentina, won the World Championship no less than five times. From a background of incredibly gruelling long-distance town-to-town races in South America, he burst upon the European scene in 1949, winning six races against the Continent's best. Alfa Romeo quickly signed up the quiet, sinewy, bow-legged Argentinian, and he won his first World Championship in a Type 159 in 1951. After two years with Maseratis he became Mercedes-Benz No. 1, taking two more Championship titles in 1954 and 1955, then he joined Ferrari to score his fourth Championship in 1956. Maserati took him to his fifth title, his victories including that awesome 1957 German GP when, despite an extra pit stop, forty-seven-year-old Fangio caught the Ferraris of Hawthorn and Collins, breaking the lap record ten times. In all, the incomparable Champion won twenty-four classic GPs and as many lesser ones; he retired in 1958.

José-Froilan Gonzalez (Arg.). (b. 1922). Portly "Pepe" Gonzalez, friend and rival of Fangio, made big news early in 1951 when he defeated the Mercedes-Benz attempt at a come-back with their 1939 GP cars and won the President and Eva Peron GPs at Buenos Aires. That earned him a Ferrari works drive in Europe, and Gonzalez fully justified it by winning the 1951 British GP, the first time the all-conquering Alfa Romeos were beaten. He won races at Goodwood with both B.R.M. and Thinwall Special in 1952, and in 1954 again won the British GP for Ferrari, this time defeating the new Formula 1 Mercedes-Benz. He won other Formula 1 races at Bordeaux, Silverstone and Bari, but crashed badly in practice for the Dundrod T.T. That virtually finished his career, although he appeared in local events for several years after.

AUSTRALIA

Jack Brabham (Australia). (b. 1926). Boldness and skill, alloyed with intimate mechanical knowledge of his car and shrewd race psychology, were the recipe for Jack Brabham's enormous success in motor racing. From a rugged background of Australian midget and speedway racing he came to Europe in 1955, joined Coopers in 1956, became Formula 2 Champion in 1958 and won his first World Championship in 1959 with Monaco and British GP wins and good placings elsewhere. In 1960 he answered critics calling it "a fluke" by winning five GPs in a row and his second Championship. By 1962 he was building his own Brabham Formula 1 car and in 1966 won both the World Championship—his third—and the Constructors' Championship with the Repco-engined Brabham. He also won the Formula 2 Championship with the Brabham-Honda; during the next four seasons he won three more GPs and lost the British GP of 1970 on the last lap for a pint or so of petrol. That year he retired from racing, but later in the decade was a frequent visitor to circuits where his son Geoff raced. Brabham was knighted in the 1979 New Year Honours list.

AUSTRIA

Niki Lauda (Austria). (b. 1949). Nikolaus-Andreas Lauda was uncompromisingly a wholly professional

racing driver of the 1970s, as skilful in business as in a single-seater racing car, his make-up lacking only the charm of archetypal Jackie Stewart. In the face of opposition from his wealthy family, Lauda had to make his own way in racing, starting in Formula Vee in 1969. He progressed through Formula 3 and sports-car racing with a Porsche 908, to Formula 2 in 1971 and to Formula 1 drives with March and B.R.M. He joined Ferrari in 1974, winning his first Grand Prix in Spain; in 1975 he won five Grands Prix, and the World Championship. After a horrifying accident at the Nürburgring in the 1976 German Grand Prix, he made an astounding return to racing in the Italian GP, but narrowly lost that year's Championship to James Hunt—in effect surrendering the title when he dispassionately adjudged the wet weather of the Japanese GP too dangerous. He regained the title in the following year, then left Ferrari in somewhat acrimonious circumstances to join Brabham. Here he enjoyed few racing successes in the next two seasons, both his 1978 victories coming in odd circumstances, with the subsequently banned "fan car" in Sweden and after the first two drivers past the chequered flag in the Italian GP had been penalised. During a largely barren 1979 season he was courted by other teams, reputedly offering very large retainers for his highly professional services. Less than professionally, he inexplicably decided to retire in the middle of practice for the 1979 Canadian GP!

Jochen Rindt (Austria). 1942–1970. A true "tiger" of indomitable courage and skill, Jochen Rindt

burst unknown upon the racing world in 1964 by winning at Crystal Palace with a private Formula 2 Brabham. A three-year contract with the waning Cooper marque retarded his progress, and a 1968 season with Brabham also proved unfruitful. However, he won Le Mans in 1965 in a Ferrari with Masten Gregory, as well as numerous Formula 2 races. His GP fortunes changed when he joined the Lotus team in 1969; that year's American GP marked his first Formula 1 win, and in 1970 he scored five more, the Monaco, Dutch, British, French and German events. Alas, during practice for the Italian GP at Monza this great driver was killed when his Lotus 72 went out of control and hit the Armco barrier head on. His lead in the World Championship was not unassailable at that time, but in fact his points score was not equalled and he was awarded the title posthumously.

Hans Stuck (Austria). (1900–1979). The famous Austrian "King of the Mountains", Hans Stuck, could

claim a racing career lasting over forty years. Beginning with a Durkopp in 1924 he graduated to Austro-Daimlers with which he won innumerable hillclimbs then to Mercedes-Benz and into GP racing with the Auto Union team in 1934. He won three GPs in his first year, one in 1935, and apart from challenges by Rosemeyer and Lang virtually dominated hillclimbing until the outbreak of war. In 1947 he successfully raced an 1100 c.c. Cisitalia then acquired a Formula 2 A.F.M., amazing Ascari by pipping his Ferrari to win heat 2 of the 1950 Monza GP, and coming first at Grenzlandring in 1951. Later he concentrated on hillclimbs again, driving B.M.W.s. In 1960 at the age of sixty, he won his final German Mountain Championship, and did not finally retire until 1965, leaving the fray to his son Hans-Joachim, who became an established Grand Prix driver by the mid 'seventies.

BELGIUM

Arthur Duray (B.). 1881–1954. The racing career of Arthur Duray, a naturalised Frenchman born in

New York of Belgian parents, lasted from the age of seventeen to forty-nine. He drove in many classic races, including the Gordon Bennett Trophy series and the early GPs. He won the Circuit des Ardennes in his native Belgium in 1906, and the St. Petersburg-Moscow Race of 1907, both times in a Lorraine-Dietrich, while with a private 3-litre Peugeot he finished a brilliant second in the 1914 Indianapolis 500 Miles. After the First World War Duray drove a Voisin without success in the 1923 French GP, and last raced in 1930 with an Ariès.

Jacky Ickx (B.). (b. 1945). Undoubtedly Belgium's finest driver in the last twenty years is Jacky Ickx, son

of a prominent motor journalist and pre-war scrambling star. From the age of sixteen he rose rapidly through motorcycle trials, saloon-car racing and Formula 3 to top-line racing. Talent-spotter Ken Tyrrell signed him in 1966, and he became European Formula 2 Champion in a Tyrrell team Matra in 1967. Ickx joined Ferrari in 1968, showing his renowned mastery of wet road racing by winning a drenching French GP at Rouen, and in 1969, moving to Brabham, he won the German and Canadian GPs and the Oulton Park Gold Cup. Back with Ferrari in 1970, he scored in the 1970 Austrian, Canadian and Mexican GPs, and in the 1971 Dutch GP, but Ferrari performance waned thereafter and the Ickx talents brought little fruit. A switch to JPS-Lotus in 1974 proved equally disappointing, apart from a typical "rainmaster" win in the Race of Champions. A superb sports-car driver, Ickx has raced Mirage, Ford GT40, Ferrari, Matra, Alfa Romeo and Gulf cars to over twenty major co-victories since 1967, including Le Mans four times (1969, 1975, 1976 and 1977), Spa, Watkin's Glen and Brands Hatch three times, Sebring, Monza and Silverstone twice, and numerous other major events. A quiet, serious-minded driver with decided opinions, who loves his native Spa and deplores the modern emasculation of classic circuits, Ickx left the G.P.D.A. in 1970. He was probably past his prime by 1976, when he signed with Frank Williams to drive the ex-Hesketh Formula 1 car. He failed to score Championship points, and was no more fortunate in occasional drives for Ensign in 1977 and 1978. In 1979 he undertook the task of re-establishing a shortened Spa as a major circuit, besides acting as a useful "stand-in" driver for the Ligier team when Patrick Depailler suffered a hang-gliding accident. Ickx then virtually retired.

Camille Jenatzy (B.). 1868–1913. The famous "Red Devil" of the heroic days of road racing, Camille

Jenatzy of the red, pointed beard and dashing style has two major claims to fame. He was the first to raise the Land Speed Record to over 65 m.p.h. and 100 k.p.h., with his streamlined electric car *La Jamais Contente* at Achères in 1899, his record of 65·79 m.p.h. standing for three years; and he won the fourth Gordon Bennett Trophy Race in 1903 for Germany with a stripped touring Mercedes 60, defeating the French, British and American teams. He finished second in the 1904 event, but had small success after that. Jenatzy met his death during a wild-boar hunt in the Ardennes forests in 1913, when he was mistaken for an animal by a friend and shot.

BRAZIL

Emerson Fittipaldi (BR.). (b. 1946). He is a national hero in Brazil, but in a racing car shows none of the

supposed Latin temperament, for Emerson Fittipaldi is one of the shrewdest drivers ever to win the World Championship. His natural talent was obvious as soon as he started racing in Formula Ford in England in 1968; two years later he won a Grand Prix, and by the time he won his first Championship was recognised as a very cool and calculating driver as well as a fast one. Fittipaldi raced karts in Brazil when he was seventeen, and within two years was a national champion (and, in partnership with his brother, a successful kart constructor). He moved on to Formula Vee, then came to Europe, swiftly passing through Formula Ford and Formula 3 to Formula 2 in 1970. That year he drove a works Lotus 49 in his first Grand Prix, at Brands Hatch, and when Jochen Rindt was killed at Monza he became Lotus team leader. Team problems and a road accident in 1971 slowed his progress, but in 1972 he took the Championship with victories in the Spanish, Belgian, British, Austrian and Italian GPs. In 1973 the young Brazilian won the Argentine, Brazilian and Spanish GPs, and was runner-up in the Championship, and in 1974 he moved to the McLaren team, to win the Brazilian, Belgian and Canadian GPs and his second Championship. He was runner-up again in 1975, when he won the Argentine and British GPs for McLaren, and at the end of the season surprised the world by moving to the Brazilian Copersucar team for 1976. Success proved elusive (he scored only three Championship points in 1976), but Fittipaldi worked hard to improve the team's record through the following seasons, sometimes showing his brilliance.

FRANCE

Robert Benoist (F.). 1895–1944. One of France's great drivers, Robert Benoist began his racing career

with 1100-c.c. Salmsons, scoring notable wins at Le Mans, Tarragona and in the 200 Miles Race at Brooklands in 1922, and at Monza, Boulogne and Le Mans in 1923. He joined the Delage GP team in 1924, winning the French GP the following year. His greatest season was 1927, when successive victories in the French, Spanish, Italian and British GPs, plus the GP de l'Ouverture at Montlhéry, established him a worthy European Champion. Driving a factory sports Alfa Romeo he won the 1929 Belgian 24-hour Race with Marinoni, then joined Bugatti, winning the 1935 Picardie GP and the Le Mans 24-Hour Race in 1937, co-driving with Wimille. As a daring liaison officer in the French Resistance during the Second World War, Benoist twice escaped from the Gestapo; captured again, he was strangled in Buchenwald Camp in 1944.

Georges Boillot (F.). 1885–1916. France's most outstanding driver of the 1910–14 era, the great

Georges Boillot drove exclusively for Peugeot, raising them to the heights by his victories in the French GP in 1912 and 1913. His desperate fight to hold off the Mercedes team and score a third victory in the 1914 race, only to retire on the last lap through engine failure, is legendary, but this brilliant, forceful driver won meritorious victories elsewhere. With the freakish Lion-Peugeot *voiturettes* he won the Normandy Cup race in 1909 and the Targa Florio and Boulogne *voiturette* races in 1910, while in larger Peugeots Boillot was successful at Ostend in 1911 and Provence and Boulogne in 1913, besides winning the Mont Ventoux hillclimb twice in 1912–13. He was killed in an aerial battle with the Germans over Verdun in 1916 when flying with the Armée de l'Air.

Louis Chiron (F.). (1899–1979). Although a Monégasque from Monte Carlo, Chiron was of French

parentage and stands as one of France's finest drivers in any era. Possessing fire, shrewdness and extreme delicacy in handling his car, his many sage victories earned him the nickname "The Wily Fox". After being chauffeur to Maréchals Pétain and Foch in the First World War Chiron began racing with Bugattis in the 1920s, switched to Alfa Romeos from 1933 to 1935, then to Talbots, Maseratis, Oscas, etc. after the Second World War. Among his greatest successes Chiron won the French GP five times, the Czechoslovakian GP three times, the San Sebastian, Comminges, Spanish and Marne GPs twice, and the German, Italian, Belgian and Monaco GPs once. He also won the Monte Carlo Rally in 1954 with a Lancia, and subsequently officiated as Race and Rally Director at Monte Carlo.

Philippe Etancelin (F.). (b. 1896). Popular Rouennais "Phi-phi" Etancelin with his reversed cap,

gritted teeth and spectacular driving style was a memorable racing figure. Competing as an amateur, he began with Bugattis and came to the fore by winning the 1930 French GP at Pau. Switching to Alfa Romeos in 1931 he won at Rheims, Comminges, Picardie and elsewhere, then bought a Maserati in 1934, defeating the proud Ferrari Alfas in the Dieppe GP. That year he also won Le Mans with Chinetti in a 2·3-litre Alfa Romeo, and in 1936 took the Pau GP with a V-eight Maserati. Thereafter he raced Talbots, always on the limit, with spinning wheels and smoking tyres. At the 1952 French GP, held in his native Rouen, Etancelin was awarded the Cross of the Legion d'Honneur for his twenty-five years' service to French motor sport. The following year, aged fifty-seven, he drove his final race, again at Rouen, finishing a fighting third in his Talbot to two works Ferraris.

Fernand Gabriel (F.). ?–1943. This unobtrusive French driver gained eternal fame for his epic

performance with an 11·2-litre 70-h.p. Mors in the disastrous 1903 Paris-Madrid Road Race. Starting in eighty-second place on crowded, dusty roads thronged with careless spectators, he moved right up into the lead, and won the Paris–Bordeaux leg at an average of 65·3 m.p.h. The race was then stopped by the authorities owing to many serious accidents, and thus Gabriel became the outright winner. Subsequently he drove Lorraine-Dietrich, Clément-Bayard, Schneider and, after the First World War, Ariès cars but never with outstanding success. He was killed during the Second World War in an Allied bombing raid on La Garenne, outside Paris.

Jules Goux (F.). 1885–1965. This talented, imperturbable French driver made his name with Peugeots,

first in the voiturette class with wins in Sicily, Catalonia, Barcelona, Normandy and elsewhere in 1909–10, then in the GP class, with victory on the Sarthe in 1912 and then with his memorable win in the Indianapolis 500 Miles of 1913. After the First World War Goux drove for Ballot, winning the 1921 Italian GP at Brescia, and later he joined the Bugatti team, placing first in both the French GP and the GP of Europe in Spain during the 1926 season. He retired that year from racing.

Victor Héméry (F.). 1876–1950. Another of the great names from the heroic age of racing, Victor

Héméry from Le Mans was a daring, colourful driver of great strength and stamina. He won both the Ardennes and Vanderbilt Cup races for Darracq in 1905, and that same year he drove the 200-h.p. V-eight Darracq to a new Land Speed Record at 109·65 m.p.h. near Arles. The year 1908 brought him another victory in the St. Petersburg-Moscow Race over atrocious Russian roads with a Benz, averaging over 53 m.p.h. for 440 miles, and the following year he took his second Land Speed Record, this time with the famous 200-h.p. Blitzen Benz at 125·95 m.p.h. on Brooklands track. In 1911 Héméry won the GP de France at Le Mans in a Fiat, and essayed a come-back after the First World War, driving a Rolland-Pilain in the 1922 and 1923 GPs, but without success. He died on the same day as Raymond Sommer, 10th September 1950.

Louis (1877–1944) and Marcel (1872–1903) Renault (F.). The most effective way to establish a new

Marcel, 1903
Paris–Madrid

make of car in pioneer days was to win motor races, as Louis Renault (see page 46), founder of the Renault marque, and his older brother Marcel proved very convincingly between 1899 and 1903. On victories gained, Louis seemed the better driver, taking the voiturette class in the Paris-Trouville, Paris-Ostend and Paris-Rambouillet races in 1899, Paris-Toulouse in 1900, and the Pau GP, Paris-Bordeaux and Paris-Berlin in 1901. With a 16-h.p. Renault light car, however, Marcel scored an outstanding success in the 1902 Paris-Vienna Race, beating all the big cars to win outright. Tragedy came in the 1903 Paris-Madrid, for while Louis was ahead, brother Marcel crashed at Couhé-Vérac and was killed. Louis Renault, who gained the light car category and second place overall when the race was stopped at Bordeaux, immediately retired from racing.

Raymond Sommer (F.). 1906–1950. The "Gay Cavalier" of French racing in the 'thirties and 'forties,

Raymond Sommer drove with tigerish determination, mostly on an amateur basis. His long list of victories includes two Le Mans 24-hour races, with Chinetti in 1932 and Nuvolari in 1933, both times in a 2·3-litre Alfa Romeo. With a private Alfa Romeo he beat the factory cars at Marseilles in 1932 and Comminges in 1935, while in 1936 he won the French GP with Wimille in a Bugatti and the Belgian 24-hour Race with Severi in an Alfa Romeo. Although he liked to win, Sommer revelled in the actual race battle, and with his flair and flamboyance was highly popular with the French public, who called him "Cœur de lion". He was French Champion in 1937, 1939 and 1946, raced Alfa Romeo, Maserati, Simca, Ferrari and other makes after the war, including a Cooper-J.A.P. 500 for the sheer fun of it. It was tragically ironic that in such a car, fitted with an 1100-c.c. J.A.P. engine, this driver of top GP quality should have been killed in a minor national race at Cadours in 1950. He was forty-four.

Léon Théry (F.). 1880–1909. "The Chronometer" to his admiring countrymen, Léon Théry was re-

nowned for his calm, consistent but very fast driving of Richard-Brasier cars. His fame was built on his quadruple success in the Gordon Bennett Trophy races. In 1904 he won the Eliminating Race in France and the Trophy itself in Germany, and in 1905 he repeated the "double" on French soil. He did not race again until 1908, when he made a come-back in the French GP with one of the old Brasiers, lying as high as third place against more modern cars when trouble forced him out with only two laps to go. Théry died from tuberculosis in 1909 at the early age of twenty-nine.

Louis Wagner (F.). 1882–1960. A great driver from the "Heroic Age", Paris-born Louis Wagner's first success came in the 1903 Ardennes race in Belgium when he won the light car class with a Darracq. He repeated this success in 1905 then moved on to greater deeds, winning the 1906 Vanderbilt Cup in the U.S.A. for Darracq and the 1908 American Grand Prize for Fiat. A consistent high performer, he scored many good placings driving Mercedes, Alfa Romeo, Ballot, Talbot and Delage cars, and in 1926 won his last victories, the British GP with Sénéchal, and the La Baule GP, both in a Delage. During the Second World War, tuberculosis of the bone cost him a leg, and he spent his last years as a supervisor at Montlhéry track.

Jean-Pierre Wimille (F.). 1906–1949. Had the World Championship been inaugurated earlier than 1950, J.-P. Wimille would surely have won the title. His quiet, aloof nature concealed tremendous enthusiasm and skill. Like many Frenchmen, he began with Bugattis, early wins coming at Lorraine and Oran in 1932. By 1934 he was a works Bugatti driver, scoring over the Alfas in the Algerian GP, took a sports car triple in 1936 in the French, Marne and Comminges GPs, won the Le Mans classic in 1937 and 1939, and in 1945 won the first post-war race, held in Paris. Driving the works 158 Alfa Romeos he placed first in the Belgian and Swiss GPs of 1947 and the French, Italian and Monza GPs in 1948; but for team orders he would have won more. He also much enjoyed driving Simca *voiturettes*, winning the Rosario GP in Argentina with one in 1948. Alas, practising for the Buenos Aires GP in a similar car a year later, J.-P. Wimille crashed fatally when avoiding a spectator, and France lost a master driver.

GERMANY

Rudolf Caracciola (Ger.). 1901–1960. For sheer consistency and weight of victories, "Rudi" Caracciola, the calm and masterly Rhinelander, must rate as one of the greatest drivers of all time. In a career lasting from 1922 to 1952 he garnered a tremendous number of victories in GPs, sports car races and hillclimbs. He won every continental GP at least once, and the German GP six times, and apart from 1932 when he drove for Alfa Romeo all were gained in Mercedes cars. A bad crash at Monaco in 1933 broke a thigh and gave him a permanent limp. Practising at Indianapolis in 1946 he struck a bird at speed, suffering head injuries and partial paralysis. In 1952 he came fourth in the Mille Miglia, but in the subsequent Swiss sports car GP at his favourite Berne circuit he again crashed, breaking another thigh—a sad ending to a magnificent career.

Hermann Lang (Ger.). (b. 1909). The phenomenal rise of Hermann Lang from Mercedes racing mechanic to the fastest driver in Europe highlighted the last pre-war GP years. He began as a trainee driver in 1935, and by 1937 had won the world's fastest track race, at Avus, at 162·61 m.p.h., and the world's fastest road race, at Tripoli, at 134·42 m.p.h. He won Tripoli again in 1938 and 1939, and in the latter year scored four other GP victories, becoming European Champion. But for the Second World War he would surely have gone on to further GP glories; as it was he made a come-back with Mercedes sports cars in 1952, winning Le Mans and the Nürburgring Sports Car Race. He remained in Mercedes-Benz employ until he reached retirement age.

Christian Lautenschlager (Ger.). 1877–1954. Christian Lautenschlager of the heavy Teutonic

moustaches and massive build was unique among racing drivers, competing in only two French GPs yet winning them both. After being riding mechanic to Salzer in the Mercedes team in 1906–07 he was entered for the classic 1908 GP at Dieppe with a 12·75-litre Mercedes. Driving for nearly 7 hours and running perilously short of tyres, he won at 69·05 m.p.h. His second race was the 1913 GP de France at Le Mans, where he was placed sixth, and his third was the 1914 GP, which he won in magnificent fashion, averaging 65·66 m.p.h. in a race lasting over 7 hours. After the First World War Lautenschlager competed in two Targa Florios and the 1923 Indianapolis 500 Miles, but could never recapture his superb pre-war form.

Bernd Rosemeyer (Ger.). 1910–1938. Three short but shattering seasons saw ex-racing motorcyclist

Bernd Rosemeyer rise like a meteor from raw Auto Union recruit to GP star. His first race was in May 1935, yet his first win in the unwieldy rear-engined car, the Czech GP, came four months later. In the next two seasons he scored nine brilliant victories—the Eifel and Pescara GPs twice, the German, Swiss, Italian and Donington GPs, and the Vanderbilt Cup in the U.S.A. Sadly, 1937 was the last season for this cheerful, fighting Saxon, his life being squandered in a record attempt early in 1938, his streamlined Auto Union leaving the road at over 270 m.p.h. and hitting a bridge.

GREAT BRITAIN

Sir Henry Birkin, Bt. (G.B.). 1896–1933. Captain "Tim" Birkin epitomised the irrepressible "Bentley

Boys" of Le Mans fame as the wealthy, colourful amateur of formidably professional ability. He won Le Mans twice, with Woolf Barnato in a Bentley in 1929, and with Earl Howe in an Alfa Romeo in 1931. He placed second in the 1930 French GP with his stripped four-seater blown Bentley, won the Brooklands Mountain Championship in 1931 with a Maserati, and set the Brooklands outer circuit lap record at 137·96 m.p.h. in 1932 with his famous Bentley single-seater. In 1933 Birkin led the 1,100 c.c. class in the Mille Miglia until his M.G. Magnette failed under him, then finished third in the Tripoli GP. That was his last race, for an arm burnt on the exhaust-pipe developed into blood poisoning, and he died at the peak of his ability.

Jim Clark (G.B.). 1936–1968. One of the great geniuses of motor racing, ranking with Fangio, Moss,

Caracciola and Nuvolari, Jim Clark "the wee Scot" from Duns, began with a D.K.W. saloon in local events in 1956. He progressed rapidly via Porsche, Jaguar, Lister, Lotus Elite and Tojeiro cars, and Lotus signed him on in 1960, driving Formula Junior, Formula 2 and Formula 1. Clark wins thereafter became profuse; his first Formula 1 win was the 1961 Pau GP, and his first Championship victory the 1962 Belgian GP. Suffice it to record that this magnificent driver won twenty-four Championship GPs and innumerable lesser events. He won his first World Championship in 1963, scoring irresistible victories in the Belgian, Dutch, French, British, Italian, Mexican, and South African GPs with a Lotus-

Climax. The year 1965 brought him his second World Championship with six great wins. That year he also won the Indianapolis 500 Miles in a Lotus-Ford, the first European to do so for forty-five years. His last Championship race victory was the 1968 South African GP; four months later he crashed inexplicably in a Formula 2 race at Hockenheim, Germany, and was killed.

Peter Collins (G.B.). 1931–1958. The 500-c.c. racing movement in Britain produced many fine drivers, including cheerful Peter Collins, who began in 1949 with a Cooper-Norton and won his way into both the H.W.M. Formula 2 and Aston Martin sports car teams by 1952. His first major win was the Goodwood Nine Hours, shared with Pat Griffith; the same pair won the 1953 T.T.; in 1955 Collins was first at Silverstone in the International Trophy with a Maserati, while in his one sensational drive for Mercedes-Benz, he shared victory with Stirling Moss in the Targa Florio. The year 1956 brought Collins a Ferrari contract and victory in the Belgian and French GPs. He won the Syracuse and Naples GPs in 1957 and the International Trophy and British GP in 1958, plus several sports car races. It was while battling for the lead in the 1958 German GP at the Nürburgring that Collins left the road and was killed.

Mike Hawthorn (G.B.). 1929–1959. The phenomenal rise to international fame of John Michael Hawthorn resembled that of Rosemeyer, Lang and Rindt. In 1951 he was an amateur racing a fast Riley; in 1952 he became Britain's white hope with a Cooper-Bristol F2, and by 1953 he had joined Ferrari, the greatest continental team, and had won the French GP from the great Fangio. Ferraris brought him other fine victories—the 1953 International and Ulster Trophy races, the 1954 Spanish GP, the 1958 French GP again, and the World Championship itself that year. He scored in many sports car races for Ferrari, too, and also Jaguars, for whom he won Sebring and Le Mans in 1955. The death of his friend Peter Collins deeply upset Hawthorn in 1958, and having won the Championship he decided, at twenty-nine, to retire. Three months later he was killed in a road accident on the Guildford By-pass in his Jaguar saloon.

Mike Hawthorn (2,488-c.c. Ferrari Tipo 625) during the 1955 British Grand Prix at Aintree, where he gained sixth place with Castellotti.

Graham Hill (G.B.). 1929–1975. Londoner Graham Hill fought his way up from looking after other

people's racing cars to the GP élite by sheer determination. In twelve seasons, seven of them driving for B.R.M. and five for Lotus, he won the Monaco GP five times—a unique record—the U.S. GP three times, and the Dutch, German, Italian, Spanish, Mexican and South African GPs. He was World Champion in 1962 with a B.R.M. and in 1968 with a Lotus. He also won the Indianapolis 500 Miles in 1966 as a "rookie" driving a Lola. He crashed badly in the 1969 U.S. GP, breaking both legs, but by tremendous pluck Hill refound his form in 1971, winning a Formula 2 race at Thruxton and a Formula 1 race at Silverstone, driving for Brabham. That proved to be his last Formula 1 victory, and he became increasingly involved in running his Embassy-Hill team. He raced for the last time in the 1975 International Trophy at Silverstone, thereafter becoming a full-time constructor. Piloting his own aircraft back from a test session at the Paul Ricard circuit on the 29th November 1975, Hill crashed on a golf course on the approach to Elstree airfield. He was killed instantly, together with driver Tony Brise and four other members of his team.

    In 1976 the Silverstone International Trophy Race was renamed the Graham Hill International Trophy as a tribute.

Identifiable by his helmet markings, Graham Hill at Silverstone in May 1971 driving a Brabham BT34.

James Hunt (G.B.). (b. 1947). James Simon Wallis Hunt was one of the most controversial of all World

Champions, from his early days in single-seater racing, through his 1976 Championship season, to his abrupt retirement from racing in the middle of the 1979 season. His extrovert manner and disregard for convention alienated some enthusiasts, but on his day he could drive with great determination and ability. In his early racing years he gained a "Shunt" nickname, although this was not wholly deserved, and he seemed to be slipping towards racing obscurity in 1972. But in that year he started to drive for Lord Hesketh, late in the season showing competitive ability in a year-old Formula 2 March. This blossomed further when the team took up Formula 1 with their own Hesketh car, and in 1975 Hunt won his first Grand Prix, in Holland. Hesketh withdrew at the end of that year, and Hunt took Fittipaldi's place in the McLaren team for an extraordinary season of victories, disqualifications (and one reinstatement) and through the second half of the year a determined onslaught on Lauda's apparently unassailable points score, which saw Hunt clinch the Championship in the last race. His defence of the title was at times spirited, but the McLaren M23 was increasingly outclassed and its successor, the M26, was not such an outstanding design. Hunt joined the Wolf team for a final season of racing in 1979, but became disillusioned at his lack of success and retired from racing in mid-season.

Stirling Moss—England's greatest Grand Prix driver. Above: With the Mercedes-Benz W.196 taking the 1955 British GP at Aintree. Centre: With the immortal Vanwall winning the historic, breakthrough British GP of 1957 (aided by Tony Brooks). Below: In Rob Walker's privately-entered Lotus 18 with which he beat the foreign "works opposition" in four Grands Prix during 1960 and 1961. (Photos: Geoffrey Goddard.)

The Ickx/Oliver Ford GT 40 sports car, winner by about 100 yards after 24 hours' racing in the 1969 Le Mans event at an average speed of 129·40 m.p.h.

The Chris Amon/Pedro Rodriguez Ferrari 312P which finished fourth in the 1969 B.O.A.C. 500 at Brands Hatch.

Winner of the 1970 Le Mans 24-Hour Race was the Attwood/Herrmann Porsche 917 at 119·30 m.p.h.

Les Vingt-quatre Heures du Mans, 1974: the Matra-Simca team won the race for the third year in succession and Henri Pescarolo achieved his personal hat-trick of victories.

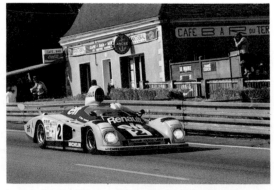

Le Mans victors, 1977 and 1978. Left: The turbocharged Porsche 936 of Barth/Haywood/Ickx. Right: The Pironi/Jaussaud Renault A442B. (Photo: Nigel Snowdon.)

Charles Jarrott (G.B.). 1877–1944. One of the few British drivers to shine in the French-dominated

pioneer period of racing, Charles Jarrott renounced a law career to go racing, beginning on motor tricycles and turning to Panhard cars in 1901. His great year was 1902, when he finished second in the Circuit du Nord, pursued his dictum "Always finish" in the Paris-Vienna by repairing his broken chassis with wood from hotel furniture and pressing on to twelfth place despite no clutch, no exhaust-pipe and only one gear, and then won the Circuit des Ardennes in Belgium. Transferring to De Dietrich in 1903, he placed fourth in the Paris-Madrid, and drove a Wolseley to twelfth place in the 1904 Gordon Bennett Trophy Race.

Stirling Moss (G.B.). (b. 1929). Although ill-fortune denied him a World Championship title, Stirling

Moss rates among the very greatest of drivers. For sheer genius, shrewdness and versatility Moss was a master indeed. He began racing in 1948 with a Cooper 500, rising by H.W.M. Formula 2 and Jaguar sports cars to GP status, first with a private Maserati, then Mercedes, Maserati, Vanwall and Rob Walker-Lotus, as well as being Aston Martin's sports car No. 1. Moss's victories in fourteen seasons exceed 100, and include seven R.A.C. T.T.s, five Oulton Park Gold Cups, four Nürburgring 1,000-kilometres races, three Monaco and Italian GPs, two British and Portuguese GPs, the German, Dutch and Argentine GPs, the Targa Florio and the Mille Miglia. A crash at Goodwood in the Formula 1 B.R.P. Lotus in 1962 ended the most brilliant career of any British driver, for on recovery he decided reluctantly to retire from mainstream racing, although he occasionally appears in historic car races and returned to saloon car racing in 1980.

Richard Seaman (G.B.). 1913–1939. Starting as an amateur in 1931, R. J. B. Seaman rose to the

highest professional racing status on sheer ability. His first win came at Berne in 1934 with an M.G. Magnette, then he bought an E.R.A. for 1935 and scored at Pescara, Berne and Brno. In 1936 he humiliated modern rivals by restoring a 1927 GP Delage and defeating them in four major races at Douglas, Pescara, Berne and Donington, besides taking the Empire Trophy in a Maserati and the Donington GP, with Hans Ruesch, in an Alfa Romeo. Mercedes-Benz hired him in 1937, and he placed second in the 1937 Vanderbilt Cup, won the 1938 German GP and was second in the 1938 Swiss GP. In the 1939 Belgian GP Seaman took the lead in pouring rain, then his Mercedes skidded, folded round a tree, and Seaman died from the resultant fire.

Sir Henry Segrave (G.B.). 1896–1930. Britain's greatest Grand Prix star of the "Golden Age" of the

1920s, Henry O'Neal De Hane Segrave secured a place in the Sunbeam-Talbot-Darracq team in 1921 by sheer persistence, and won that year's 200 Miles Race at Brooklands. His greatest victory, the French GP at Tours, came in 1923 when he also scored at Boulogne. He won the 1924 San Sebastian GP, and both the GP de Provence and 200 Miles Race twice in 1925 and 1926, and many lesser events. Segrave broke the Land Speed Record three times, in 1926 with a 4-litre Sunbeam at 152·33 m.p.h., in 1927 with the 1000-h.p. Sunbeam at 203·79 m.p.h., and in 1929 with the *Golden Arrow* at 231·44 m.p.h., a feat for which he was knighted. Britain lost a hero when Segrave died in 1930 on Lake Windermere after *Miss England II* struck a floating obstruction and capsized after setting a new Water Speed Record at 98·76 m.p.h.

Jackie Stewart (G.B.). (b. 1939). Jackie Stewart came from Dunbartonshire, Scotland, younger

brother of racing driver Jimmy Stewart and a clay pigeon shooting champion, to drive Formula 3 racing cars for Ken Tyrrell's Cooper-B.M.C. team in 1964. An obvious "natural", he won twelve races, also did well in Formula 2, and inevitably was snapped up for Formula 1 in 1965, B.R.M. just beating Lotus and Cooper in the rush. Stewart's first Formula 1 win was the Silverstone International Trophy, then he won the Italian GP, the Tasman Championship "down under" and, in 1966, the Monaco GP. A bad crash at Spa broke the spell, but he won four Formula 2 races with a Matra-Ford and for 1968 signed to drive Formula 1 Matras for Ken Tyrrell. A wrist broken in Spain spoiled his Championship chances that year but he won three GPs, and in 1969 made no mistakes. He took the South African, Spanish, Dutch, French, British and Italian GPs and won the Championship. He gained his second World Championship in 1971, and his third in 1973, both in Tyrrell cars. He retired at the close of the 1973 season with a record twenty-seven Grand Prix victories in his scintillating career. After retirement he continued to centre his activities on motor racing, as a counsellor and in the "political" and commercial aspects of the sport, and television commenting.

John Surtees (G.B.). (b. 1934). John Surtees came to car racing in 1960 with seven motorcycle World

Championships behind him, amply fulfilling expectations by his formidable skill and total dedication. From Formula Junior in 1960 he drove Formula 1 Lotuses, Coopers and Lolas, then joined Ferrari in 1963, winning the World Championship the following year through victories in the German and Italian GPs and other good placings. He also shared in several sports car wins for Ferrari, and took the 1966 Belgian GP just before leaving them. Then he won the Mexican GP for Coopers, and became the first CanAm Champion with a Lola. The year 1967 saw him driving for Honda and winning the Italian GP by a stupendous last-minute dash. Two largely fruitless seasons with Honda and then B.R.M. decided Surtees to launch out as a manufacturer himself, first in the Formula 5000 Class and then Formula 1. His only Formula 1 successes were in the Oulton Park Gold Cup, and since his retirement from racing his team and company had mixed fortunes—no Surtees car managed to win a Grand Prix, but in 1972 Mike Hailwood won the Formula 2 Championship for the team. After further fruitless Formula 1 efforts, John Surtees became increasingly disillusioned with modern Grand Prix racing—at least with its "political" and business aspects—and did not attend some of the later races. At the end of the 1978 season he abandoned his GP efforts, though keeping Team Surtees alive at a secondary level.

ITALY

Antonio Ascari (I.). 1888–1925. This superb Italian driver began driving on a De Vecchi in 1911

but only became well known after the war, first driving a Fiat with which he did well in hillclimbs, then a works Alfa Romeo. His first race victory came at Cremona in 1923, and he won the Alfa Romeo P2 its first race, again at Cremona, in 1924. Appalling bad luck cost him Targa Florio and French GP victories that year, but he won the Italian GP, and in 1925 led the GP of Europe at Spa from start to finish. In his next race, the French GP at Montlhéry, Ascari had a 4-minute lead when, encountering sudden rain on a fast corner, he slid slightly and entangled a hubcap in the paling fence. The Alfa Romeo overturned and Ascari, aged thirty-six, died in the ambulance taking him to hospital.

Alberto Ascari (I.). 1918–1955. Famous son of a famous father, Alberto Ascari was Italy's greatest ace of the 1950s, a driver of immense skill and shrewdness. Like many of his countrymen, he began racing on motorcycles, but took to four wheels in 1940 and won his first car race in 1947, at Modena. Teaming with Villoresi, first with Maserati, then Ferrari, Ascari soon outpaced his teacher and by 1949 had won his first classics—the Swiss and European GPs. Many victories in Ferraris ensued—ten in 1950, six in 1951, eleven in 1952 and eight in 1953, clinching a World Championship double in 1952 and 1953. The following year he signed with Lancia and won the Mille Miglia, while in 1955 with the new GP Lancia he won at Turin and Naples, then crashed into the harbour when about to lead the Monaco GP. Back in Italy four days later and eager to "limber up", Ascari took a 3-litre sports Ferrari out on to Monza track, only to crash inexplicably and fatally.

Pietro Bordino (I.). 1887–1928. Rated by Segrave and many other authorities as the fastest road-racing driver of the 1920s, Pietro Bordino—"Il Diavolo Rosso"—began racing for Fiat in 1908 at the Château-Thierry hillclimb in France. He made the fastest lap in the 1921 Italian GP and 1922, 1923 and 1924 French GPs, but retired each time. His great year was 1922, when he won both the GP di Vetturette and the Italian GP at the newly opened Monza track. In 1927 Bordino made a come-back with a new 1·5-litre twelve-cylinder Fiat, winning the Milan GP at Monza. He changed to a Bugatti for 1928, and was practising for the Alessandria race when he hit a large dog at full speed; Bordino crashed into the River Tanaro and was drowned.

Giuseppe Campari (I.). 1892–1933. Employed as mechanic and tester by the original A.L.F.A. Company, big burly Giuseppe Campari began racing in 1913, and helped to put the new name "Alfa Romeo" well on the map in post-war years. He won races at Mugello in 1920 and 1921, and was victorious in the 1924 French GP at Lyons with an Alfa Romeo P2. His great stamina helped him to two Mille Miglia wins in 1928 and 1929, and other successes with Alfa Romeo included three Acerbo Cup races and the 1931 Italian GP, sharing the drive with Nuvolari. Campari's last great win came in the 1933 French GP with a 2·9-litre Maserati, for this colourful driver was killed at the ill-fated Monza meeting later that year, when Borzacchini and Czaykowski also lost their lives.

Luigi Fagioli (I.). 1899–1952. Ranking close to Varzi and Nuvolari among Italy's master drivers of the 1930s, massive-shouldered Luigi Fagioli was a carefree individualist not always amenable to discipline. Graduating from Salmsons to Maseratis by 1930, then to the Alfa Romeo team by 1933, his several victories impressed Mercedes-Benz sufficiently to hire him for their new GP team in 1934. He won six races for them—the Spanish, Pescara and Italian GPs in 1934, and Monaco, Avus and Barcelona in 1935, but had constant brushes with team control and left after 1936. He raced but little thereafter until 1950 when he joined the Alfa Romeo 158 team sharing victory with Fangio in the 1951 French GP. He also won the 1100 c.c. class in the 1951 Mille Miglia with an Osca, and placed third over all in this race in 1952 with a Lancia. Sadly, when practising for the Monaco sports car GP he crashed his Aurelia, dying three weeks later from his head injuries.

Giuseppe Farina (I.). 1906–1966. "Nino" Farina's formative years were the 1930s, when he raced

Maseratis and then joined Alfa Romeo in 1936. Somewhat remote, temperamental and impetuous, Farina at his best was brilliant, and in the new Type 158 1·5-litre Alfa Romeo he scored three pre-war wins, won the GP of the Nations at Geneva in 1946, and took five first places in 1950, when he became the first World Champion. Farina also drove Maseratis and Ferraris with success, though overshadowed by Alberto Ascari's brilliance in 1952–53. However, he won the 1953 German GP and also had a fine record in sports car racing. His career was marred by several serious accidents, and he died in a road crash when driving a private Lotus near Chambéry in France in 1966.

Vincenzo Lancia (I.). 1881–1937. Honoured both as a fearless racing driver and a car-manufacturer,

Vincenzo Lancia was an eighteen-year-old mechanic with Ceirano when their company became Fiat in 1899. From testing he quickly advanced to racing for the new marque, and his massive build and tempestuous pace made him one of the great characters of the "Heroic Age". Ill luck and sometimes his own impetuousness, robbed him of several victories, but he scored in many early hillclimbs, won the Florio Cup Race in 1904, was second in the 1906 Vanderbilt Cup and won the unique Coppa d'Oro regularity event around Italy the same year. He founded the Lancia marque in November 1906, but continued racing for Fiat until 1908.

Felice Nazzaro (I.). 1881–1940. One of the great masters of Italian motor racing, Felice Nazzaro of the

smooth gait and delicate touch sprang to the forefront with his remarkable triple victories in the 1907 Targa Florio in Sicily, Kaiserpreis in Germany, and French GP, all in Fiat cars. The following year he won the Florio Cup Race at Bologna, and in 1911 he left Fiat to manufacture the Nazzaro car. Driving his own marque he won the 1913 Targa Florio and the 1914 Florio Cup, but after the war Nazzaro returned to Fiat to score an outstanding victory in the 1922 French GP at Strasbourg. He lost the 1923 European GP on the last lap through a broken oil-pipe, and drove his last GP in 1924, when his car failed him. He remained on the Fiat staff almost to his death in 1940.

Tazio Nuvolari (I.). 1892–1953. "Il Maestro" to numberless admirers, Nuvolari of Mantua was the

greatest racing driver of his era, if not of all time. Possessing indomitable will and courage, tremendous fire and devilish skill, he stood out even from other great masters. With his small, wiry physique he cultivated the practice of four-wheel drifting through corners, and whatever he drove—Bianchi, Chiribiri, Bugatti, Alfa Romeo, Maserati, M.G., Auto Union, Cisitalia or Ferrari, he always drove to win. Of his major race victories, totalling over fifty, the 1935 German GP, when he routed nine modern German cars with his outdated Alfa Romeo, was outstanding, but he also beat the Germans at Barcelona, Budapest and Leghorn in 1936, and won three GPs in 1938–39 for Auto Union. After the war he took the Albi GP in 1946 and, at fifty-six, led the 1947 Mille Miglia in his little Cisitalia until rain killed its electrics 90 miles from victory. His last race was at Monte Pellegrino in 1950 when he won his class with a Cisitalia. There was much sadness in Nuvolari's private life, for he lost both his sons, while he himself died a lingering death in 1953.

Tazio Nuvolari (Ferrari) at the start of the 1948 Mille Miglia.

Achille Varzi (I.). 1904–1948. Traditionally the fierce rival of Nuvolari, Achille Varzi was the very antithesis of the dynamic Mantuan, having a cold, calculating, nerveless style, spectacular only for its sheer ferocious speed. Lacking Nuvolari's sheer dedication, Varzi's career was more erratic, though punctuated by many brilliant victories in Alfa Romeo, Bugatti, Maserati and Auto Union cars. They included four Alessandria GPs, three Tripoli GPs, two Monza GPs, two Acerbo and Ciano Cups, and single Monaco, Spanish and Mille Miglia wins. Becoming engrossed with girl-friends and drugs, Varzi gave up trying after 1936, but reappeared invigorated after the war to drive for Alfa Romeo. He won at Turin in 1946, and at Bari, Rosario and Interlagos in 1947, only to meet his death during practice for the 1948 Swiss GP when his car skidded in the wet and overturned on him.

NEW ZEALAND

Denis Hulme (N.Z.). (b. 1936). Tough, competent, quiet and wholly professional, Denny Hulme of New Zealand came to Europe in 1960 under the "Driver to Europe" scheme. It took him five hard years of slogging in Formula Junior and Formula 2 before getting a foot on the Formula 1 ladder by 1965, driving for Jack Brabham. Victory eluded him until 1967, when he won the Monaco and German GPs which, combined with three seconds, three thirds and a fourth, made him World Champion. Then he left Brabhams to join his countryman Bruce McLaren, dividing his activities between Formula 1 and the CanAm Group 7 series in North America. He won four more Formula 1 races—the 1968 Italian and Canadian GPs and the Silverstone Trophy, and the Mexican GP of 1969, and created an enviable record in CanAm by winning the Championship in 1968 and 1970. He continued to show consistency in GP racing from 1971 until the end of 1974, when he retired. His last Championship victory was gained in Argentina in 1974. During 1975 he was still active around the circuits as President of the G.P.D.A., then he retired to New Zealand.

Bruce McLaren (N.Z.). 1937–1970. Brilliant driver/manufacturer from New Zealand, Bruce

McLaren came to Coopers of Surbiton in 1958 under the New Zealand Grand Prix Association's "Driver to Europe" scheme. He won the 1959 U.S. GP and the 1960 Argentine GP, and the Monaco and Rheims GPs of 1962, but by 1963 his interests widened to sports car racing. Group 7 McLarens won the CanAm Championship four years in succession from 1967 to 1970, Bruce himself winning the title in 1967 and 1969. He also won Le Mans in 1966 with his countryman Chris Amon in a Ford GT40, and in that year built the first Formula 1 McLaren. He won the 1968 Race of Champions and the Belgian GP, and it was a bitter blow when this quiet, clever New Zealander was killed at thirty-two while testing a new CanAm car at Goodwood in 1970.

SOUTH AFRICA

Jody Scheckter (Z.A.) (b. 1950). Like many drivers of the present generation, Jody Scheckter started his

racing career driving karts, graduating to a Renault saloon when he was nineteen. He won the Sunshine Series Formula Ford title in 1970, and with it a "Driver to Europe" award. For some time he appeared to live up to his "sideways Scheckter" reputation—which belied a natural talent—but piled up an impressive success score in Formula Ford and Formula 3. After a period in Formula 2 with McLaren's less-than-successful car, Scheckter made his Grand Prix début in a McLaren at Watkins Glen in 1972. In 1973 he won the U.S. Formula 5000 Championship, running in only a few GPs but achieving fame—or notoriety—when a rash manœuvre in the British GP at Silverstone started an enormous chain-reaction accident. The Tyrrell team provided Scheckter's GP finishing school; driving for this team, he scored his first championship victory in Sweden in 1974 (he scored a unique victory in the same event in 1976, driving the six-wheeled Tyrrell P34). In 1977 he joined the new Wolf team, winning three GPs, but a second season with the same team was less rewarding. With the announced conviction that it would give him the best chance of winning the Championship, he joined Ferrari in 1979. The Italian cars gave him race victories, and almost as important consistent points-scoring places, and he clinched the Championship by winning the Italian GP. A dour individual—sometimes almost surly—Scheckter is his own man. As he became an experienced driver, accumulated racecraft complemented talent, but this maturity was not reflected in a changed public image; the wealth that came with racing success was not paid for in charm for average racing enthusiasts.

U.S.A.

Mario Andretti (U.S.A.). (b. 1940). The most versatile driver ever to win the World Championship,

Andretti moved to Formula 1 when he already had a highly successful career in U.S. racing behind him. In his Italian background, heavily influenced by his hero-worship of Alberto Ascari, lay the roots of his ambition to succeed in the Grands Prix, but he came to them by a most unusual route, having never competed in any of the international road race categories for single-seaters. His family emigrated to the U.S.A. when he was nineteen, and Andretti soon started racing stock cars, and on dirt and paved ovals. By 1964 he had graduated to U.S.A.C. single-seaters, becoming National U.S.A.C. Champion in 1965, 1966 and 1969. That same year, driving a Brawner Hawk Ford, his U.S.A.C. career peaked with victory in the Indianapolis 500 Miles—the race in which he took the Rookie prize in 1965, and pole position in 1966 and 1967. His first Formula 1 drive came with a Lotus in the

1968 U.S. GP, when he shook the establishment by setting fastest practice lap, though retiring in the race. He again drove for Lotus in 1969 and for March in 1970, but division of his talents between GPs, prototype sports cars and U.S.A.C. have all too often affected Andretti's race record.

He was co-victor at Sebring in 1970, won the South African GP and the Questor GP in 1971, and shared four 1972 prototype wins with Jacky Ickx at Daytona, Sebring, Brands Hatch and Watkins Glen, all in Ferraris. In 1974 he won the Monza 1,000 kilometres with Merzario in an Alfa Romeo, and raced an F 5000 Lola for the Vel's Parnelli team in U.S. events, winning at Watkins Glen, Elkhart Lake and Riverside but losing the Championship title to Brian Redman. The year 1975 saw him putting in almost a full World Championship Formula 1 season with the Parnelli-Cosworth, when his best placing was fourth in the Swedish GP.

In 1976 Andretti tried the Lotus 77 in the Brazilian GP, returned to the Parnelli team until its Formula 1 effort suddenly expired, then rejoined Lotus. He worked hard with Chapman and the team to pull Lotus out of a depressed period, at the end of the year winning the Japanese GP. In 1977 Andretti won more GPs than any other driver, but the Lotus 78 was plagued with unreliability, especially in its Cosworth development engines, and he placed only third in the Championship table. In the following year the only question soon became whether the Championship would go to Andretti or his Lotus team-mate Ronnie Peterson—in fact, Andretti had undisputed Number One status in the team, and this was appreciated by the Swede. The Lotus 79 ground effects car gave the team an enormous advantage, and Andretti's single point earned on a sombre afternoon at Monza put the issue beyond dispute.

David Bruce-Brown (U.S.A.). 1890–1912. This young American's racing career was brilliant but lamentably brief. His love for motor racing led him to run away from college to the 1908 Daytona Speed Trials, where he broke the Amateur Mile Record by 3 seconds in a borrowed Fiat. In 1909 he won two events at Daytona with a 120-h.p. Benz. In 1910 he won the American Grand Prize with a factory Benz; in 1911 he won it again with a factory Fiat. In 1912 he led the French GP almost to ¾-distance, then refuelled away from the pits and was disqualified. Practising for the 1912 American Grand Prize at Milwaukee, Bruce-Brown was killed when his Fiat burst a tyre and overturned.

Ralph De Palma (U.S.A.). 1882–1956. One of America's finest and shrewdest drivers, Italian-born Ralph de Palma rose the hard way, through the familiar mechanic and motorcycle-racing route to his first car event in 1908. By 1912 he was near the pinnacle, winning the Elgin Trophy and Vanderbilt Cup races and losing the Indianapolis 500 Miles 5 laps from the end with engine failure. He raced for twenty-seven years, driving Mercedes, Fiats, Packards, Ballots, etc., highlights including two more Elgin Trophies, another Vanderbilt Cup, the 1915 Indianapolis 500 Miles, a new Land Speed Record in a V-twelve Packard at 149.87 m.p.h. in 1919, and second place in the 1921 French GP with a Ballot.

Dan Gurney (U.S.A.). (b. 1931). Tall, sinewy, and with a huge, ready grin, Dan Gurney stands as one of America's greatest all-round drivers of all time. He was scarcely known in Europe when Ferrari nominated him a team member in 1959; he gained invaluable experience but little success that season, moved to B.R.M. in 1960, won the Nürburgring 1000-kilometres Race with Moss in a sports Maserati, joined Porsche in 1961–62 and Brabham in 1963–64. He won the French GP twice in 1962 and 1964, the 1962 Solitude GP and the 1964 Mexican GP. Like other drivers he hankered after building his own cars, and by 1966 Anglo-American Racers Inc. was turning out Eagle-Weslake Formula 1 cars and Eagle Fords for U.S. racing. Gurney won the Race of Champions and the Belgian GP—his greatest victory— in 1967, also the Le Mans 24-hour Race with A. J. Foyt in a Ford. At Indianapolis he was second both in 1968 and 1969, but after a half-hearted come-back to GPs early in 1970, he retired from race driving to concentrate on his Eagle cars.

Early in his racing career, Dan Gurney (Ferrari) during the 1959 Tourist Trophy Race.

Phil Hill (U.S.A.). (b. 1927). The first American to win the World Championship, lean, nervy Phil Hill from California had much experience and many fine performances in sports cars to his credit when Ferrari invited him to join their team in 1956. He accepted, winning sports car races in Sweden, Sicily, Venezuela, Buenos Aires and elsewhere. In 1958, almost reluctantly, Ferrari let him drive in the last two Formula 1 GPs of the season and he placed third in both. He scored two seconds in 1959, won his first GP at Monza in 1960, and in 1961 took the Belgian and Italian GPs, which with high placings elsewhere gained him the Championship. Driving subsequently for other teams, he never equalled his 1961 GP form, but he was a consistently brilliant sports car driver, with three Le Mans victories to his credit, in 1958, 1961 and 1962, each time shared with the Belgian Olivier Gendebien, while in 1966 he confounded "has been" critics by winning the Nürburgring 1000-kilometres Race with Joakim Bonnier, then the B.O.A.C. 500 Miles Race at Brands Hatch in 1967, co-driving with the late Mike Spence, both times in a Chaparral-Chevrolet. He then retired from racing to concentrate on his car restoration business.

Section 3

SPRINTS, HILLCLIMBS AND RALLIES

Compiled by F. Wilson McComb
and John Davenport

Photo: W. J. Brunell.

The first speed hillclimb in the world was held on 31st January 1897, over the 10·3-mile course from Nice to La Turbie, just outside Monte Carlo, and formed the concluding stage of the race from Marseilles to Nice. It was won by M. Pary driving André Michelin's 15-h.p. De Dion Bouton steam car, which averaged just under 20 m.p.h., from an 18-h.p. De Dion Bouton steamer driven by the Comte de Chasseloup-Laubat, and the 6-h.p. petrol-driven Peugeot of Lemaître, which took more than 20 minutes longer to cover the course than the winning car. The success of Michelin's car over Chasseloup-Laubat's similar but more powerful machine was attributed to the fact that the first was using pneumatic tyres, the second running on solid tyres.

The first hillclimb organised as a separate contest was held on 27th November 1898 at Chanteloup, near Paris, and sponsored by *La France Automobile*. The course, a little over a mile in length, included several tight bends on a steep gradient and was in poor condition owing to heavy rain, but only three of the fifty-four competitors failed to climb the hill. Fastest was Camille Jenatzy's electric car with a time of 3 minutes 52 seconds. This was not his famous record car, *La Jamais Contente*, but an earlier machine of his own manufacture.

The first sprint meeting in the world was held on 18th December 1898 at Achères Park, near Paris, and was also organised by *La France Automobile*. The course was flat but very wet, and competitors were timed over 2 kilometres from a standing start, thus providing two sets of figures, for the standing-start kilometre and the flying-start kilometre. The Comte de Chasseloup-Laubat covered the first in 72·6 seconds and the second in 57 seconds. His average speed over the flying kilometre, 39·3 m.p.h., automatically became the world's first Land Speed Record figure. It was achieved with a Jeantaud electric car weighing almost 1½ tons. This was followed by a series of duels between the Count and Jenatzy for the Land Speed Record (see pages 29 and 182).

The first of the famous Nice Speed Trials was held on the Promenade des Anglais on 23rd March 1899, when cars were timed over 1 mile from a standing start. Fastest was Lemaître's 20-h.p. Peugeot with a time of 95·6 seconds (37·5 m.p.h.), which thus became the first petrol-driven car to win a sprint event. The following day Lemaître also won the La Turbie Hillclimb at 25·4 m.p.h. This is almost certainly the first hillclimb success by a petrol-driven car: the De Dion Bouton of Spitz won the first Semmering Hillclimb in Austria, also in 1899, but the exact date is not recorded and the De Dion Bouton could have been either a steam or a petrol-driven model of that period.

The first American car to win a sprint or hillclimb was almost certainly a Stanley steamer, which is said to have won a hillclimbing contest at Charles River Park, Boston, Mass., in 1897. A Stanley has also been recorded as achieving 27·4 m.p.h. over a timed mile at Charles River Park in 1898. The first event organised by the newly formed Automobile Club of America was a 7-mile run on 4th November 1899 which included a climb of Riverside Drive in New York City, a test that defeated all but a dozen of the thirty-eight competitors. Also in 1899, Freelan O. Stanley succeeded in driving his steam car to the summit of Mount Washington, New Hampshire. The first of the classic Gaillon Hillclimbs in France, over a 1,096-yard course in the Seine Valley, was won in 1899 at 21·6 m.p.h. by an American steam car of unknown make, which was probably a Stanley.

The first hillclimb in England was held on a 325-yard course at Petersham Hill, near London, on 9th June 1899, as part of a series of contests organised in and around the Old Deer Park, Richmond. Most of the drivers were employees of the dealers and manufacturers concerned, and only the more prominent names are recorded. The fastest climb was made by a Barrière tricycle at about 14 m.p.h., closely followed by a Leitner dog-cart. A Benz is said to have "torn up the hill" at 9·7 m.p.h., and the Hon. Charles Rolls averaged 8·75 m.p.h. with his "racing" 6-h.p. Panhard.

The Hon. Charles Rolls in his 6-h.p. Panhard at Petersham Hill. (Photo: Radio Times Hulton Picture Library.)

The first sprint meeting in England was arranged for 14th June 1899 on a public road outside Colchester, Essex. Only one car was entered, a Delahaye which covered the flying-start mile at just under 27 m.p.h. **The first successful sprint meeting** was held on 11th May 1900, as part of the Thousand Miles Trial arranged by the Automobile Club of Great Britain and Ireland. The course, a flying-start mile, was not quite level, so cars were timed in both directions; it was on one of the drives at Welbeck Park, belonging to the Duke of Portland. The winner was the Hon. Charles Rolls, whose two-way average was 37·63 m.p.h. with a 12-h.p. Panhard.

The Duke banned motor cars from his estate when one of them caused him to fall off his bicycle shortly after, but he eventually relaxed his ban. Welbeck Park became a popular sprint venue, meetings being held there at intervals until 1924. It was also used in 1903 for the Gordon Bennett Cup eliminating trials.

At the first hillclimb held in the twentieth century, the runner-up for best performance was Herbert (later Lord) Austin, driving one of the Wolseleys which he designed at that time. The event was a minor club meeting at Mucklow Hill, near Birmingham, late in January 1900. It was held in heavy snow, and the fastest car took nearly 10 minutes to cover a timed distance of little over a mile.

The first competitor killed on a hillclimb course was the German driver, Wilhelm Bauer, whose Daimler crashed during practice for the La Turbie event held on 30th March 1900. For the following year's event the course was shortened by 1 kilometre.

It was also at La Turbie that the **first fatality occurred during a hillclimb**. The Polish Count Eliot Zborowski, father of the creator of the "Chitty-Chitty-Bang-Bangs" (see page 198), crashed his Mercedes there on 1st April 1903 and was killed instantly. The event was abandoned, and the course subsequently reduced to less than half its former length.

Pelzer in his Serpollet steamer at the Gaillon course in 1904.

The first Englishman to win a continental hillclimb was E. T. Stead, whose 40-h.p. Mercedes climbed La Turbie at a record 34·73 m.p.h. on 7th April 1902. The following year he drove in the notorious Paris-Madrid Race, and in 1904 and 1905 he drove Brasiers in the French Gordon Bennett Eliminating Trials.

The first hillclimb held in Italy was the Consuma Cup event near Florence on 15th June 1902, in which Nourry's 8-h.p. De Dion Bouton averaged 23 m.p.h. over a 9·4-mile course. This was quickly followed on 22nd June by the 2·8-mile Sassi-Superga Hillclimb, near Turin, and on 27th July by the first of the classic Susa-Mont Cenis meetings, over a timed 16·8-mile course. Vincenzo Lancia (Fiat) won both of these, and both at an average of about 27·5 m.p.h.

Mont Ventoux, 1934: the holder, Whitney Straight (Maserati), who took second place to Stuck's fastest-ever Auto Union.

The longest hillclimb series in Continental Europe was at Mont Ventoux, France, where the first event was held in 1902 and the last (over a shortened course) in 1976. Until 1973 the original course of 13·48 miles was still in use, making it **the longest hillclimb course in the world.** In 1902 the first winning car, Chauchard's 13·7-litre Panhard, covered the distance in 27 minutes 17 seconds, which represents an average speed of 29·65 m.p.h. **The fastest-ever climb over the original distance** was made in little more than one-third of that time, Jimmy Mieusset's 2-litre March 722 clocking a record 9 minutes 3·6 seconds in 1973 to average 88·41 m.p.h. This was 47·5 seconds better than the previous record, achieved in 1972, but the course had been completely resurfaced.

The fastest pre-war climb at Mont Ventoux was made by Hans Stuck, who returned a time of 13 minutes 38·6 seconds to average 59·3 m.p.h. with a 4·4-litre Auto Union in 1934.

The only American who ever won at Mont Ventoux was Whitney Straight, a member of the well-known Vanderbilt family of Long Island, New York. In 1933, driving his 2·6-litre Maserati, he took more than 40 seconds off Caracciola's 1932 record for the hill. A few weeks later, he broke Stuck's three-year-old record for Shelsley Walsh in England.

The longest hillclimb now held (1980) is at Trento Bondone, Italy. With a measured distance of 10·75 miles, it is just one kilometre more than the Montseny course in Spain, but it is little more than one-quarter the length of the climb from Cuneo to the Col of the Madalena, which was **the longest course ever used for a speed hillclimb.** Held from 1925 to 1930, this featured a timed distance of no less than 41·5 miles.

The first seaside speed trials in England were held on 19th May 1902 on the promenade at Bexhill-on-Sea, Sussex, and won by Léon Serpollet with his famous Gardner-Serpollet steam car known, because of its curious shape, as "The Easter Egg". His time for the flying-start kilometre was 41·8 seconds (54·53 m.p.h.) despite a downhill start from a specially built ramp. At the Nice Speed Trials five weeks earlier, with a longer start, Serpollet had established a world record in the same car by covering the kilometre in only 29·8 seconds (75·06 m.p.h.). Despite local opposition, the Bexhill Speed Trials were held annually until 1907, then again from 1922 to 1924.

The first speed trials at Daytona Beach, Florida, were held on 28th March 1903. Alexander Winton, one of the instigators of the Gordon Bennett Cup Race, made the fastest run with a speed of 69·0 m.p.h. over the flying-start mile. His low-built Winton Bullet had a 17-litre engine placed on its side to reduce the height of the car.

The first Irish Speed Trials were held on 4th July 1903, two days after the Gordon Bennett Cup Race, in Phoenix Park, Dublin. Over the flying kilometre, Baron de Forest's privately owned Paris-Madrid Mors beat Gabriel's works Mors, and an 80-h.p. Panhard driven by the Hon. Charles Rolls. Two hill-climbs were also included in the so-called "Irish Fortnight", at Bally-bannon Hill, Co. Down, and Killorglin, near Killarney. Rolls won at Killorglin, but was beaten at Ballybannon by Campbell-Muir's Mercedes.

The last Nice Speed Trials on a straight course were held on 28th March 1904, when Rigolly and Duray both drove the 13½-litre Gobron-Brillié over the standing-start mile in exactly the same time, 53·6 seconds. But the flying-start kilometre went to Rigolly with a time of 23·6 seconds (94·78 m.p.h.). Later in the year, the Gobron-Brillié was the first car to exceed 100 m.p.h.

From 1905 to 1914 the Promenade des Anglais was used for a variety of timed manœuvrability tests. True speed events recommenced in 1932 with a circuit race that became known as the "Nice Grand Prix".

The first "Climb to the Clouds" contest at Mount Washington, New Hampshire, U.S.A., is believed to have been held on 12th July 1904 over a timed distance of 8 miles. Harry Harkness made the fastest climb at an average of 19·5 m.p.h. F. E. Stanley, twin brother of F. O. Stanley who had reached the summit in 1899, averaged 15·2 m.p.h. with a Stanley steamer.

The first speed trials held on sand in the British Isles were not staged at Southport but at Port-marnock, Dublin, on 17th September 1904. The Southport event on 2nd–3rd October 1903 was held on the Promenade; it was not until 1920 that the Southport sands were first used for sprint meetings and eventually for circuit racing.

The first speed hillclimb in the Isle of Man was held at Port Vuillen on 11th May 1904 as part of the eliminating trials for that year's Gordon Bennett Cup Race. The following day, cars were timed over a flying kilometre on Douglas Promenade. Fastest in both was S. F. Edge (80-h.p. Napier), who climbed the ½-mile hill at 47·0 m.p.h. and averaged 57·3 m.p.h. over the flying kilometre. The Promenade was so unsuitable for speed events that Clifford Earp's Napier, returning from its second run, skidded and hit a wall, after which the trials were abandoned.

The first recorded hillclimb at Giant's Despair, Wilkes-Barre, Pennsylvania, U.S.A., was in 1905 when H. J. Koehler won with a Buick. Meetings were held regularly until· 1910, an unsuccessful event was run in 1916, and the series restarted in 1951.

The World's Land Speed Record was equalled on Blackpool Promenade at the second sprint meeting held there, on 28th July 1905. Driving his 90-h.p. Napier, Clifford Earp covered the flying kilometre in 21·4 seconds (104·53 m.p.h.), exactly the same time as Baras had returned with the 100–h.p. Darracq at Ostend Speed Trials the previous November.

The first supercharged car to win a speed hillclimb was a Chadwick Six which broke the record at Giant's Despair, Pennsylvania, on 30th May 1908. It was also the first supercharged car to compete in a hillclimb.

John Boyd Dunlop, inventor of the pneumatic tyre, was one of the class winners at a hillclimb held near Enniskillen in July 1908 by the Motor Yacht Club of Ireland. This was not the only Irish hillclimb held by a nautical organisation; the Royal North of Ireland Yacht Club held several events at Cultra, Co. Down, in 1910 and 1911.

H. G. Day corners his Talbot during the South Wales A.C. and Cardiff M.C. Hillclimb at Caerphilly in June 1913. (Photo: Radio Times Hulton Picture Library.)

Harry Ferguson, manufacturer of the Ferguson tractor and advocate of four-wheel-drive for passenger cars, won the first hillclimb held at Craigantlet, near Belfast. It was organised by the Irish section of the Society of Motor Manufacturers and Traders, and held on 24th May 1913. Half a century later, a four-wheel-drive Ferguson car won the R.A.C. Hillclimb Championship of Britain.

Percy Lambert (25-h.p. Talbot), about to establish a climb record during the 1913 Leicester A.C. Beacon Hill meeting. (Photo: Radio Times Hulton Picture Library.)

The first Czechoslovakian hillclimb was the Zbraslav-Jiloviste event in 1908. The Prague series started in 1921, and the Ecce Homo in 1924.

W. O. Bentley's first motor-car competition was the Aston Clinton Hillclimb of 8th June 1912. He drove a modified D.F.P., the French car for which the Bentley brothers held the British concession, and broke the 2-litre class record.

W. O. Bentley finishing his climb on the D.F.P. at the Herts A.C. Open Hillclimb, Aston Hill, May 1914. (Photo: Radio Times Hulton Picture Library.)

The last hillclimb held in England before the First World War was won by W. R. Morris, the future Lord Nuffield, driving a Morris Oxford. It was held on 29th August 1914 by the Coventry and Warwickshire Motor Club at Style Kop, Staffordshire—not to be confused with the better-known Kop Hill in Buckinghamshire.

The last Irish hillclimb before the First World War, and the last before the Second World War were both held at the same venue, Ballinascorney, near Dublin. The event on 28th May 1914 was won by J. T. Wood (G.W.K.), and that on 23rd September 1939 (strictly, after war had been declared), by A. P. MacArthur (M.G.).

An early Shelsley Walsh meeting. J. A. Barber Lomax (and three passengers) in his Vauxhall during the June 1913 Midland A.C. Hillclimb. While occupants strive to overcome the centrifugal force, a rear door succumbs!

The only car named after a hillclimb is the Aston Martin, but it was not so called because the marque gained many successes at Aston Clinton, as commonly supposed —the early cars seldom appeared there and scored only a few class wins. Lionel Martin chose the "Aston" prefix while his car was still little more than a pipe-dream, and many years before it actually reached production, because he had won several trophies at Aston Clinton with a modified Singer 10 before the First World War. The marque's first hillclimb success was at the Hampshire A.C.'s Spread Eagle event in 1921, when Kensington-Moir won his class with the famous prototype, *Bunny.*

Hillclimbing in the 'twenties. M. Chalmers sets off in his Beardmore at Aston Clinton in 1925. (Photo: A. R. and J. A. Twentyman.)

The only hillclimb named after a car is the Duryea Drive event at Reading, Pennsylvania. The Duryea (which first appeared in 1892/93) was for some time built at Reading, and the name of Duryea Drive commemorates the fact that cars were frequently tested on that stretch of road, which is now used for speed hillclimbs.

The grounds of Palace House, Beaulieu, where the National Motor Museum is situated, were used for a ¼-mile hillclimb by the Royal Automobile Club on 22nd May 1909, and again on 26th June by the Hampshire A.C.

At the first post-war speed trial in England, held on 23rd July 1919 on the seafront at Westcliff, Essex, competitors included Malcolm Campbell (12-h.p. Talbot), Woolf Barnato (10-h.p. Calthorpe) and Yvonne Arnaud (10-h.p. Eric-Campbell).

Tony Vandervell, the man behind the successful Vanwall G.P. car, was runner-up at the Shelsley Walsh Hillclimb on 3rd July 1920, the first meeting there after the First World War. With a Clement-Talbot he was only 2·2 seconds behind the works driver, C. A. Bird, whose Indianapolis Sunbeam made the fastest climb of the day.

The fastest run ever made in a hillclimb was achieved half a century ago. At Gaillon in 1920, René Thomas averaged 109·25 m.p.h. with the 350-h.p. Sunbeam which was to gain the Land Speed Record three times. The classic French hillclimb course was not only a fast one, but featured a flying start from 1901 to 1921; in 1923 it was changed to a rolling start, 50 metres before the line.

    The famous 18·3-litre Sunbeam reappeared in several English sprints driven by Malcolm Campbell. It was the fastest car at the Saltburn Sands meeting, Redcar, Yorkshire, on 17th June 1922—less than a month after setting the Land Speed Record at 133·75 m.p.h. at Brooklands in the hands of Kenelm Lee Guinness. At Skegness two years later, Campbell again had the fastest run, and at the 1924 Saltburn Speed Trials he matched the Sunbeam against another Land Speed Record contender, Ernest Eldridge's 21·7-litre Fiat. Eldridge won the standing-start kilometre with 76·09 m.p.h. to Campbell's 61·38 m.p.h., but Campbell reversed the order in the flying kilometre by averaging 145·26 m.p.h. to the 139·81 m.p.h. returned by Eldridge. Campbell's speed was actually higher than the Land Speed Record at that time, although unrecognised as such. However, Eldridge made the record his at Arpajon three weeks later with a two-way average of 146·01 m.p.h.

The first Southsea "Speed Carnival" brought together two strangely different vehicles on 23rd August 1922—Count Louis Zborowski's huge 23-litre "Chitty-Chitty-Bang-Bang" and J. A. Joyce's little 1½-litre A.C., the first small car to achieve 100 m.p.h. Zborowski's monster won the flying-kilometre event at 73·1 m.p.h., but Joyce's record car returned 69·5 m.p.h. for the standing-start mile. In addition to many hillclimb successes, Joyce won at Brighton Speed Trials in 1923 (over a standing ¼ mile), made the fastest run at the 1923 Southsea meeting, and won again over a standing ½ mile at Brighton in 1924.

H. O. D. Segrave's first sprint success came on the Southport sands in 1920, when he was fastest over the standing-start mile with a G.P. Opel. He also competed successfully in some hillclimbs, and made the fastest climb at Shelsley Walsh on his only appearance there, on 23rd May 1925 with a works 2-litre G.P. Sunbeam. But he disliked short-distance events, as did many road-racing drivers. One of Nuvolari's few hillclimb victories was gained in the Cuneo-Maddalena event of 1930, but this course was over 40 miles long. Juan-Manuel Fangio drove once in the 1953 Swiss Vue des Alpes Hillclimb; his Maserati easily broke the three-year-old course record, and the runner-up was Ken Wharton, Hillclimb Champion of Britain. Mike Hawthorn, in the whole of his career, never took part in a hillclimb. Jim Clark won the Scottish Bo'ness Hillclimb in 1959, and also competed in the Ollon-Villars Hillclimb, Switzerland, in 1962 and 1965.

The slowest-ever success for Ralph DePalma, leading American driver for twenty years, Land Speed Record contender and winner at Indianapolis in 1915, was his victory in the Mount Wilson Hillclimb near Los Angeles on 16th July 1924. Driving a Chrysler, he averaged 22·1 m.p.h. over the $9\frac{1}{2}$-mile course to win the event.

Four-in-a-row victories in major continental hillclimbs have been gained by three outstanding experts in this branch of the sport. Every Semmering (Austria) event from 1903 to 1906 was won by Hermann Braun with a Mercedes. Every Stelvio (Italy) Hillclimb from 1933 to 1936 was won by Mario Tadini with an Alfa Romeo. Every La Turbie (France) Hillclimb from 1936 to 1939 was won by Hans Stuck with an Auto Union.

Hat-tricks have been achieved by many hillclimb specialists. Alfieri Maserati won Susa-Mont Cenis (Italy) from 1921 to 1923; Emilio Materassi won Capodistrada-Collina (Italy) from 1924 to 1926; Hans Stuck won Kesselberg (Germany) from 1928 to 1930; Luigi Fagioli won Tolentino-Paterno (Italy) from 1928 to 1930; Clemente Biondetti won Scansano (Italy) from 1929 to 1931; Eugenio Castellotti won Bolzano-Mendola (Italy) from 1953 to 1955; Ferdinando Pagliarini won Castell'Arquato-Vernasca (Italy) from 1956 to 1959 (event not held in 1957); and Odoardo Govoni won Pontedecimo-Giovi (Italy) from 1959 to 1961.

An unusual double hat-trick went to Giovanni Bracco in the Biella-Oropa Hillclimb. He won every event there from 1939 to 1956—but only six meetings were held there during that time: in 1939, 1947, 1948, 1949, 1953 and 1956.

The last speed hillclimb held on a public road in Britain was the Essex M.C. meeting at Kop Hill, Buckinghamshire, on 28th March 1925. It was stopped when a spectator was slightly injured by the ex-Mays Brescia Bugatti, *Cordon*

A lady driver (accompanied by lady passenger) climbs Caerphilly Hill during a South Wales Auto Club meeting between the wars. (Photo: W. J. Brunell.)

Bleu, driven by Francis Giveen, an Oxford undergraduate. The last Spread Eagle and South Harting hillclimbs were held the previous year, on 28th June and 26th July 1924 respectively. The last Aston Clinton Hillclimb was on 28th February 1925. However, two public-road sprints were run on 4th April 1925: one on Whitecross Road, near Hereford, and one on Brentner Straight, Tavistock. The ban did not apply to Ireland, the Isle of Man or the Channel Islands.

The only woman to win a major European hillclimb outright was Madame Jennky, whose 2-litre Bugatti made the fastest climb at Gaillon in 1927. Understandably, she is often confused with Madame Junek, a Czechoslovakian girl driver who drove in several major races—also with a Bugatti—in 1927 and 1928.

A new ladies' record was established at Shelsley Walsh in August 1957 when Miss Roberta Cowell climbed in 40·14 seconds with an Emeryson-Alta. This same driver, a war-time fighter pilot and ex-P.O.W. known as Bob Cowell, had been a successful male competitor at Shelsley Walsh and other speed events ten years before.

Enzo Ferrari won the Italian Bobbio/Penice Hillclimb with a 2·3-litre Alfa Romeo on 14th June 1931. This was his last season as a regular competitor before taking up full-time team management for the Alfa Romeo factory and eventually designing his own cars.

The Mont Ventoux Hillclimb was run from 1902 to 1976, making it the longest hillclimb series in Continental Europe, and for many years the timed distance of 13·48 miles was the longest in the world. A Type 35 Bugatti is seen here being driven by Delmo during 1934.

The British Mountain Championship was not a hillclimb contest, but the title of a series of Brooklands races held from 1931 to 1938 on the so-called "Mountain Circuit" (see also page 195).

Dick Seaman and Whitney Straight both made their début in speed events at the same Shelsley Walsh Hillclimb, on 11th July 1931. Both drove Rileys and neither of them gained an award.

The first consistently successful "Shelsley Special" was Basil Davenport's *Spider*, which cost less than £150 to build, but made the fastest climb at every meeting from September 1926 to May 1929 inclusive—a total of six victories, with four new course records.

With a 1½-litre V-twin engine in a G.N. chassis of the early 'twenties,

Basil Davenport in his replica Spider *at Shelsley Walsh after the Second World War. (Photo: Guy Griffiths Motofoto.)*

Spider was fitted with bodywork so disreputable in appearance that it was once refused admission to Shelsley Walsh, on the grounds that such a shabby device could not possibly be one of the competing cars.

In July 1930 the two finest hillclimb drivers in the world came to Shelsley Walsh: Hans Stuck with his 3·6-litre Austro-Daimler and Rudi Caracciola with his 7-litre Mercedes-Benz SSK. Stuck shattered the Shelsley Walsh record with a climb in 42·8 seconds, and Caracciola returned a time of 46·4 seconds. Between the two came the humble *Spider*, with 44·6 seconds.

Not long after, Davenport retired from hillclimbing until 1946, when the first Shelsley Walsh meeting was held after the Second World War. Despite an absence of some fifteen years, he took the ancient *Spider* up in 45·65 seconds to record the fastest climb by any unsupercharged car. Davenport and *Spider* reappeared at Shelsley Walsh in October 1946— but this was not, as many imagined, the same car. It was a replica with a 2-litre engine in a modified H.R.G. chassis.

Rudi Caracciola in his Mercedes-Benz 38/250 at Shelsley in 1929. (Photo: Autocar.)

Twin rear wheels were first used on a hillclimb car in 1929, when Raymond Mays had them fitted to his Vauxhall-Villiers for the September Shelsley Walsh meeting to reduce wheelspin on getaway. But this was not, as has been stated, the first time that twin rears had been fitted to *any* competition car. Parry Thomas had experimented with them on his Leyland-Thomas at Brooklands in 1924–25.

The first four-wheel-drive car entered for a hillclimb was the special 4·9-litre Bugatti with which Louis Chiron won his class at the Swiss Klausen Hillclimb on 7th August 1932. The following month it was brought to Shelsley Walsh by Jean Bugatti, who crashed the car during practice. Subsequently the special Bugatti gained several successes, the most notable at La Turbie in 1934 when René Dreyfus reduced the course record by 6·6 seconds.

The worst accident in the history of speed hillclimbs occurred at Château-Thièrry, France, where competitors were required to stop their cars on the finishing-line. At the 1935 meeting, Cattanéo's 1½-litre Bugatti spun under braking, slid off the course, and killed eight spectators.

The fastest pre-war runs on three leading Italian hillclimbs were all made by the same driver, Mario Tadini, with an Alfa Romeo. In 1936 he averaged 37·4 m.p.h. at Stelvio (8·7 miles); in 1937 he covered Susa–Mont Cenis (13·8 miles) at 54·5 m.p.h., and Parma-Poggio di Berceto (31·5 miles) at 64·0 m.p.h. average.

The winner of the last pre-war sprint meeting in England, Sydney Allard, overturned his 3·9-litre Allard after crossing the finishing-line in the Southsea M.C.'s 1939 Horndean event. Neither he nor his passenger (William Boddy, the future Editor of *Motor Sport*) was injured.

Alec Issigonis, designer of the Mini, drives his Lightweight Special up Prescott Hill in April 1948. (Photo: Guy Griffiths Motofoto.)

Sir Alec Issigonis was one of the class winners at the first English sprint meeting held after the Second World War, a ½-mile event at Filton Aerodrome, near Bristol, on 28th October 1945. Issigonis returned 32·0 seconds with the Lightweight Special, built by himself and George Dowson shortly before the war. The fastest run was made by Bob Gerard (1½-litre E.R.A.) in a time of 26·3 seconds.

The Filton meeting was not, however, the first English speed event after the war. On 18th August 1945 the Bristol club held a timed climb for cars and motor cycles at Naish House, near Portishead, on a grass and earth course almost ½ mile long.

The first post-war speed event in Germany was a hillclimb at Ruhestein on 21st July 1946. It was won by Hermann Lang, driving a 2-litre B.M.W. which had been built for the substitute Mille Miglia run on a closed circuit in 1940.

Colin Strang during his winning climb at Prescott in August 1946 with the rear-engined pioneer Strang 500. (Photo: Guy Griffiths Motofoto.)

The first 500-c.c. car to win a hillclimb outright was Colin Strang's pioneer special with a Vincent-H.R.D. engine. At Prescott, near Cheltenham, on 31st August 1946, Strang climbed in 54·88 seconds. Second came John Bolster's 1,962 c.c. *Bloody Mary* (55·32 seconds) and third was Paul Emery's supercharged 4,168 c.c. Hudson Special (55·4 seconds).

The first-ever success for a Cooper was gained at the Brighton Speed Trials on 7th September 1946, the first meeting held there after the Second World War. Driving his original 500 c.c. prototype, John Cooper recorded 35·81 seconds to win the 850 c.c. class. Best performance of the day was made by Raymond Mays in a 2-litre E.R.A. with a run in 24·47 seconds (91·03 m.p.h.).

The first overseas success by a Cooper came in April 1949, when one of the marque won a hillclimb in Ceylon.

John Cooper climbing Prescott in his Cooper 500 during September 1947. (Photo: Guy Griffiths Motofoto.)

The first success by Stirling Moss was at Stanmer Park, near Brighton, on 5th June 1948. He won the 500 c.c. class with his Cooper with a run in 58·78 seconds over the course, which was being used for the first time. With a gradient of only 1 in 10, it was sometimes rated as a hillclimb, sometimes as a speed trial. Bob Gerard made the fastest run (50·87 seconds) with his 2-litre E.R.A., then crashed into several parked cars beyond the finishing-line, after which the meeting was stopped.

This event also marked the first appearance of the long-chassis Cooper with 1,000 c.c. J.A.P. engine, in which John Cooper won the 1,100 c.c. class and made the fourth fastest run of the day.

The start of it all. Stirling Moss winning his class in the Stanmer Park event in a Cooper 500 on 5th June 1948. His time of 58·78 seconds earned him an award of five guineas. (Photo: Guy Griffiths Motofoto.)

Another one from the family album! Colin Chapman conducts his Lotus 2 on a 1949 trials event.

The first speed event in which Mike Hawthorn competed was the Brighton Speed Trials on 2nd September 1950. He won the 1,100 c.c. sports-car class with a time of 35·99 seconds in his Riley Nine. The fastest run was by Raymond Mays with his 2-litre E.R.A., which covered the standing-start kilometre in 24·40 seconds. This was the last sprint event in which Mays competed.

Mike Hawthorn's Riley at Brighton on 2nd September 1950. Here his father, Leslie Hawthorn, is trying the car. (Photo: Guy Griffiths Motofoto.)

The 500 c.c. class record was broken three times in successive runs by Les Leston in a Cooper-Norton at Prescott Hillclimb on 27th July 1952. This was not only Leston's first appearance at Prescott; it was the first time he had ever competed in a hillclimb. The runner-up was Stirling Moss, driving a Kieft.

The biggest car ever to appear at a Brighton Speed Trials made the slowest run in its class. On 5th September 1953 F. W. Wilcock appeared with the *Swandean Spitfire Special*, which had a supercharged 27-litre Rolls-Royce Merlin engine installed in a special chassis with a wheelbase of 14 ft. 6 in., and transmission to all four wheels via the gearbox from a Stoke-on-Trent Corporation bus.

First, second and third fastest climbs of the day were all made by the same driver, with three different cars, at the Rest-and-be-Thankful meeting on 3rd July 1954. Michael Christie returned 63·87 seconds with a supercharged Cooper 1100, 65·67 seconds with an unsupercharged Cooper, and 66·03 seconds with a 2-litre E.R.A.

Michael Christie in a 2-litre Kieft during a 1953 Prescott meeting. (Photo: Guy Griffiths Motofoto.)

Christie was runner-up for the R.A.C. Hillclimb Championship of Britain five times from 1953 to 1958 but never actually won the title. He was virtually runner-up in 1955, but displaced to third position because of a tie for the Championship.

The oldest car to win a major British sprint or hillclimb outright is the ex-Mays 2-litre supercharged E.R.A. known by its chassis number, R4D. With it Ken Wharton made the fastest Shelsley Walsh climb in June 1956 and broke the Brighton course record in September. Its exact age at that time is uncertain, R4D being a late 'thirties conversion of an earlier E.R.A., but it was undoubtedly about twenty years old.

Up to June 1950, R4D won at Shelsley Walsh at least ten times in the hands of Raymond Mays. The next owner, Ron Flockhart, broke the Bo'ness Hillclimb record in 1953. Ken Wharton won Shelsley Walsh three times with R4D from 1954 to 1956, setting up two new records for the hill. Tom Norton took several awards with the old E.R.A. in the late 'fifties, and the next owner, Jim Berry, finished sixth in the Hillclimb Championship of Britain in 1960.

Surprisingly, R4D never won the Brighton Speed Trials before the war, but it made the fastest run there four times, driven by Mays, from 1946 to 1950, with three new course records. Ken Wharton used the E.R.A. to win three times at Brighton, with new records in 1954 and 1956. The fastest winning run made by R4D at Shelsley Walsh was 35·80 seconds (Wharton, August 1954); and at Brighton, 23·34 seconds (Wharton, September 1956).

Marshal Tito's personal chauffeur, Milivoj Bozic, was one of the competitors at the Freiburg Hillclimb in Germany on 7th August 1960. Driving a Porsche RS1500, he made ninth fastest climb of the day.

Jack Brabham made third fastest climb of the day at Ollons-Villars, Switzerland, with a Formula 2 Cooper on 28th August 1960.

Pike's Peak, the American hillclimb course in the Rocky Mountains, is named after a man who failed to reach the summit. Lieutenant Zebulon Pike was commissioned by President Jefferson to carry out a survey in July 1806, but eventually abandoned as "utterly impossible" his attempt to scale the 14,110-ft. mountain. A carriage road was built about 1890, and a Loco-mobile steamer reached the top in 1901, taking 10 hours. Nowadays the fastest climbs are made in less than 12 minutes, rounding 156 corners and ascending 4,708 ft. in the timed distance of 12·42 miles.

It is **the second oldest speed event in America**, only the Indianapolis 500 Miles Race having a longer history. The first Pike's Peak Hillclimb was held on 12th August 1916 to publicise a new toll-road built by

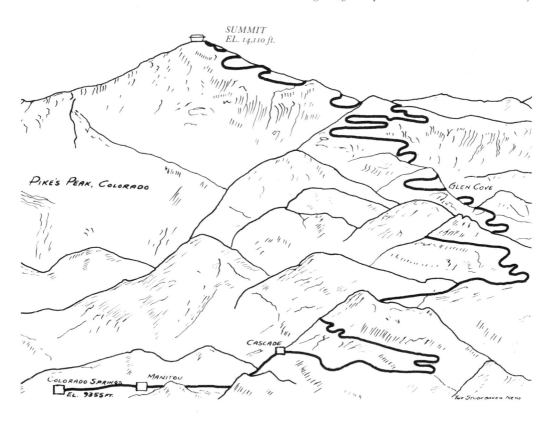

SUMMIT
EL. 14,110 ft.

PIKE'S PEAK, COLORADO

GLEN COVE

CASCADE

COLORADO SPRINGS
EL. 9355 FT.

MANITOU

THE STUDEBAKER NEWS

Spencer Penrose, and the Penrose Trophy, a mammoth 60-lb. silver cup which was made in England, is still the premier award. **Its first winner** was Rea Lentz, who climbed in 20 minutes 55·6 seconds with a Romano Eight Special, beating such experienced drivers as Eddie Rickenbacker, Ralph Mulford and Barney Oldfield. Another famous American driver, Glen Schultz, won seven times between 1923 and 1933.

Pike's Peak has been called "Unsers' Mountain" because of its close associations with the remarkable American racing family of that name, three generations and nine members of which have now competed on the hill. Three motorcycling brothers named Louie, Jerry and Josef Unser attended the first event as spectators in 1916, competed for the first time in 1926, and in 1936 Louie achieved the first of nine victories with a record-breaking climb; his last, in 1953, was also a new record for the hill.

The four sons of Jerry Unser were Jerry Junior (who gained several class wins before being killed at Indianapolis), his twin brother Louie (who also won his class several times at Pike's Peak before retiring due to ill-health), Al Unser (another class-winner, and Indianapolis winner in 1970) and Bobby (Indianapolis winner in 1968, and fastest at Pike's Peak on nine occasions between 1956 and 1968). Bobby's son, Bobby Junior, competed at Pike's Peak for the first time in 1976. Al's son, Al Junior, made his first appearance at the hill in 1979 but non-started because of axle failure in practise.

The present hill record is 11 minutes 54·18 seconds by Dick Dodge, jnr., whose Chevrolet-powered Wells Coyote took just 0·72 second off Bobby Unser's eleven-year-old record when he made the fastest climb in 1979. The event is promoted by the Colorado Springs Chamber of Commerce, whose ninety-nine-year lease of the hill will expire in AD 2040.

The European Mountain Championship was instituted in 1930, when the racing category was won by Hans Stuck in an Austro-Daimler and the sports class by Rudi Caracciola in a Mercedes-Benz. The last pre-war winner was Hermann Lang in a Mercedes-Benz in 1939.

The Championship was reinstituted in 1957, restricted to 2-litre sports cars, and won by Willy Daetwyler with a works Maserati. From then until 1968 it was won nine times with a Porsche. A Ferrari was the winning car in 1962, 1965 and 1969.

Patsy Burt, in a McLaren Oldsmobile, at the Wiscombe Hillclimb in May 1970. (Photo: Guy Griffiths Motofoto.)

A German driver has won the title seven times since 1957, a Swiss four times; the only Italian winner was Ludovico Scarfiotti (1962 and 1965), who was killed at the Rossfeld Hillclimb in 1968. Edgar Barth won in 1959, 1963 and 1964, and Gerhard Mitter in 1966, 1967 and 1968. The 1970 title-holder was Johannes Ortner, an Austrian resident in Italy, who drove an Abarth. Subsequent contests had no overall winner, being split into several different categories. The only title-holder who could claim to be "Hill-climb Champion of the World" was the late Edgar Barth, for in 1959 the qualifying events included the Pike's Peak Hillclimb in America.

The only privately owned toll road in the U.S.A. is the course of the Mount Equinox Hillclimb near Manchester, Vermont, which is also **the longest paved hillclimb course in America** with its timed distance of 5·2 miles, incorporating 31 corners and an ascent of 3,140 feet. Once owned by the late Dr. J. G. Davison, the inventor of vinyl, it was left by him to the Carthusian Order whose first monastery was established 900 years ago on a mountain-top at Chartreuse, where the monks first distilled the liqueur of that name. At Mount Equinox, the toll road is now operated by the monks, and a Carthusian monastery is being built half-way up the hill, but the event is still held annually.

The Guinness hop-farm at Bodiam, Sussex, has been the site of several speed hillclimbs on one of the service roads. It has no connection with Corkscrew Hill in Ireland, where hillclimb meetings are also held.

The first Sprint Championship of Britain was won by a woman driver, Patsy Burt, who was awarded the title for 1970. Driving a 4·4-litre McLaren Oldsmobile, she won the first six of the nine qualifying events in which she entered, setting up four new course records. She also gained the highest place ever achieved by a woman in the British Hillclimb Championship when she finished fourth overall in 1959 with a Formula 2 Cooper-Climax.

Miss Burt competed in sprints and hillclimbs from 1953 to 1970. She made the best performance 42 times, was runner-up 24 times, and won the Ladies' Award 151 times. She established 13 new course records, 46 new ladies' records in Britain, and 12 new ladies' records in continental events. She gained 172 class awards and 118 special awards.

The Hillclimb Championship of Britain was instituted in 1947 with a total of five qualifying events in England, Scotland, Ireland and the Channel Islands. There are now sixteen events at eleven venues, the longest of which is Craigantlet, near Belfast (1,833 yards); the shortest is Fintray (725 yards), south-west of Edinburgh. The title was first won by Raymond Mays with his veteran 2-litre E.R.A.

Ken Wharton, who had been Trials Champion of Britain in 1948, 1949 and 1950, followed his hat-trick by winning the British Hillclimb Championship four times, from 1951 to 1954. In 1955 he tied with Tony Marsh, who was awarded the title for that year. Marsh won again in 1956, 1957, 1965, 1966 and 1967. Another very successful contestant was David Boshier-Jones, who won the Championship in 1958, 1959 and 1960.

The first four-wheel-drive car used by a British Hillclimb Champion was the 2½-litre Ferguson-Climax driven by Peter Westbury in 1964, when he won the title for the second successive year. The 1978 Champion, David Franklin, drove a B.M.W.-powered March 772 and also won the British Sprint Championship.

The oldest sprint meeting still held regularly in Britain is the Brighton Speed Trials, which was first run as a four-day event on 19th/22nd July 1905 over what was then known as Madeira Road (it was not called Madeira Drive until 1910). Due to local opposition it was not held again until 1923; two meetings were held in 1924, but it lapsed again until 1932, after which it became an annual event interrupted only by the Second World War. The 1969 meeting was cancelled because of a fatal accident the previous year, when the fastest competitors were crossing the finishing line at more than 160 m.p.h., and for 1970 the course was shortened to ¼ mile. It reverted to 1 kilometre in 1971.

Contrary to popular belief, the Brighton course has not always been a standing-start kilometre. In 1905 the cars were timed over a standing-start mile and flying-start kilometre, running in the opposite direction (east to west) to that used nowadays. The 1923 and 1924 meetings were run on ¼-mile and ½-mile courses. From 1932 to 1938 a standing-start ½ mile was used. The standing-start kilometre did not, in fact, come into use until the first Brighton meeting after the Second World War, held on 7th September 1946.

Only three records were ever established on the pre-war ½-mile course. The first was 23·6 seconds (76·27 m.p.h.) by Sir Malcolm Campbell with his Land Speed Record Sunbeam on 17th September 1932; the second was 22·68 seconds (79·36 m.p.h.) by Dick Shuttleworth with a 2·9-litre Alfa Romeo on 14th September 1935; the third was 22·45 seconds (80·18 m.p.h.) by Geoffrey Taylor with his 2-litre Alta on 2nd July 1938.

On the standing-start kilometre used after the Second World War, the winning run of 1946—24·47 seconds (91·03 m.p.h.) by Raymond Mays with his 2-litre E.R.A.—was almost as fast as the winning run over the *flying* kilometre in 1905: 24·2 seconds (92·88 m.p.h.) by Clifford Earp with his 90-h.p. Napier. **The only lady driver ever to win at Brighton** was Miss Patsy Burt, who on 14th September 1968 covered the kilometre in a record-breaking 20·21 seconds (110·69 m.p.h.) with a McLaren Oldsmobile.

Record holder: Alastair Douglas-Osborn's Pilbeam R.22. This combination achieved six F.T.D.s in eight Shelsley meetings during 1976/77.

The Maestro. Raymond Mays (supercharged 2-litre E.R.A.) climbing Shelsley Walsh on 12th June 1948. (Photo: Guy Griffiths Motofoto.)

Only two drivers have ever scored a Brighton hat-trick: Raymond Mays (1946, 1947 and 1948) and Ken Wharton (1954, 1955 and 1956). Both achieved it with the same car, R4D, the veteran 2-litre E.R.A. The period from 1948 to 1954 was the longest in which the Brighton record has gone unbroken, and when Wharton bettered May's figure in 1954 he did so with a broken supercharger drive; it sheared 100 yards before the finishing line.

The record for the Brighton course was established by three different competitors on the same day. It is 17·48 seconds, which represents an average speed over the standing-start kilometre of 127·98 m.p.h. This time was recorded by two car drivers (Terry Smith with a Brabham BT35X and Dave Harris with a McRae GM1) in a run-off for the National Sprint Championship in September 1978, and also by Henk Vink of Holland with his supercharged 1,000-c.c. Kawasaki motorcycle. The motorcycle's terminal speed was approximately 165 m.p.h.; the two cars, having less initial acceleration, were crossing the finishing-line at about 177 m.p.h. to record the same time.

The oldest speed hillclimb still held regularly in Britain is Shelsley Walsh, Worcestershire. The first meeting was run on 12th August 1905, and the course was a resurfaced farm track 992 yards in length with an average gradient of 1 in 8; it was won by E. M. C. Instone, who covered the distance in 77·6 seconds driving a 35-h.p. Daimler. In 1907 the now-traditional 1,000-yard course was used for the first time and the best performance was made by J. E. Hutton (Berliet), who recorded 67·2 seconds. The present record is 27·35 seconds, established by Alastair Douglas-Osborn's Pilbeam R.22 in July 1977.

Until 1913, competing cars had to be of fairly standard specification and climbs were made complete with passengers. Not until July 1927 were competitors allowed to make two attempts at the hill, the faster of the two to count.

The first meeting after the First World War was held on 3rd July 1920, not—as has often been stated—in 1921. Similarly, two meetings were held annually from 1926, not from 1933 (but only one in 1952 and 1957). Two meetings were also held in 1909.

The "tie" of 67.2 seconds in 1907 is a long-perpetuated myth arising from the fact that J. E. Hutton was the winner on a scratch basis, and T. W. Bowen (Talbot) on handicap. In 1923, M. C. Park (Vauxhall) and Raymond Mays (Bugatti) both recorded 52.80 seconds and were declared joint winners, although Mays returned a time of 51.80 seconds later the same day, in a special team event. The only other tie was in August 1962, when Philip Scragg (Lister-Jaguar) and Peter Boshier-Jones (Lotus) both recorded 37.24 seconds.

The closest-ever win was in June 1949 when Joe Fry (Freikaiserwagen) beat Raymond Mays (E.R.A.) by one-hundredth of a second to establish the first new Shelsley record for ten years.

The first winning climb in under 60 seconds (34.09 m.p.h.) was made by J. Higginson's 30/98 Vauxhall in 1913; the first under 50 seconds (40.90 m.p.h.) by Basil Davenport's *Spider* in September 1926; the first under 40 seconds (51.14 m.p.h.) by Raymond Mays's E.R.A. in May 1935; the first under 30 seconds (68.18 m.p.h.) by David Hepworth's Hepworth FF 4WD in June 1971. To break the half-minute barrier at Shelsley, Hepworth had to cross the finishing-line at about 120 m.p.h.

No Shelsley Walsh competitor has ever approached the success of Raymond Mays, who made the best performance twenty-one times between 1923 and 1950. He broke the course record officially five times, and also did so unofficially in 1923. His fastest climb was made in 37.36 seconds with R4D on 3rd June 1939; surprisingly, although he made best performance seven times after the Second World War, he never succeeded in getting closer than 37.52 seconds (September 1948) to his pre-war figure. Ken Wharton and Tony Marsh both made best performance at Shelsley on eight occasions, Wharton with five new course records and Marsh with two.

The longest unbroken run of Shelsley successes—nine victories in a row—was also achieved by Raymond Mays. Of the sixteen meetings held from September 1934 to September 1948, the only one in which Mays did *not* make best performance was that of September 1937, when A. F. P. Fane won with a Frazer Nash.

Fastest ever on British soil: Slam'n Sammy Miller's Vanishing Point *blasts off at Santa Pod. His record terminal velocity is 317.4 m.p.h.*

Visiting American Firemen at Santa Pod: Raymond Beadle's Blue Max *holds the British "funny car" record at 6.24 secs and 221 m.p.h., beating last-year's holder, Gene Snow, during 1979.*

The shortest elapsed time that any dragster has achieved over the standing-start ¼-mile is 3·9 seconds. This was recorded at Miami Speedway in 1979 by Sammy Miller with his hydrogen-peroxide-powered car, *Vanishing Point*. His average speed was 230·77 m.p.h., and his terminal velocity was 360 m.p.h. Miller was also **the first driver to exceed 300 m.p.h. on British soil.** At Santa Pod Raceway, Bedfordshire, he was timed at 4·20 seconds, with a terminal velocity of 307 m.p.h., in July 1979. **The highest speed ever achieved on British soil** is 317·4 m.p.h., which was Miller's terminal velocity in his 4·31 second run at Santa Pod on 15th September 1979.

The highest terminal velocity by any dragster is 377·754 m.p.h. (elapsed time 4·65 sec.) by Craig Breedlove's rocket-powered *English Leather Special* at Bonneville in 1973.

Only four drivers in the world have exceeded 250 m.p.h. with a piston-engined dragster, and **one of the four is a woman,** Shirley Muldowney of the U.S.A. **Only seven times has this speed been exceeded,** and on four of these occasions it was Shirley who did so. Her highest-recorded terminal velocity was 255·58 m.p.h., which is only 0·1 m.p.h. slower than the highest-ever figure returned by Jerry Ruth at Englishtown, New Jersey, in July 1977. The remaining two drivers in the élite 250 m.p.h. category are Gary Beck and Don Garlits.

The shortest elapsed time by a piston-engined dragster is 5·637 seconds, representing an average speed over the standing-start ¼-mile of 159·66 m.p.h. This was recorded by Don "Big Daddy" Garlits at the Ontario Motor Speedway in October 1975. The terminal velocity of his supercharged 7,984 c.c. V-eight-engined car was 250·69 m.p.h.

RALLIES
by John Davenport

Like most specialised occupations, rally driving has its own terminology and sometimes if you hear two rallymen talking, you may have difficulty in understanding them. In order to try and help you, here are some explanations of the more common terms. A special stage, special test, *épreuve* or hillclimb are usually run flat out against the clock with the fastest man taking the smallest penalty, while a selective or regularity section has a set time but an average speed higher than will be encountered elsewhere on the rally.

Ordinary sections between normal time controls are called "liaison sections", though "pruning" by the organisers may make them difficult. "Pruning" can comprise any of the following: saying that there are fewer miles in a section than there really are, or allowing fewer minutes in the official times than the legal average would permit for the distance, or just simply setting the clock at the finish of the section a few minutes fast. You may come across the expression "yump" or "to yump"; this is merely a crest or bump from which the car is flung into the air, or the action of being flung in the air. "Studs" or "spikes" are small pins of steel with carbide tips with are fitted to winter tyres for driving on snow or ice, and it is useful to know that in French they are *clous*, in Italian *chiodi* and in Swedish *dubb*, as they don't often get used on British rallies.

You may have heard about "pace notes"; the simplest way to define them is that they are an artificial representation of the rally road written out on paper in shorthand. An inter-com is a system using two-way amplifiers plus microphones and earpieces fitted to crash-helmets in order to communicate the pace notes from co-driver to driver. Crash-helmets are normally called just that—the more flowery terms are left to other branches of the sport.

Within the field of international rallying, very little common vernacular has been created as Italian teams tend to have Italians in them, and so on. On the British scene, however, because of the greater dependence on navigation from maps there is a much wider range of unusual terms. If you heard the following: "Graham wrong-slotted on the three-ply at Bwylch. He looked up that goer—dotted white becomes yellow—and reckoned it wasn't on and then got boxed in the farm"; you might be forgiven for not knowing what it was all about. The gentleman was trying to say that Graham had taken a wrong turning (or made a wrong decision) near the Welsh hamlet of Bwylch while being driven down a road that comprised two strips of tarmac with grass growing in the middle. He had told his driver to turn up a track which was marked without colours and with a dotted margin on the one-inch

Above: *Champion drag record-holder "Big Daddy" Garlits in his Dodge-powered Wynn's Jammer. He achieved the highest terminal velocity recorded by a piston-engined dragster at 250·69 m.p.h. in 1975.*

Right: *One of the most beautifully situated hill-climb venues is Prescott in Gloucestershire, belonging to the Bugatti Owners' Club. A single-seater GP Bugatti is shown here climbing in 1971.*

Below: *Rally Super-Car of the mid 'seventies was the Lancia Stratos which helped Lancia to win a hat-trick of World Championships and four victories on the Monte Carlo Rally. The Italian firm was not content just to win tarmac rallies with this car but the toughest of the African rallies as well as the more demanding of the European ones: Sandro Munari with co-driver Mario Mannucci in their Stratos at the Col du Turini, 1975 Monte Carlo Rally.*

Ligier JS11 (Patrick Depailler), U.S. GP West. (Photo: Nigel Snowdon.)

Brabham BT46 (Nelson Piquet), Argentine GP. (Photo: Nigel Snowdon.)

Saudia-Williams FW07 (Alan Jones), British GP. (Photo: Diana Burnett.)

Renault RS10 (Jean-Pierre Jabouille), French GP. (Photo: Nigel Snowdon.)

Lotus 80 (Mario Andretti), Race of Champions, Brands Hatch. (Photo: Nigel Snowdon.)

Ferrari 312T4 (Giles Villeneuve), Monaco GP. (Photo: Diana Burnett.)

1979 FORMULA 1 CARS

Ordnance Survey map, which a little further up turned into a metalled road marked in yellow on the map, but his decision was not to use it as he could not be certain that their vehicle would make it across the unsurfaced portion to the tarmac, so he ordered his driver to turn round in a farmyard— where they got stuck! (Incidentally, the implication of the speaker in calling the road a "goer" in the first place was that Graham's mistake was in not trying to go through.)

Obviously, not all the terms in use have been covered by any means, but you have enough to give you reasonable entrée at the finish of a rally.

The first rally ever to be held was perhaps the annual Herkomer Trophy event, initiated in Germany in 1904. A complicated event, in which the competitors often failed to understand what was required of them and consequently were very much out of sympathy with the judge's decisions, the Herkomer Fahrten had many features which modern rally drivers would find familiar. There were even specially timed tests on public roads, and these fell foul of speed restrictions which were introduced by the German Parliament in 1908, and led to the end of the Herkomer Trophy in that year. Pluto-cratic opinion within Germany, however, persuaded royalty in the person of Prince Heinrich of Prussia to lend his name to the Prince Heinrich Fahrt, which started in that same year and was run upon similar lines.

Prince Heinrich of Prussia.

Prince Heinrich at the wheel of his Benz during the 1906 Herkomer Fahrt.

One of the earliest marathon rallies was held in 1908—before the term "motor-car rally' had even come into vogue. The Peking-Paris Rally, organised by *Le Matin*, a Paris newspaper, was not really a rally as such, in that Prince Borghese did not have to check in at successive controls with his 40-h.p. Itala; but there was a prescribed route to which the competitors had to stick, although the regulations did permit deviations. For the record, Borghese left Peking with the other four starters on 10th June at 8.30 a.m., and he reached Paris on 10th August having waited at Meaux, 30 miles from Paris, for his reception to be prepared.

Three of the other competing cars finished some three weeks later, and the other one broke down 10 miles from the start.

Many people use the expression "Rally Car", but there was actually a make of car called a "Rally". It was made in France in the late 'twenties and was a typical French sporting *voiturette*. The first car was made in 1921. It was powered by a twin-cylinder Harley Davidson engine and used many of that motorcycle's running gear. The following year a new model was fitted with a water-cooled, four-cylinder engine which came from various suppliers (Chapuis-

High flying on the 1000 Lakes Rally in this Toyota Celica of Finnish driver Tapio Rainio.

Dornier, SCAP, CIME and Ruby) and this continued to be made for some years. Examples were entered in circuit races but strangely they gained most of their success in—*rallies*. They won their class in the Criterium Feminin Paris-Saint-Raphaël Rally, and even the Tour de France. Before production ceased in 1933, several prototypes featuring such power units as a straight-eight 1,100 c.c. and a supercharged twin-cam four cylinder had been tried, but the advent of the mass production M.G. Midget had captured the demand for small sports cars.

The name "Messerschmitt" is more often associated with the Battle of Britain than with British rallies, but at one time a car made by the German firm was very competitive in British events. It was a version of the familiar three-wheeler "bubble car" called the *Tiger*, whose stripes comprised a 500-c.c. engine and four wheels independently sprung. It was owned and driven by Ken Piper, who created a mild sensation when he won the National Cat's Eyes Rally with it in 1958. He later cut off the bubble top and autocrossed it as an open car.

Mathis (Fiat) in the 1908 Prince Henry Trials.

Rallying during the 'twenties. A Salmson in the Glencoe deer forest during a Scottish Rally. (Photo: W. J. Brunell.)

Pace notes are a form of shorthand used by rally co-drivers to note down and read back the severity of bends on roads used as special tests during rallies. However, one of the first instances when these were developed professionally and used to win an event was on the Mille Miglia of 1955 when Stirling Moss took Denis Jenkinson with him in a works Mercedez-Benz 300 SLR. During the recce trips that they did round the route, they noted bend speeds and hazards on a long roll of paper from which Jenkinson read back the information during the race. Nowadays, pace notes are even used on events like the East African Safari where rally crews from Europe have discovered that one can locate bumps and holes with greater accuracy using pace notes than with a mileage counter.

It was unusual for a marque to win both the Liège-Rome-Liège and the Monte Carlo rallies within twelve months, but Lancia have this to their credit, with the Aurelia B20 Third Series. In August 1953 Johnny Claes won the Liège-Rome-Liège in such a car, while in January 1954 Louis Chiron, similarly mounted, won the Monte Carlo Rally.

Belgium is not famed today for its automobiles, but before the Second World War the armaments firm of F.N. used to make cars. It was one of their products, with a 3,250 c.c. eight-cylinder engine, that has the distinction of being the only home-grown product ever to win the Liège-Rome-Liège which it succeeded in doing in 1933.

Rally drivers' nicknames are usually straightforward and refer to some peculiarity of appearance. For instance, "Tiny" Lewis stands well over six feet, but sometimes the derivation is more obscure. Harry Källström is known as "Sputnik" as he rose to fame so quickly by finishing third over all on his second event, and becoming champion in his second year of the sport. Roger Clark was nicknamed "Porky" by the Ford mechanics because of his habit of gleaning everything eatable from the service cars and consuming it. Legend has it that on one occasion he even ate some dog biscuits and pronounced them excellent. The admirers of Sandro Munari call him "Drago" but his fiery temperament only comes out when he is behind the wheel and away from it he is the most equable of men. Ove Andersson, who won the 1971 Monte Carlo for Renault, acquired the nickname "Paven"—the Swedish word for "the Pope"—after he had gone from relative obscurity in Sweden to a works drive for the Italian firm of Lancia in 1966. Finally, also from Sweden, there is Erik Carlsson's title of "Pa taket"—which simply means "on the roof" and originated as a comment on his style of driving!

Large entries are a rally organiser's dream and in its heyday the Monte Carlo used to attract over 300 cars and crews. The Swedish Rally to the Midnight Sun in the late 1950s also used to have entries of about that size and, with cars running at 2-minute intervals, the controls had to be kept open for well over 12 hours.

The most successful of modern rally cars is without doubt the B.M.C. Mini, which as the 850, the Mini Cooper and finally as the Mini Cooper S had a very distinguished career in the 1960s. Its first big victories came in 1962 when the 998-c.c. Mini Cooper first won the Swedish Rally to the Midnight Sun with Bengt Soderström; then Pat Moss won both the Tulip Rally in May 1962 and the German Rally (Baden-Baden in September) in a similar car. The Mini Cooper S first won the Monte Carlo Rally in 1964 with a car powered by a 1,071-c.c. engine and driven by Paddy Hopkirk and Henry Liddon; then Timo Makinen/Paul Easter won in 1965 with a 1,275 c.c. version, and won again in 1966 but were disqualified. It was left to Rauno Aaltonen/Henry Liddon to belatedly complete the hat-trick in 1967. Aaltonen was European Rally Champion in 1965 driving a Mini Cooper S, and his victories included the R.A.C. Rally—which is the only time a Mini has won the event.

A convenient lorry provides a grandstand for Welsh spectators watching the DTV Chevette HS 2300 of Pentti Airikkala.

Delahayes in the Monte Carlo Rally. Left: Lebegue's Type 135 in the 1937 event. Below: Trefaux's Type 175 at Grasse in the 1951 Rally. (Photos: The Motor.)

The Ford Escort and the Lancia Fulvia have confirmed the success and popularity of the saloon car in rallying since the Mini charged on to the rally scene, but in the 1970s there has been a trend towards specialised sports cars. The Alpine Renault is just such a car. It started life as a fibreglass special based on the Renault 4CV and designed by a young man called Jean Redele. It made its first competition appearance in the Mille Miglia of 1955 and went through a succession of models and engine sizes until Redele evolved the A110 Berlinette based on the Renault R8. It was this model which was destined to win the Coupe des Alpes with Jean Vinatier in 1968 and 1969 but it had to wait until 1971 for its greatest moment, victory in the Monte Carlo Rally with the Swede Ove Andersson at the wheel. Two years later it was to carve another first in the record books by being part of the only all-French win in the Monte Carlo for fifteen years when Jean-Claude Andruet and Mlle "Biche" won in an Alpine A110 in 1973.

The Lancia Stratos is another specialised sports car manufactured with rally victories in mind. The original concept appeared at the Turin Motor Show of 1970 as a Bertone styling exercise on a "back-to-front" Fulvia chassis with the engine at the rear. The final version adopted the 2·4-litre Ferrari Dino engine and

Fierce concentration as Jean-Pierre Nicolas wonders if his light-weight Renault Alpine will float or sink on the approach to a special stage during the 1973 RAC Rally. He could have done with the water later in the event for the car caught fire and burnt out.

gearbox in a new chassis under the same Bertone styling. After helping Sandro Munari to become European Rally Champion in 1973 while it was still a prototype, it emerged from the chrysalis as a perfect imago, and four days after being recognised as a production sports car by the F.I.A. on the 1st October 1974, it won its first World Championship rally, the San Remo. Not more than three weeks later, it had won its second such event, the Rideau Lakes in Canada, and handed Lancia the World Championship. In 1975, still with Sandro Munari at the wheel, it won the Monte Carlo Rally and later repeated its win in San Remo but this time with Bjorn Waldegaard driving.

Munari went on to win the Monte Carlo Rally for the next three years with the Stratos, but its main achievement for Lancia was to help them complete a hat-trick of three consecutive World Championship titles (1974, 1975 and 1976). In 1975, Lancia very nearly achieved a most remarkable success with the Stratos when they finished second (Waldegaard) and third (Munari) on the East African Safari.

The Lancia Stratos ceased production late in 1977 which means that under current International Rules it may still be rallied until 1982.

The Italian driver, Sandro Munari from Cavarzare is the only man ever to have won the Monte Carlo Rally four times. He first won that event in 1972 when he profited from the demise of the entire Alpine Renault team, who had started as favourites, to take the honours with a Lancia Fulvia Coupé. Since then, he has won that Rally three times in a Lancia Stratos making it a hat-trick both for him and the car in 1975, 1976 and 1977.

The only man to come close to this record on the Monte Carlo is Frenchman, Jean Trevoux. He won twice immediately after the Second World War driving a 3·5-litre Hotchkiss in 1949 and a 4·5-litre Delahaye in 1951. Before the war, he had finished equal first in 1939, again in his faithful Hotchkiss, while in 1934 he was the second nominated driver in the winning Hotchkiss of Gas. It would thus need a pedant to be able to say whether M. Trevoux had won the rally just twice, or three times or perhaps even four!

Sandro Munari announced his retirement from active rallying on the East African Safari on 1979 where he drove a Fiat 131 Abarth. Bjorn Waldegaard who won the Monte in a Porsche 911 in both 1969 and 1970 is the only active rallyman with a good start towards Munari's total. Waldegaard was involved in a remarkable tie for third place over all on the 1971 Monte Carlo Rally when, driving a Porsche 914/6, he finished equal third with Jean Claude Andruet in an Alpine Renault. Not only did they finish on exactly the same number of points after more than 5,000 kilometres of motoring but they had exactly the same results, second for second, over the last three special stages of the Rally.

Hotchkiss and Lancia have enviable records in the Monte Carlo Rally having both won it six times. The French firm of Hotchkiss was the first to achieve this and it was also first to win the rally three times in succession, with its victories in 1932, 1933 and 1934. The driver in 1932 was Vasselle driving a 3·5-litre AM80; the following year he won again, driving a 3·5-litre, 6-cylinder car, thereby becoming the first man to win the Monte twice. Hotchkiss seemed to be associated with unique events for, in 1939, their driver Jean Trevoux tied for first place with Paul in a Delahaye—the only time there has ever been such a tie; while after the war they returned with the Type 686 (with the same 3·5-litre engine) to win the Monte twice more in 1949 and 1950.

The Italian firm of Lancia first won the Monte with an Aurelia GT driven by Louis Chiron in 1954. Sandro Munari's four victories in the 1970s were then complemented by the efforts of another Frenchman, Bernard Darniche who won the Monte Carlo Rally in a Lancia Stratos in 1979.

Handicaps have been used in an attempt to equate the widely differing performances of touring cars since the earliest days of rallying. At times they became quite ridiculous, and never more so than in 1961 when Geoff Mabbs won the Tulip Rally in a Triumph Herald by virtue of the retirement of his team-mate, Tiny Lewis, so that Mabbs would have a bigger "improvement" on the next finisher in his class. Similarly, the handicap imposed upon G.T. cars during the 1966 Monte Carlo Rally brought all handicaps into disrepute, and nowadays it is not fashionable for organisers to employ them.

A legendary figure in post-war rallying was the Belgian band-leader, Johnny Claes. He not only won the Liège-Rome-Liège twice but, on the first occasion—1951, when he drove a Jaguar XK120 with Jacques Ickx—he became the only man ever to finish such an event unpenalised on the road section. The rally that year was 3,000 miles long and reduced 126 starters to 58 finishers. Claes won the rally again in 1953 driving a Lancia Aurelia G.T., and on this occasion his co-driver, Jean Trasester, fell ill during the rally, so that Claes drove unaided for 52 hours having had about 4 hours' sleep in 90. That year there were 28 finishers from 92 starters.

New arrival and new name on the 1979 rally scene is this Talbot Sunbeam Lotus seen here on the 24 hours of Ypres, driven by Tony Pond.

The Mini-Cooper of Bengt Soderström and Henry Liddon on the Col de Luens during the 1963 Monte Carlo Rally. (Photo: The Motor.*)*

Normally in a rally the cars leave the start at 1-minute intervals, but there are exceptions to this. On the East African Safari Rally, in which dust can be one of the greatest hazards the drivers must face, the cars are started at 2-minute intervals, while the same interval used to be employed in the Swedish Rally to the Midnight Sun. The 2-minute gap is also used on the final mountain circuit of the modern Monte Carlo Rally (in which only the top-placed sixty cars take part) so that cars running in the same team may be better spaced for service.

The most unusual—and most exciting—system was used on the Liège-Rome-Liège in which three cars were started together, each group of three leaving at 3-minute intervals. Presumably the organisers felt that drivers needed company on such a long event.

Perseverance is often rewarded in rallying as is shown by the experiences of Paddy Hopkirk in the Acropolis Rally. In the mid 1960s, after the last Liège-Sofia-Liège was run in 1964, the Acropolis replaced it to some extent as a tough, non-stop event, and B.M.C. had struggled even to finish it with their Mini Coopers. In 1966, however, Hopkirk not only got through to the finish but had less penalties than anyone else, and would have undoubtedly won had there not been an eleventh-hour penalty imposed for servicing inside a control area.

Returning the following year, Hopkirk not only outdrove a strong challenge from Lancia and Ford to win the event, but judged the longevity of his mount to a nicety—as it expired on crossing the finishing-line!

One of the toughest events was, without doubt, the post-war series of rallies which was generically termed "Marathon de la Route", and which were organised by M. Garot of the Royal Motor Union in Liège. They were originally called the "Liège-Rome-Liège", but later the rally no longer visited the Italian capital, and went instead to Zagreb in Yugoslavia, and finally to Sofia in Bulgaria. The year 1955 was the last time it went to Rome, although this name was often mentioned in its title after that date.

The event was first held in 1931 when it was unique in that its route of 2,800 miles was run virtually non-stop. The last time it was held was in 1964, after which the Yugoslav and Italian authorities would no longer give permission for such a fast event to be staged on their roads.

To finish a Liège-Rome-Liège was sufficient achievement for the organisers to award a Gold Cup to anyone who managed to finish three in a row. Very few of these coveted awards were ever made, but the last one went to an Englishman, Bill Bengry, who managed to finish in the last three events ever held, in 1962, 1963 and 1964.

On the first two occasions he drove a works-owned 3-litre Rover, and on both occasions finished eighteenth overall with David Skeffington and Barry Hughes respectively as co-drivers. In 1964 Rover decided not to give him a car, so he borrowed a Sunbeam Rapier from Alan Fraser's racing team and, with Ian Hall as co-driver, finished fourteenth.

One particular bend or one particular stage will frequently claim a host of victims during the same rally. The best-remembered example must be the 1963 Acropolis Rally in which the routes converged on Serrai in northern Greece, where the rally proper was to start. It was raining hard and the first special stage started almost immediately. On the slippery tarmac, first Erik Carlsson went off the road and broke his front suspension; he was soon joined by fellow Saab driver Olle Dahl who rolled, the Anglo-American team of Fred Hogan/Murray Smith, two Greeks in an Alfa Romeo, Bertil Soderström who hit a donkey with his Volvo, and finally Bob Neyret/Jacques Terramorsi who fell 100 feet in their Citroën and had to be taken to hospital. Even the eventual winner, Eugen Böhringer, went off the road in his Mercedes 300SE but he continued on down to a track that regained the main road—and drove on.

The most successful crews to drive Alfa Romeo cars in rallies have for some strange reason always been French. In 1958, for example, Bernard Consten and Jean Hebert won the Liège-Rome-Liège in a Giulietta Sprint, this being the only time the event was won by a car of less than 1,300 c.c. In that same year Consten won the Coupe des Alpes and the touring category of the Tour de France in similar cars, while in the same car that he used in the Liège-Rome-Liège he won the German Rally.

In the 1960s, Jean Rolland and Gabriel Augias practically made the Coupe des Alpes their own possession with an Alfa Romeo Zagato

The Saab of Erik Carlsson and Gunnar Palm descending the Col de Turini in the 1963 Monte Carlo Rally. Carlsson is shown cornering by bouncing his car off a snowbank—a technique positively confined to the expert!

Tubolare, though the coveted Coupe d'Or eluded Rolland when he crashed on the 1965 event, having won *coupes* in 1963 and 1964. He did, however, win a Coupe d'Argent in 1966 for three non-consecutive *coupes*. Jean-Claude Andruet joined Alfa Romeo at the beginning of 1974 to drive for their Autodelta team in European Championship rallies. His forceful and acrobatic style has gained many adherents among the spectators but too often the car has not finished. One of his best drives was on an event that he had previously won in a Lancia Stratos, the Tour de Corse where he finished third over all in an Alfetta GT in 1975.

The smallest car ever to win the European Rally Championship was the Austrian Steyr-Puch which took Sobieslaw Zasada, the Polish driver, to victory in 1966. He did not win any events outright in this 650 c.c., Steyr-engined version of the Fiat 500 while actually gaining the Championship, although back in 1964, when he started driving for Steyr, he won the Polish Rally from no less a person than Erik Carlsson in a Saab.

Incidentally, when Steyr-Puch first entered these remarkable little cars in an international event—the Monte Carlo Rally of 1963—both got to the finish but were not classified *as someone had forgotten to homologate them with the F.I.A.*

In 1963 Ford of America entered examples of their Falcon Futura Sprint in the Monte Carlo Rally to boost the publicity surrounding the release of this new car. Among the drivers they chose an almost unknown Swedish racing driver, Bo Ljungfeldt, who at that time was forty-one years of age and had won the Swedish Track Championship five times with Ford products. He lost much time with mechanical trouble on the concentration run, but once on the special stages he set the rally world on its feet with fastest time on every stage. His earlier penalty precluded a good position, but it encouraged Ford of America to return and the next year, 1964, he repeated the performance—except that on Saint-Apollinaire Paddy Hopkirk equalled his time with a Mini Cooper S. Finally it was Hopkirk who won the rally as the times were subject to a handicap based on engine capacity.

The lady driver who is best known and most successful in the world of rallying is Pat Moss. She is unique in that, while other ladies count their victories in the Coupes des Dames, Pat has a list of outright victories in major internationals, and can be reckoned as serious competition by even the most skilful of the men. Her greatest victory was winning the Liège-Rome-Liège in 1960, driving an Austin Healey 3000 with Anne Wisdom, but she also won both the

Rallying can be expensive. The moment of impact between a wall and C. T. Cox's Rover during the 1963 R.A.C. Rally. (Photo: John Davenport.)

Three times winner of the R.A.C. Rally, Timo Makinen has a driving style all his own. Here, on the 1974 1000 Lakes Rally in his native Finland, he approaches a hairpin bend with the Ford Escort RS1600 travelling totally sideways.

Tulip and German rallies in 1962 with a Mini Cooper, as well as the Sestrière Rally with a Lancia Fulvia. Today, Pat has retired from the hurly-burly of professional rallying and though she occasionally emerges to drive an event for fun, her major preoccupation is with her family, husband Erik Carlsson and daughter Susie. So far, no lady has emerged to emulate her driving success, though Michele Mouton, the young French driver, has won the Ladies' European Championship title twice—in 1975 with a Renault Alpine and in 1977 with a Porsche Carrera—and delighted the rally world by winning the 1978 Tour de France outright with a Fiat 131 Abarth.

The most famous rallying policeman was the late John Gott who, for so many years, drove with great success in the B.M.C. team. Until his death, John was Chief Constable of Northamptonshire. In the early 1950s he was one of the few Englishmen to compete regularly in continental events, driving such cars as open Frazer Nashes in the Liège-Rome-Liège. It was his enthusiasm that led to increased British participation in such events, and thus it was a fitting reward that he should drive one of the three Austin Healey 3000s that finished first, fifth and tenth in the 1960 Liège-Rome-Liège, and which took all the team awards.

Incidentally, John is not the only "copper" whose name appears on the victory rolls, for the two Norwegians, Per Malling and Gunnar Fadum, who won the Monte Carlo Rally in 1955 driving a Sunbeam Mark III, were members of the Norwegian Police Force.

Claudine Trautmann is France's most successful lady rally driver, having won the Ladies' Championship of France no less than nine times—four with Citroën and five with Lancia. She started driving for Citroën in 1960 as a works driver and finished three times on the Liège-Sofia-Liège—winning the Coupe des Dames twice, the other occasion being in 1960 when Pat Moss won the event outright. Perhaps her most consistent performance in any event has been the Criterium Feminin Paris-Saint-Raphaël which she has won five times—every time in a Lancia, but each time in a different model.

On the Coupe des Alpes—more commonly known in England simply as the "Alpine Rally"—it used to be that an unpenalised run on the road sections and selectifs resulted in the award of a coupe. Very few of these were awarded, and even the recently instituted system of awarding them on a percentage basis makes it a very coveted award. René Trautmann, the French rally driver, has won no fewer than six coupes in the last decade, and thus has two Coupes d'Argent which are awarded for three non-consecutive coupes. In 1960 he nearly joined an even more select group of drivers—namely those who have finished a Liège-Rome-Liège unpenalised, when his Citroën emerged from Yugoslavia as the only unpenalised car, but then transmission failure caused him to retire.

Motor sport is normally associated with young men, but there are always exceptions. The best example in rallying is that of Eugen Böhringer, who came into international rallying at the age of thirty-seven when he drove a works Mercedes to second place on the Monte Carlo Rally of 1960, and later in the year, with a similar car, he won an Alpine Coupe. In 1962 he won the Acropolis Rally, the Polish Rally and the Liège-Sofia-Liège for Mercedes, and also collected the European Championship after a year-long struggle with Erik Carlsson.

In 1963 he drove one of the then-new 230SL Mercedes into first place on the Liège-Sofia-Liège, becoming one of the few men to win it twice; he then won the Acropolis Rally in a Mercedes 300SE.

Despite a couple of appearances for Porsche—which included a brilliant second place overall with a 904 on the very snowy Monte Carlo Rally of 1965—he entered very little competition after Mercedes stopped rallying, and has spent his time with his hotel and vineyards outside Stuttgart.

Until 1968 Porsche had never won the Monte Carlo Rally, largely because in the immediate post-war years—when they might easily have won it—the handicap was not favourable to G.T. cars. Since 1967 the rally has been run on a scratch basis, and in that year Vic Elford finished third in a Porsche 911S, despite the imposed handicap of a restricted number of tyres per car. Since then there has been no type of handicap in any form and Porsche have won the rally three times, with Elford in 1968, and with Bjorn Waldegaard in 1969 and 1970.

The largest number of outright victories by one driver in European Rally Championship events in one year must surely be those of the Finnish driver, Pauli Toivonen who, in the course of winning the 1968 Championship, won the San Remo, the East German, the West German, the Danube, the Spanish and the Geneva rallies. On the Monte Carlo Rally of that year he was second overall, while he finished third in the Acropolis Rally. His only mistake occurred on his home event in which he crashed in the 1000 Lakes. In all these events he drove a Porsche 911S.

The top rally drivers of the 1960s were the Scandinavians. It is not surprising therefore that on the result list of the Swedish Rally we find only Swedes in the winning position, while the same is true about the succession of home wins on the Finnish 1000 Lakes. Moreover, consecutive wins seem to be very common: on the Swedish Rally Carl-Magnus Skogh (Saab) won in 1960 and 1961, Tom Trana (Volvo) won in 1964 and 1965, and Bjorn Waldegaard (Porsche) managed the hat-trick in 1968–70. Even more remarkable was that on the 1000 Lakes Simo Lampinen (Saab) won in 1963 and 1964, and that was followed by *two* hat-tricks: Timo Makinen (Mini Cooper S) in 1965–67, and Hannu Mikkola (Ford Escort T/C) in 1968–70. The 1971 1000 Lakes saw a Swede winning this Finnish event for the first time when Stig Blomqvist won it for Saab, but then it was Lampinen who took his third victory in 1972—also with a Saab. Not to be outdone, Makinen won it with a Ford Escort in 1973 while Mikkola took his fourth win in 1974 with a similar car. In 1975, he astounded everyone by beating all his rivals in a 1,600 c.c. Toyota Corolla thus bringing his personal score of 1000 Lakes victories to five. The new Finnish superstar, Markku Alen, has now won the 1000 Lakes Rally three times for Fiat in 1976, 1978 and 1979. Thus, the score sheet for the 1000 Lakes Rally is: Mikkola 5, Makinen 4, and Lampinen and Alen 3 each.

The biggest scandal in rallying occurred on the Monte Carlo Rally of 1966 when four British cars, three Mini Coopers and one Lotus Cortina, finished in the first four places and, after nearly a day of scrutineering, all four were disqualified and the winner was announced as a French Citroën DS21.

The rally that year had very much favoured cars prepared to the new Group 1 of Appendix J, because cars of higher groups had a very heavy handicap on their special-stage times. It was popularly supposed that this was done to favour Citroën whose big, front-wheel-drive cars had long been kings of the Group 1 category. The apple-cart was, however, upset by the British teams who managed to get the Mini Cooper S and the Lotus Cortina homologated into Group 1. During the scrutineering these cars were stripped to the last nut and bolt to find something wrong with them and, when everything was found to be in order, they were disqualified on the grounds that their headlamp dipping system—using four single iodine bulbs in four separate lenses—did not comply with international lighting regulations. Protests were made explaining that the British team managers had checked this very point with the F.I.A. in Paris before the event, but to no avail. Nevertheless, two matters arose from this: the British discovered that there is as much publicity in failure as in success, while the Monte Carlo Rally organisers have been scrupulously fair ever since.

A scandal was instrumental in the disappearance from the International Calendar of the second oldest rally in the world—the Austrian Alpine.

This rally, which was first held in June 1910, had been reborn in Austria once the partition of that country, established after the Second World War, ceased. By the 1970s, it was a round of the World Rally Championship which, in 1974, was being led—and eventually won—by the Renault Alpine team. At the finish of the 1974 Austrian Alpine, three cars emerged as potential winners; Achim Warmbold's B.M.W. 2002 seemed to have the least penalties until the organisers excluded it for allegedly approaching a control from the wrong direction. He counter-claimed that the control was in the wrong place and further alleged that, on a section where the rally organisers had allowed the possibility of using two routes, the Renault Alpine Team Manager had deliberately blocked the road not used by his own team. Bernard Darniche in a Renault Alpine was announced as the winner just one second ahead of Per Eklund in a Saab. However, the Saab Team Manager then pointed out that the regulations stated that timing was to be to the whole second and that during the rally the organisers had been given stage times to a tenth of a second. If all these tenths were ignored, then Eklund would win by a second.

The uproar and protests went on for months and, in the absence of a satisfactory outcome, the rally was excluded from the World Championship results that year. The organisation split up and the rally was never held again.

Scrutineering can produce some strange decisions, but none more peculiar than that which caused Peter Harper to be disqualified from the Coupe des Alpes in 1966. He was driving a Sunbeam Tiger, powered by a 4·2-litre Ford of America V-eight engine, and not only finished but was leading the highly competitive G.T. category. The scrutineers discovered that his exhaust manifold was fractionally *undersize*, and promptly disqualified the car—though what possible advantage there could be in a smaller emission diameter no one could explain.

Protests on rallies are never welcomed, but they occur more frequently than in other branches of the sport, as so much of the competition takes place away from the sight of officials. It is unfortunate that when they do occur they tend to give the general public an idea that rallying is decided other than by driving skills.

For example, when Tony Fall was disqualified from the 1969 T.A.P. Rally in Portugal as a result of having his wife—an unauthorised passenger —in the car when it crossed the finishing-line, the story made the headlines.

High retirement rates can be a feature of rallying, and it was often said that the aim of M. Garot, who used to organise the Liège-Rome-Liège, that he would never be satisfied until just one car got to the finish. However, the worst year on the Liège-Rome-Liège was 1961 when only 8 cars survived from 85.

This has been beaten twice by the East African Safari Rally. On that event, the rainy years of 1963 and 1968 have seen 7 cars finish from 84 starters, and 7 out of 91 respectively. The Polish Rally has twice had 3 finishers; the first time in 1967 when local man Sobieslaw Zasada headed home two local drivers in his Porsche 912 after the Lancia team failed to finish and again in 1973 when Achim Warmbold won the rally in a Fiat 124 Spyder after Jean-Luc Therier's Alpine Renault had been disqualified for missing a special stage. Perhaps the record in smallest number of finishers should go to the South African Total Rally which had just 2 finishers in 1971 when Chris Swanepoel/Gus Krause won in a Toyota 2000 from husband and wife team, Hein and Ronel Dahms in a Renault 12.

Paddy Hopkirk is one of Ireland's best-known sportsmen, and he is at the same time probably the best-known rally driver in the world. Among his rallying achievements are a Coupe d'Argent on the Alpine Rally which resulted from Coupes gained with a Triumph TR3 in 1956, a Sunbeam Rapier in 1959, and a Mini Cooper in 1965. As well as being the man who started the great string of successes for the Mini Cooper S by winning the Monte Carlo Rally in 1964, he also won the Acropolis Rally and the Alpine Rally in 1967—at the end of the Mini Cooper's rallying career.

Over the years he has also made the Circuit of Ireland a Hopkirk speciality, winning it no less than five times: with a Triumph TR3 in 1958, Sunbeam Rapiers in 1961 and 1962, and with Mini Coopers in 1965 and 1967.

The hazards of special sections. Rauno Aaltonen and Tony Ambrose, leading crew of the award-winning Datsun team, on a remote "road" in the Lake District during the 1969 R.A.C. Rally. (Photo: Hugh W. Bishop.)

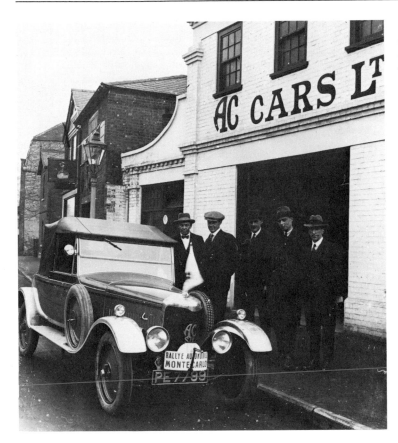

The 1926 Monte-winning A.C. Six outside the Thames Ditton Works. Hon. Victor Bruce is second from the right.

The first-ever British success in the Monte Carlo Rally was gained by the Hon. Victor Bruce and W. J. Brunell driving their A.C. Six in the 1926 event.

The only man ever to win the Monte Carlo Rally in a car bearing his own name was Sidney Allard who won that event in 1952 driving an Allard P Type Saloon. The chassis and body were constructed in England in Allard's workshops, but the engine was an American Mercury V-eight of 3,622 c.c., developing 140 b.h.p. Following this sporting success, Allard put the P2 Monte Carlo Saloon on the market but he had a very hard time selling it against the emergent Jaguars.

The closest anyone else came to equalling this feat was Jacques Bignan, who had one of his 2-litre Bignan saloons win the rally in 1924 and then won the event himself in 1928 driving a Fiat 509A. Another well-known car-constructor who has himself won the Monte Carlo Rally was Donald Healey who came first in 1931 at the wheel of an Invicta S-type powered by a 4½-litre Meadows engine.

Rivalling Allard's place in the history books is the Austrian Wolfgang Denzel who, between 1948 and 1960, built his own two-seater sports cars based on a Volkswagen chassis fitted with Porsche 1·3- or 1·5-litre engines. It was driving one of these cars that he made best performance in the Coupe des Alpes in 1954.

One of rallying's most coveted awards is the Coupe d'Or awarded on the Alpine Rally for gaining *coupes* in three successive years. In the whole career of the Alpine Rally which was last held in 1971, only three such awards were ever made and two of them went to Englishmen. Ian Appleyard won the first with his Jaguar XJ120 on the 1951, 1952 and 1953 events while no less a person than Stirling Moss gained the award in the events of 1952, 1953 and 1954 driving different models of the Sunbeam Talbot. The third driver to win a Coupe d'Or was Frenchman, Jean Vinatier, who won *coupes* in 1968 and 1969 and again in 1971. These were, of course, non-consecutive years but it must be remembered that the Coupe des Alpes was not held in 1970 and it was for this reason that an exception was made in Vinatier's case.

The famous rallying twins, Donald and Erle Morley very nearly pulled off a fourth with *coupes* in 1961 and 1962 driving Austin Healey 3000s, but a broken differential put them out in 1963; nevertheless, they went on to win a Coupe d'Argent in 1964, also with a big Austin Healey. Another B.M.C. crew, Rauno Aaltonen and Tony Ambrose, almost made it in 1965, having won *coupes* with a Mini Cooper in 1963 and 1964, but a misdirection by a gendarme on what should have been an easy liaison section, cost them a *coupe* and the higher award.

One of the shortest events in the rally calendar is also one of the toughest, and is rated by rally drivers as a true test of their skill. Nicknamed the "Rally of ten thousand corners", the Tour de Corse was originated in 1956, and since there is a fairly limited number of roads on the island of Corsica it seldom lasts more than 24 hours. However, the sinuous roads and the impossible time schedule make it a very tough event, and at the time when it is run—at the beginning of November—the weather can be very unkind. Frequently held in rain, the rally has been stopped by snow—as in 1961, when Trautmann was awarded the victory as he was leading when the event was halted.

Since 1969, the format of the rally has changed and the emphasis is now upon the special stages and the road sections are not so difficult. Before then, there had been a prize fund which increased every year and was to be given to the man who first finished a Tour de Corse with no road penalty. It was never attributed but Sandro Munari came closest to winning it when he won the rally in 1967 losing just one minute at one time control—and that by a mere nine seconds!

Austin Healeys during their heyday. Peter Riley and Tony Ambrose in the 1961 Alpine Rally.

The original title of the East African Safari Rally was "The East African Coronation Safari", so called after its inauguration in 1953—the year of the coronation of Queen Elizabeth II. One of its most original ideas, which has since been dropped, was to run the cars in classes determined not by capacity (as is normal in international events), but by price in East Africa. Since the cars were rallied practically in standard form, the results of the rally then meant a great deal to the prospective car-buyers of Africa, while this system of classes was also an inducement to car-importers to reduce the delivered price of their cars on Mombasa dock in order to get into a lower class.

What the best-dressed long-distance rally car should wear. The J. Greaves/T. Fall Ford Escort sets out on the 1970 World Cup Rally. The cage in front of the head lamps is affectionately known as a "roo-bar" while the two bars on either side of the windscreen are to strengthen the windscreen pillars.

One of the fastest success stories in rallying is that of Hannu Mikkola who not only won the World Cup Rally for Ford in 1970 but became the first European driver to ever win the East African Safari in 1972. He started rallying when he bought a second-hand Volvo just before going to college in 1963. He finished fourth in his first event and continued to drive Volvos for several years. In 1968, he made quite a name for himself by having several contracts going at once; he drove the Monte Carlo, Tulip and Acropolis rallies with Datsun, the Austrian Alpine and R.A.C. Rally for Lancia, the Finnish championship with a Volvo. But the most significant thing was that Ford lent him an Escort for the 1000 Lakes and he won the rally for them, thus starting his association with that company. In addition to his two great long-distance victories, he won the 1000 Lakes four times for Ford before leaving them at the end of 1974 to go to Fiat and then to Toyota. He has driven many times for Peugeot and in 1975 he won the Moroccan Rally for them despite running out of tyres in the desert and having to wait for a team mate to bring him some new ones. In 1977, Hannu Mikkola rejoined the Ford team and had had an impressive list of victories in British International Rallies. From time to time, he still freelances with other teams for long-distance events and, for instance, finished second on the 1979 East African Safari driving a Mercedes 450 SL.

When it was first rallied some drivers rather unkindly nicknamed the Peugeot 504 "the Paris taxi". It was Peugeot who had the last laugh, however, for in 1975 they won all three of the long-distance African rallies—the Bandama, the Safari and the Moroccan.

Rally cars frequently carry quite a lot in the way of spares, and it is not unheard of for a car to weigh twice as much in rally trim as the manufacturers' listed weight. Jacques Bignan's Fiat 509, with which he won the Monte Carlo Rally in 1928, allegedly weighed over 30 cwt. with the crew aboard, while the catalogue weight was a mere 16¾ cwt. Although M. Bignan probably carried plenty of heavy de-ditching gear, which is rendered less necessary nowadays by studded tyres and service crews—modern rally cars still carry essential spares.

The late Paul Hawkins could have saved himself a long walk if he had remembered this during the 1965 Targa Florio in which he drove with Timo Makinen. He had a rotor arm break on his works Austin Healey 3000, and he ran all the way back to the pits for a spare—only to be told that it was in the car. It had been prepared by the Abingdon rally mechanics.

There are many stories about people rallying in borrowed cars, hired and partly-paid-for cars but perhaps the nicest concerns a gentleman called John Patten who, in the company of John Sprinzel, finished third overall in an Austin Healey Sprite on the very tough Liège-Rome-Liège of 1960. He had only paid the deposit on the car before leaving to compete in the rally, and his comment at the finish was to the effect that as it didn't seem such a bad car he might pay off the rest of the price!

Incidentally, John Sprinzel's distinguished rallying career started when he borrowed his mother's Austin A30 and entered the R.A.C. Rally in it.

The Nicolas/Roure Renault Alpine being night driven in the Forest of Lente on the 1970 Monte Carlo Rally. (Photo: Hugh W. Bishop.)

The Solomon/Saintigny Citroën on the Col de Perty during the 1970 Monte Carlo Rally. This car crashed on the very last épreuve. (Photo: Hugh W. Bishop.)

The longest rally held to date is the 1977 version of the London to Sydney Rally, run on that occasion over 19,329 miles from Covent Garden in London to the Sydney Opera House. The route passed through seventeen countries and finished on 28th September 1977 when the sponsors, Singapore Airlines, presented the winner's spoils to a Mercedes 280E crewed by a British team comprising Andrew Cowan, Colin Malkin and Mike Broad.

Joginder Singh made history in 1965 when he became the first man of non-European race to win a major international rally. Pictures of him and his brother Jaswant wearing their turbans and sitting on the bonnet of their Volvo PV 544 appeared all over the world. Since then, the Safari has twice been won by non-Europeans; Shekhar Mehta brought off a sensational victory in 1973 when he won in his Datsun 250Z after being declared equal on points with Harry Kallstrom in a Datsun 180B. Mehta had in fact beaten Kallstrom by a

The only man to have won the Safari Rally three times is the diminutive Sikh, Joginder Singh, seen here with co-driver, David Doig and their Colt 1600 at the end of the 1974 event. Singh first won as long ago as 1965 when he and his brother, Jaswant, drove an old PV 544 Volvo.

The winning Escort T.C. of Chris Sclater and John Davenport on the 1970 Manx Trophy Rally. (Photo: Hugh W. Bishop.)

single minute but was penalised one minute at the final scrutineering for having a headlamp missing. In fact, the whole front wing was missing where he and co-driver Lofty Drews had cut it free after an accident. The tie between the two cars was finally resolved on the principle of who had gone furthest in the rally from the start without losing points. The third non-European victory went again to Joginder when he won the 1974 Safari with David Doig as co-driver in a factory-prepared Colt 1600. The same pair won the 1976 Safari in a Mitsubishi Lancer.

Many rally team managers have followed the tradition set by Norman Garrad of Rootes in reaching their positions after actually competing in the sport. Examples are Stuart Turner of Ford and Cesare Fiorio of Lancia, but it is interesting that they came from "different sides of the car". Turner started out as a navigator in British events, and was *Autosport* Champion Navigator three years running before joining *Motoring News* as a journalist and starting to co-drive in international events—when he was equally successful, winning the R.A.C. Rally in 1960 with Erik Carlsson.

On the other hand Fiorio was a driver, starting out on the Rally of the Dolomites in a Triumph TR 2, and at the same time racing a Fiat 500. He became Italian G.T. Champion in 1961 driving a Lancia Appia Zagato; the next year he drove a Flaminia both on rallies such as the Monte Carlo and at races like the *Motor* Six Hours at Brands Hatch, in which he won the class and finished fifth over all.

Tony Fall is one of the "personalities" to emerge from international rallying. Hailing from Bradford in Yorkshire, Fall initially drove Mini Coopers at the time when he worked for the former Coupe d'Or winner, Ian Appleyard, and after some success Appleyard started to help in financing his rallying.

Eventually, he came to the notice of Stuart Turner, then B.M.C. Competitions Manager, when he emulated the exploits of his boss by winning a *coupe* on the Alpine Rally of 1965. He won the Circuit of Ireland and Scottish rallies in 1966 with a 1,275 c.c. Mini Cooper, and on the Polish Rally he won outright as a result of choosing the smaller 999 c.c. Mini Cooper which had a better handicap. He also became the only driver ever to win an international rally with a B.M.C. 1800 when he won the Danube Rally in 1967.

Since then he has rallied in a variety of cars, including Lancia, for whom he won the T.A.P. Rally in Portugal in 1968 and finished third in the R.A.C. Rally in 1969. With Ford, he travelled far afield to win the Rally of the Incas in Peru as part of his World Cup Rally recce with a Ford Escort Twin-Cam. He retired from active rallying to run the Opel Dealer Team in Britain. In 1977 he was invited to go to Germany to head the International Opel Competition Department where one of his first major projects has been the homologation of the special Opel Ascona 400 especially developed for competitions.

True international rallying: Walter Rohrl from Germany driving for Fiat and winning the Quebec Rally in Canada, 1978.

Breaking a thirteen-year-old duck is not easy but Roger Clark and Tony Mason did it for British drivers when they won the R.A.C. Rally of Great Britain in 1972 with a Ford Escort. The last time that a British driver won the rally was in 1959 when Gerry Burgess survived a very snowy session in Scotland to win with a Ford Zephyr. Since Clark's victory the emphasis has switched back to the Scandinavians and Timo Makinen has scored an impressive hat-trick, winning the rally in 1973, 1974 and 1975. On each occasion he was sponsored by a different firm; in the first rally it was the Milk Marketing Board, then Colibri lighters and on the more recent win, by Allied Polymer Group.

North American Rallying used to be more of a strain on the brain than a strain on the supplies of adrenalin but the advent of special stage rallies has changed that for good. In its third year, the S.C.C.A.'s Pro-Rally Series was a great success and the 1975 Champion was a man from Vermont called John Buffum. For years, he had suffered the nickname of "Stuff'em Buffum" but in 1975 he and his ex-wife, Vicki Dykema kept their Ford Escort/Porsche Carrera on the road and won five of the seven events outright. In 1977, John signed a contract to rally the Triumph TR7 in North America and in that year he won the American Series outright. This success was repeated in 1978 when he won all three of the major North American Championships, including the Canadian, with this Triumph sports car.

Most amazing example of the Tortoise and Hare in modern rallying was Ove Andersson's win on the East African Safari in 1975. His Peugeot 504 was one of the slowest cars in the rally with 165 b.h.p. in some 30 cwt. and its major rivals were two works Lancia Stratos with 240 b.h.p. in about 18 cwt. Nevertheless, the Peugeot was extremely strong and could be driven flat-out over the worst roads while the Lancias had to be more circumspect. Many times they got ahead only to stop for lengthy repairs and finally the Peugeot defeated them both.

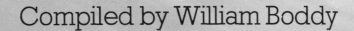

Section 4
TRACK RACING AND RECORD BREAKING

Compiled by William Boddy

The late John Cobb (Napier-Railton) on the banking at Brooklands during the 1937 Broadcast Trophy Handicap Race which he won at 136·07 m.p.h. (Photo: Radio Times Hulton Picture Library.)

WORLD SPEED RECORDS

The beginnings of the World's Land Speed Record date back to 18th December 1898, when the Comte Gaston de Chasseloup-Laubat was timed to cover a one-way kilometre on his special electric racer at the Agricole Park at Achères, near Paris, at a speed of 39·24 m.p.h. Great fears were expressed for the health of automobilists who were so foolish as to endeavour to go faster and faster. They were expected to die of heart failure or to be unable to breathe.

The first time 60 m.p.h. was exceeded on land was in April 1899, when the Comte de Chasseloup-Laubat's existing speed of 57·6 m.p.h. was bettered by Camille Jenatzy who set up an official record of 65·79 m.p.h. on the Achères road, near Paris, in France. Jenatzy drove an electric car with rudimentary streamlining, called *La Jamais Contente* (see page 29). The motors ran at up to 900 r.p.m.

100 miles per hour was first officially achieved in July 1904 by Louis Rigolly, who was timed to cover a flying kilometre at Ostend in a big 100-h.p. Gobron-Brillié at 103·56 m.p.h.

A speed of 150 m.p.h. was first reached by Captain (later Sir) Malcolm Campbell of Great Britain in 1925. In March that year he was credited with the Land Speed Record, which he broke on Pendine Sands driving the old 350-h.p. V-twelve Sunbeam at 150·87 m.p.h.

Malcolm Campbell in the V-twelve Sunbeam on Pendine Sands in 1925.

The honour of being the first man to exceed 200 m.p.h. on land belongs to Sir Henry Segrave. He took the twin-engined 1,000-h.p. Sunbeam out to Daytona Beach in America in 1927 and established the Land Speed Record at 203·79 m.p.h. on 29th March at just after 8 a.m., Florida time. His fastest one-way run was at a speed of over 207 m.p.h.

Sir Henry Segrave's 1,000-h.p. Sunbeam record-breaking car, after its return from Florida in 1927.

Sir Malcolm Campbell was the first driver to officially exceed 250 m.p.h. This he did at Daytona in 1932 in one of his many *Bluebirds*—this one powered by a supercharged Napier Lion engine. A head-wind in one direction held the great car back, but the record fell at 253·968 m.p.h., the best run in one direction being 267·459 m.p.h.

Malcolm Campbell with the 1933 Rolls-Royce-engined Bluebird (R-type, V-twelve, 36·5 litres, 2,300 b.h.p.) with offset body. He took the Land Speed Record at 272·46 m.p.h.

The 300 m.p.h. goal was attained by Campbell in September 1935, using *Bluebird* with a 2,500-h.p. Rolls-Royce R-type racing aeroplane engine. He made his bid at Bonneville Salt Flats, Utah, U.S.A.; despite the 4,000-foot altitude drastically reducing the maximum power of the engine, the Land Speed Record was raised to 301·13 m.p.h. The best run, at 304·311 m.p.h., meant that *Bluebird* was in the timed section of the course—a distance of a mile—for only 11·83 seconds.

The first to motor at more than 350 m.p.h. was John Cobb of Britain, whose Railton Mobil Special, with two 1929 supercharged Napier Lion aero-engines, recorded a mean speed of 350·20 m.p.h. at Utah, U.S.A., in September 1938.

The World's Land Speed Record exceeded 400 m.p.h. after the Second World War, when the admission of gas-turbines and jet-propelled cars confused the issue to some extent. But in 1947, before this new era of fastest-ever records, John Cobb had exceeded 400 m.p.h. in one direction in the Napier-Railton at Utah in September, when he left the record at 394·196 m.p.h. His speed over the mile from south to north of the course was 403·135 m.p.h.

The fastest officially recognised two-way average speed on land stands to the credit of Gary Gabelich of the U.S.A., whose rocket-powered four-wheeler holds the Land Speed Record at 630·38 m.p.h., the first time 1,000 km./hr. has been exceeded. The fastest speed in one direction was 631·36 m.p.h., and he beat the previous fastest-ever speed of 600·60 m.p.h. held by Craig Breedlove's jet-propelled four-wheeler *Spirit of America Sonic 1*. Breedlove had previously broken the existing four-wheeler Land Speed Record with a jet-propelled three-wheeler in 1964, thus prompting the F.I.A. to rewrite the rules governing these records, which now include categories for (*a*) vehicles with at least four road wheels and driven through any pair of wheels, (*b*) vehicles with at least four road wheels driven other than through the wheels, and (*c*) vehicles with less than four road wheels driven other than through the wheels.

The fastest man on earth, however, is Hollywood stuntman Stan Barrett in his rocket-powered *Budweiser* (an American beer) three-wheeler, with assistance from the propulsion unit of a Sidewinder air-to-air missile. He achieved 739·666 m.p.h., over a time trap of but 52 feet, on a one-way run over Rogers dry lake in the Californian Mojave desert on 18th December 1979. Barrett thus became **the first man to drive faster than the speed of sound on land**, under the temperature conditions prevailing at the time.

The ultimate motorcycle speed record is held by Donald A. Vesco of California. On 28th September, 1975 at Bonneville Salt Flats, Utah, U.S.A., riding his 21-foot-long, 1,500 c.c. *Silver Bird* streamlined machine, he achieved an average of 303·810 m.p.h. for his two-way runs. On the same day he covered a flying ¼-mile in 2·925 seconds—307·692 m.p.h., and the highest speed ever recorded by a motorcycle. *Silver Bird* is powered by two Yamaha TZ750 engines developing 180 b.h.p.

Stan Barrett's Budweiser *rocket car which broke the "sound barrier".*

Goldenrod

The highest speed achieved by a piston-engined car is 418·50 m.p.h. over 666·686 yards after a flying start. The car, called *Goldenrod* on account of its long slim shape, was driven by the American, Robert Summers, on the Bonneville Salt Flats on 12th November 1965. It had four petrol-injection Chrysler engines giving a total capacity of 27,924 c.c., and developing about 2,400 b.h.p.

The Mercedes-Benz C111-IV, driven by Dr. Hans Liebold.

The World's Record for a closed circuit lap was broken in 1979 by Dr. Hans Liebold, driving the experimental Mercedes-Benz C111-lV, with a new aerodynamic body, when he was timed at 251 m.p.h. at the 7·5-mile Nardo track in Southern Italy. The engine was a twin turbo-charged V-eight petrol unit developing about 500 b.h.p.

The first electric car to break the Land Speed Record was Chasseloup-Laubat's Jeantaud which did 39·24 m.p.h. in 1898. Camille Jenatzy raised this to 65·79 m.p.h. in 1899. The most exciting of the electric Land Speed Record cars was Walter C. Baker's Baker Torpedo electric of 1902. A fully streamlined, enclosed-cockpit vehicle—very low built—it was powered by an Elwell-Parker motor behind the cockpit, fed from forty Gould cells. Drive was by chains, while the body was of white pine covered with oil-cloth, and the tyres were 40 × 3 inch

Battery Box with driver Roger Hedlund (left) and Ted Brown, crew.

Goodrich on disc wheels. The driver, Baker, was accompanied by his mechanic, C. E. Denzer. Unfortunately, the Baker Torpedo crashed at Staten Island Boulevard, New York Bay, while attempting to break the Serpollet steam-car record, running into the crowd and killing two people.

The electric car two-way flying-start kilometre and mile World Records stand to Roger Hedlund's lead-acid-powered *Battery Box* in Class 2 (500–1,000 kg.), which achieved 175·061 m.p.h. at Bonneville in 1974; and in Class 1 (under 500 kg.) to Miss Cissy Johnson with her *Golf Car Special*, at 83·955 m.p.h.

The fastest electric motorcycle is *Quicksilver* which, ridden by Mike Corbin at Utah, clocked 165 m.p.h. in 1974.

The Land Speed Record was first broken by a petrol-engined car in August 1902 when W. K. Vanderbilt used a Paris-Vienna Race Mors and set the record to 76·08 m.p.h. at Ablis, near Chartres, France. His time beat Serpollet's steamer by two-fifths of a second.

The first steam car to break the Land Speed Record was driven by Léon Serpollet at 75·06 m.p.h. on Nice Promenade in 1902—the first time 75 m.p.h. had been exceeded.

The fastest steam car of all was Fred Marriott's boat-shaped Stanley which put the record up to 121·57 m.p.h. for the kilometre in 1906. The Stanley steamed over the mile at 127·56 m.p.h., but this was never officially recognised. The Stanley steamer in which Fred Marriott had his sensational accident while trying to beat the Land Speed Record at Daytona in 1907 was known as the *Wogglebug* (later renamed *Rocket*). It was a red car, also shaped like an inverted boat, with a steam pressure of 1,300 lb./sq. in. It was unable to equal the earlier Stanley record of 1906 on its first attempts on 25th January 1907, and crashed on its final attempt, driver and boiler rolling along the sands. The facts of this accident have been grossly exaggerated (see page 27).

World Diesel-car Records were set by Mercedes-Benz at the Nardo track in Italy in 1978 using their experimental, streamlined C111-III car powered by a five-cylinder 3-litre compression-ignition engine with turbo-charger, claimed to develop 230 b.h.p. The drivers were Paul Frère, Rico Steinemann, Dr. Hans Liebold and Guido Moch. They broke some records previously held by petrol-engined cars, C111-III averaging 199·8 m.p.h. for one hour and 191·8 m.p.h. for twelve hours. Altogether the Mercedes-Benz set up nine fresh *World's* honours with this diesel-powered car, whereas for many years such records were some of the slowest in the record books.

Diesel Mercedes-Benz C111-III.

The World's Land Speed Record was broken for the last time on a special track, as distinct from a beach course, in May 1922 when K. Lee Guinness took it at 133·75 m.p.h. at Brooklands in the 350-h.p. Sunbeam. The banked track presented difficulties at this speed, especially as it had to be negotiated in two directions.

The Land Speed Record was broken for the last time on an ordinary (tree-lined) road by Ernest Eldridge in July 1924. He took a passenger with him in his hybrid 300-h.p. Fiat at Arpajon, near Paris, and, in spite of tyres in poor condition, took the record at a speed of 146·01 m.p.h. Prior to this, Eldridge had achieved 147·03 m.p.h. but a protest by his rival, René Thomas (Delage) that the old Fiat had no reverse gear—as required by the regulations—had caused Eldridge to be disqualified.

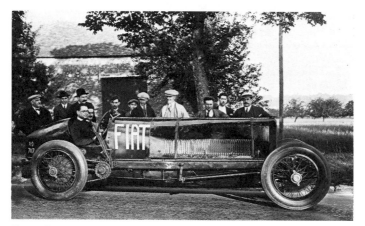 

Ernest Eldridge in the 1924 record-breaking Fiat, and the notice with which Turin announced their achievement.

Between the wars many British attempts on the Land Speed Record were made at Pendine Sands, Carmarthenshire, in Wales. In 1926, however, H. O. D. Segrave preferred Southport Sands, on which he drove the 4-litre V-twelve Sunbeam at 152·33 m.p.h. for a two-way run, establishing a new record.

The first twenty-four-hour motor race ever staged was run in Columbus, Ohio, U.S.A. on 3rd–4th July 1905 on a one-mile oval horse-racing track. Three cars started and all survived the race, which was won by the brothers Charles and George Soules driving their Pope-Toledo, with a Frayer-Miller second and a Peerless third. The winning car covered 828·5 miles in the twenty-four hours, an average speed of 34·5 m.p.h.

S. F. Edge celebrated the opening of Brooklands Track on 17th June 1907 by driving a 60-h.p. Napier single-handed for 24 hours on 28th–29th June, resting only when the car had to be refuelled or provided with fresh tyres. Edge covered 1,581 miles 1,310 yards at an average speed of 65·905 m.p.h. and afterwards drove back to his hotel at Cobham. During the run twenty-four tyres were changed. The record stood until 1924.

The first car to exceed a speed of 100 m.p.h. for an hour was the 25-h.p. Talbot driven at Brooklands by Percy Lambert. This was achieved in 1913. Later, in trying to retake his record from a Peugeot, Lambert had a tyre burst and was killed when the Talbot rolled down the banking.

S. F. Edge (1903 Gordon Bennett 60-h.p. Napier) setting out in 1937 on a lap commemorating his inaugural 24-hour run at Brooklands in June 1907.

One hundred miles an hour was exceeded for 24 hours for the first time by a Renault 45 specially streamlined fabric saloon at the Montlhéry track in 1926. It averaged 107·9 m.p.h. and, to show that this was no fluke, it was timed over the last lap at 118·74 m.p.h.

The World Hour Record was a covetable target, being a record calling for high speed for a duration long enough to test the skill and endurance of the driver, the mechanical stamina of the machinery—and particularly the tyres—in the between-the-wars era. After Percy Lambert had exceeded 100 miles for this duration in 1913, the Hour Record was first raised to over 120 miles in 1926 by Ortmans driving a Panhard-Levassor. An 8-litre Panhard-Levassor single-seater was also the first car to set the Hour Record to over 130 m.p.h., at Montlhéry in 1932. (Incidentally, Panhard-Levassor dispensed with a steering wheel on their 1926 record-breaking single-seaters, the driver steering with a ring through which he sat. The idea was abandoned after a fatal accident during testing of the idea.)

The Brooklands authorities were obliged to ban attempts on the 24-hour Record after the First World War because of complaints from the St. George's Hill residents at Weybridge, near the track, of sleepless nights due to the noise.

Henry Segrave's Sunbeam at Southport, Lancashire, in 1926. He broke the Land Speed Record on 16th March at 152·33 m.p.h.

But they substituted a "Double-Twelve" Record, the contesting cars being officially locked up during the hours of darkness—to resume the attempt, albeit with cold oil, the next morning. S. F. Edge bet *The Motor* a bronze medal that he could beat his 1907 Napier record in two 12-hour spells. This he did in 1922, with a Maybach-engined Spyker, averaging 74·27 m.p.h.

The first light car "Double-Twelve" Record was established by A. G. Miller's Wolseley Moth in 1922, at a speed of 61·06 m.p.h. In 1924, at Montlhéry, T. G. Gillett bettered the 1907 continuous 24-hour Record, in a 2-litre A.C.

A car or motorcycle could claim a duration record even if it was unable to remain in action for the full period of time, providing the distance it had set out to beat was covered and the vehicle remained at the track for the required time, even though it was stationary at the pits.

Ordinary saloon cars have been used quite frequently in International class record bids, aiming for those of such endurance that the speeds at which they stood were suitably low. Singer Ten, Riley Nine and flat-twin Jowett were among the closed utility cars to be thus employed. The Hon. Mrs. Victor Bruce and her husband used a Jowett saloon in this manner and, to obviate frequent stops for refuelling, it towed a trailer carrying a petrol bowser from which fuel could be pumped to the engine while on the move. Many years later Morris Motors staged a demonstration of a long non-stop run at Goodwood with Minors, which were serviced while on moving trucks, so that they could claim a non-stop performance by the car concerned. But this sort of performance is outside the scope of official International record-breaking.

The Stutz twin 1½-litre Miller-engined Black Hawk *of Frank Lockhart at Daytona in 1928.*

Ice-cooling was successfully employed in the Stutz *Black Hawk* record-breaker with which Frank Lockhart attempted the Land Speed Record in 1928. The ice was used in special surface containers, the idea being to reduce the wind-drag of external water-radiators. Lockhart went into the sea on his first bid at Daytona, and later, after a one-way run at 203·45 m.p.h., the car rolled over and he was flung out and killed. The Stutz was the smallest car to attempt the Land Speed Record, its capacity being only 3 litres; the engine was a twin-supercharged V-sixteen with two crankshafts, and the car weighed only 2,800 lb. (Ice-cooling was also used on Kaye Don's *Silver Bullet* (1929) and John Cobb's Railton of 1938.)

Kaye Don's unsuccessful twin 12-cylinder-engined Sunbeam Silver Bullet, *1930. In spite of a claimed 4000 h.p. it was over 40 m.p.h. short of Segrave's 1929 record in "Golden Arrow".*

THE WORLD'S LAND SPEED RECORD

Year	Driver	Car	Speed (m.p.h.)	Course
1898	G. de Chasseloup-Laubat	Jeantaud (electric)	39·24	Achères, nr. Paris
1899	C. Jenatzy	Jenatzy (electric)	41·42	Achères, nr. Paris
	G. de Chasseloup-Laubat	Jeantaud (electric)	43·69	Achères, nr. Paris
	C. Jenatzy	Jenatzy (electric)	49·62	Achères, nr. Paris
	G. de Chasseloup-Laubat	Jeantaud (electric)	57·60	Achères, nr. Paris
	C. Jenatzy	Jenatzy (electric)	65·79	Achères, nr. Paris
1902	C. S. Rolls*	Mors	63·10	Achères, nr. Paris
	W. K. Vanderbilt, Jr*	Mercedes-Simplex	65·79	Achères, nr. Paris
	L. Serpollet	Serpollet (steam)	75·06	Nice, France
	W. K. Vanderbilt, Jr*	Mercedes	67·78	Ablis, nr. Chartres
	W. K. Vanderbilt, Jr*	Mercedes	69·04	Ablis, nr. Chartres
	P. de Caters*	Mors	75·06	Bruges, Belgium
	W. K. Vanderbilt, Jr	Mors	76·08	Ablis, nr. Chartres
	H. Fournier	Mors	76·60	Dourdan, France
	M. Augières	Mors	77·13	Dourdan, France
1903	C. S. Rolls*	Mors	82·84	Clipstone, Nottinghamshire
	A. Duray	Gobron-Brillié	83·47	Ostend, Belgium
	Baron de Forest*	Mors	84·09	Phoenix Park, Dublin
	C. S. Rolls*	Mors	84·73	Clipstone, Nottinghamshire
	A. Duray	Gobron-Brillié	84·73	Dourdan, France
1904	H. Ford	Ford	91·37	Lake St. Clair, Michigan
	W. K. Vanderbilt, Jr	Mercedes	92·30	Daytona, Florida
	L. E. Rigolly	Gobron-Brillié	94·78	Nice, France
	P. de Caters	Mercedes	97·25	Ostend, Belgium
	L. E. Rigolly	Gobron-Brillié	103·55	Ostend, Belgium
	P. Baras	Darracq	104·52	Ostend, Belgium
1905	A. Macdonald	Napier	104·65	Daytona, Florida
	H. L. Bowden*	Mercedes	109·75	Daytona, Florida
	V. Hémèry	Darracq	109·65	Arles, France
1906	F. H. Marriott	Stanley (steam)	121·57	Daytona, Florida
1909	V. Hémèry	Benz	125·95	Brooklands, England
1910	B. Oldfield	Benz	131·72	Daytona, Florida
1911	R. Burman*	Benz	140·87	Daytona, Florida
1913	A. Duray*	Fiat	132·37	Ostend, Belgium

* These speeds were not officially recognised (see text).

The World's Land Speed Record—*continued*

Year	Driver	Car	Speed (m.p.h.)	Course
1914	L. G. Hornsted	Benz	124·10	Brooklands, England (2-ways)
1919	R. de Palma	Packard	149·87	Daytona, Florida
1920	T. Milton†	Duesenberg	156·03	Daytona, Florida
1922	K. Lee Guinness	Sunbeam	133·75	Brooklands, England
1924	R. Thomas	Delage	143·31	Arpajon, nr. Paris
	E. Eldridge	Fiat	146·01	Arpajon, nr. Paris
	M. Campbell	Sunbeam	146·16	Pendine, Carmarthenshire
1925	M. Campbell	Sunbeam	150·87	Pendine, Carmarthenshire
1926	H. O. D. Segrave	Sunbeam	152·33	Southport, Lancashire
	J. G. P. Thomas	Thomas Special	169·30	Pendine, Carmarthenshire
	J. G. P. Thomas	Thomas Special	171·02	Pendine, Carmarthenshire
1927	M. Campbell	Napier-Campbell	174·88	Pendine, Carmarthenshire
	H. O. D. Segrave	Sunbeam	203·79	Daytona, Florida
1928	M. Campbell	Napier-Campbell	206·96	Daytona, Florida
	R. Keech	White-Triplex	207·55	Daytona, Florida
1929	H. O. D. Segrave	Irving-Napier	231·44	Daytona, Florida
1931	M. Campbell	Napier-Campbell	246·09	Daytona, Florida
1932	Sir Malcolm Campbell	Napier-Campbell	253·97	Daytona, Florida
1933	Sir Malcolm Campbell	Campbell Special	272·46	Daytona, Florida
1935	Sir Malcolm Campbell	Campbell Special	276·82	Daytona, Florida
	Sir Malcolm Campbell	Campbell Special	301·13	Bonneville, Utah
1937	G. E. T. Eyston	Thunderbolt	312·00	Bonneville, Utah
1938	G. E. T. Eyston	Thunderbolt	345·50	Bonneville, Utah
	J. R. Cobb	Railton	350·20	Bonneville, Utah
	G. E. T. Eyston	Thunderbolt	357·50	Bonneville, Utah
1939	J. R. Cobb	Railton	369·70	Bonneville, Utah
1947	J. R. Cobb	Railton	394·20	Bonneville, Utah
1963	C. Breedlove§	Spirit of America††	407·45	Bonneville, Utah
1964	D. Campbell	Bluebird-Proteus	403·10	Lake Eyre, Australia
	T. Green§	Wingfoot Express	413·20	Bonneville, Utah
	A. Arfons§	Green Monster	434·02	Bonneville, Utah
	C. Breedlove§	Spirit of America††	468·72	Bonneville, Utah
	C. Breedlove§	Spirit of America††	526·28	Bonneville, Utah
	A. Arfons§	Green Monster	536·71	Bonneville, Utah
1965	C. Breedlove§	Spirit of America Sonic 1	555·48	Bonneville, Utah
	A. Arfons§	Green Monster	576·55	Bonneville, Utah
	R. Summers	Goldenrod	409·27	Bonneville, Utah
	C. Breedlove§	Spirit of America Sonic 1	600·60	Bonneville, Utah
1970	G. Gabelich§	Blue Flame	630·38	Bonneville, Utah

Note *As from January, 1911, the A.I.A.C.R. (now the F.I.A.) required that, for a record to be recognised, an average would be taken of the speeds of runs in both directions.*

* These speeds were not officially recognised (see text).

  † Timed in one direction only, over a mile.

†† Three-wheeled car.

§ **Not a Wheel-Driven Car.**

The wreck of the Higham Special Babs *in which Parry Thomas met his death on the Pendine Sands in Wales in 1927. It was believed that he was killed when a driving chain broke loose, probably after the collapse of a rear wheel.*

TRACK RACING AND RECORD-BREAKING

Class record-breaking was mainly a pre-war pursuit, when drivers and entrants could earn good bonuses from various sources for each important record taken. By the time Hitler stopped play in 1940, some notable speeds had been achieved:

Class (c.c.)	Driver and Car	Highest Speed (m.p.h.)	Date	One Hour (m.p.h.)	Driver and Car	Date
Over 8,000	Cobb (Railton)	369·7	23.8.39	177·05	Jenkins (Mormon Meteor)	8.9.37
5,001–8,000	Caracciola (Mercedes-Benz)	268·9	28.1.38	152·15	Jenkins (Duesenberg)	6.8.35
2,001–3,000	Caracciola (Mercedes-Benz)	248·3	9.2.39	124·68	Divo (Bugatti)	10.3.32
1,501–2,000	Mrs. Stewart (Derby-Miller)	147·7	25.7.34	121·75	Mrs. Stewart (Derby-Miller)	15.10.31
751–1,100	Major Gardner (M.G.)	204·3	2.6.39	119·01	Veyron (Bugatti)	11.11.33
501–750	Kohlrausch (M.G.)	140·7	10.10.36	113·99	Dodson (Austin)	21.10.36
351–500	Count Lurani (Nibbio)	106·7	31.5.39	74·44	de Rovin (de Rovin)	16.10.27
Up to 350	Cecchini (Moscerino)	91·3	25.5.39	73·04	Gush (Vitesse Special)	27.9.34
Compression-ignition	Eyston (Flying Spray)	159·1	29.4.36	105·6	Eyston (A.E.C.)	27.4.37

The first time 100 m.p.h. was officially exceeded was in 1904 by Rigolly's Gobron-Brillié. **A 1½-litre car first attained this speed** in 1921, the distinction belonging to Harry Hawker in an A.C. **The first 1,100 c.c. car** to do this was Morel's Amilcar, and the **first 750 c.c.-class car** to exceed "the ton" was an M.G. driven by George Eyston in 1931. By 1935 Count Lurani's *Nibbio* had exceeded 100 m.p.h. in **the up-to-500 c.c. category.**

The first time 100 miles were exceeded in the hour was by Percy Lambert's Talbot in 1913. This was accomplished **by a 1½-litre car**, J. A. Joyce's A.C., in 1922. **In the 1,100 c.c. category** this honour was Prince Ghica's with his Cozette in 1926, while George Eyston managed it in **the 750 c.c.-class** in 1931.

Two miles a minute was first achieved by Fred Marriott's Stanley steamer in 1906. By 1925 E. A. D. Eldridge had exceeded this speed in his 1½-litre Eldridge Special, and the following year Morel's Amilcar was in the 120 m.p.h. bracket in the 1,100 c.c. category. G. E. T. Eyston followed for M.G. in the 750 c.c. division in 1932.

The first driver to exceed 120 m.p.h. for the hour run was Ortmans in a Panhard-Levassor at Montlhéry in 1926—a very considerable feat at that period of motor-car development. The first man to achieve this feat in Britain was J. G. Parry Thomas in his Leyland-Thomas at Brooklands in the same year. By 1932 Eyston in the 8-litre Panhard-Levassor had exceeded 130 m.p.h., for one hour.

THE GREAT RECORD-BREAKING VENUES
BROOKLANDS

Brooklands Track was built in 1906–07 by Hugh Fortescue Locke-King on his Brooklands estate at Weybridge in Surrey, England, at a cost of £150,000 in the money of the day. It was the builder's intention that the Motor Course would give British motor-manufacturers a place where their products could be tested, with immunity from the 20-m.p.h. speed limit. Work was started in the winter of 1906 and the new track was opened on 17th June 1907. The completion had been delayed because the cement surface would have been affected by late winter frosts. To construct the track, 30 acres of woodland were felled, the River Wey was diverted in two places, and 350,000 cubic yards of earth were shifted. The track surface took 200,000 tons of concrete, and 200 carpenters were engaged on making fences, stands, etc. The consulting engineer responsible was a Mr. Donaldson, a skilled railway technician, and the plans were drawn up by

The Brooklands Track under construction early in 1907.

Colonel Holden, R.E. The steeper banking was carried over the River Wey on a ferro-concrete structure designed by L. G. Mouchal, C.E., an early form of this type of concrete construction. The Motor Course had a lap distance of 2 miles 1,350 yards, measured on the 50-foot line, and a finishing straight of 991 yards, making the total length 3¼ miles, of which 2 miles were level; the track was 100 feet wide. Of the two bankings the steeper, called the "Home" or "Members'" banking, was at a radius of 1,000 feet and it was 28 feet 8 inches high. The other banking, the Byfleet banking, was struck at a radius of 1,550 feet and was 21 feet 10 inches high.

Mr. Locke-King died in 1926 without any recognition having been given to him for his generosity in building the world's first closed motor track. His wife had been created Dame of the British Empire, but this honour was bestowed in recognition of her work for the Red Cross during the First World War, and had nothing to do with the Motor Course. The Locke-Kings were avid motorists, using big Itala motor cars, but Mr. Locke-King did not himself drive. They took frequent continental tours, and it was from watching the superiority of Italian cars at foreign race-meetings that he decided to build a British test

Some famous pioneers at the Brooklands Track; left to right, Hutton, Napier, Edge, Orde, Lord Lonsdale, Lord Montagu and Rodakowski.

course. Mr. Locke-King was a master of the jigsaw puzzle and bred pedigree French poodles. Dame Ethel was a considerable traveller, a fast driver who used a Ford V-eight in later years, and a great humanitarian. She died, in her ninetieth year, in 1956.

The newly formed Brooklands Automobile Racing Club had as its first Clerk of the Course Mr. E. de Rodakowski. Its President was Lord Lonsdale and the first Committee Meeting was held on 12th December 1906. When the track was first opened the offices of the B.A.R.C. were in Regent Street, London, and the Secretary for the entire life of the track was Mr. Kenneth L. Skinner. After the first Clerk of the Course had retired, the position was taken over by Colonel Lindsay Lloyd, and later by Percy Bradley. The famous Brooklands handicapper and starter for almost the life-span of the track was the legendary A. V. Ebblewhite, who kept a musical-instrument shop before turning to the handicapping, starting and timing of motor and aviation races. When the Brooklands Automobile Racing Club was disbanded in 1940, H.M. the King was its Patron and the Earl of Lonsdale its President.

The first race-meeting at Brooklands took place on 6th July 1907 for prize-money totalling nearly £5,000. **The first race was won** by H. C. Tryon's Napier, twenty-two different makes of cars having been entered.

A dead-heat occurred at the first Brooklands meeting, between Newton on Edge's 45-h.p. Napier and Jarrott's De Dietrich. The stakes of 450 sovereigns were divided. Two more dead-heats occurred during the track's history.

The first fatal accident to occur at Brooklands Track came in the opening season. Vincent Herman, driving J. T. C. Moore-Brabazon's Minerva, turned too quickly into the Members' banking after crossing the finishing-line and the car overturned, pinning the driver beneath it. His mechanic was thrown clear. The second fatal accident marred racing at Brooklands in 1908. Lane, in Burford's 76-h.p. Mercedes, swerved down the Members' banking in the first O'Gorman Trophy Race and hit the parapet of the river bridge. The wrecked car's engine fell into the water and the mechanic, William Burke, was flung out and fatally injured.

In the first (1907) racing season at Brooklands Mercedes cars earned £2,800 in prize-money, Napier cars £1,760 and Darracq cars £1,000.

Charles Jarrott (De Dietrich) at Brooklands in 1908. (Photo: Radio Times Hulton Picture Library.)

A. J. Hancock (Vauxhall)
during a record attempt at
Brooklands in 1913.
(Photo: Radio Times
Hulton Picture Library.)

The first records to be made on Brooklands Track, apart from S. F. Edge's 24-hour run, appear
to have been those established by Newton and Tryon, also with Napier
cars. Newton's 25·6-h.p. Napier covered a flying ½-mile at 77·92 m.p.h.
on 6th November 1907. Tryon, in a 38·4-h.p. Napier, covered a flying
½-mile at 86·75 m.p.h. on the same day.

The last record to be taken at Brooklands before it closed for ever in 1939 was Forrest Lycett's
British Class B Standing-start Mile Record in his 8-litre Bentley, at
92·9 m.p.h.

**Apart from F.I.A.-homologated records, officially observed runs were recognised at
Brooklands by the Brooklands Automobile Racing Club.** The Club
issued the first such certificate on 20th September 1907 in respect of Sir
Algernon Guinness's 200-h.p. Darracq V-eight, which covered 20 chains
(440 yards), first at 112·2 m.p.h., then at 115·4 m.p.h. The last such
certificate to be issued prior to the outbreak of the First World War in 1914
was No. 738 in respect of an Indian motorcycle which covered a flying
kilometre at 93·48 m.p.h. When the system was revived after the Armistice,
the first certificate went to Burgerhout's V-eight Cadillac tourer which
had lapped the track at 61·38 m.p.h.

The first Brooklands lap record was established in June 1908 by Felice Nazzaro with a big 89·5-h.p.
Fiat, *Mephistopheles*. The speed by electrical timing was given as 121·77
m.p.h., but this was later disputed as not agreeing with the hand-timing,
and subsequently this record was not officially recognised. In its place was

Felice Nazzaro at the
wheel of the Fiat,
Mephistopheles, *June 1908.*

substituted the lap at 123·39 m.p.h. put up by Kenelm Lee Guinness in the 350-h.p. single-seater V-twelve Sunbeam during the 1922 season. The next car to break the lap record was the 8-litre straight-eight Leyland-Thomas driven by J. G. Parry Thomas. It was timed to lap at 128·36 m.p.h. in 1924, and improved on this in 1925 with a lap at 129·36 m.p.h. Kaye Don then took this coveted Brooklands record, his Sunbeam lapping at 131·76 in 1928 and taking the lap record to 134·24 m.p.h. with the 4-litre V-twelve car in 1929. Henry Birkin replied with 135·34 m.p.h. in the

With characteristic polka-dot scarf astream, Sir Henry Birkin in the blower-4½ single-seater Bentley at Brooklands

blower-4½ single-seater Bentley in 1930, but Kaye Don recaptured the record with a speed of 137·58 m.p.h. in the Sunbeam the same year. Sir Henry Birkin, Bt., replied with 137·96 m.p.h., using the same Bentley, in 1932.

The next uplift in the lap record came in 1934 when John Cobb's new 24-litre Napier-Railton contrived to lap at 139·71 m.p.h. That was in April, and in August Cobb put the big Napier-powered car round at 140·93 m.p.h. The following year Oliver Bertram took the record from Cobb in the specially constructed 8-litre Bentley-engined Barnato-Hassan, with a speed of 142·60 m.p.h.

John Cobb had the last word, taking the record for the last time, on 7th October 1935, at a speed of 143·44 m.p.h. The Napier-Railton's time was 1 minute 9·44 seconds, or 0·41 second quicker than Bertram's time. The record nearly fell to the Multi-Union of Chris Staniland, on the eve of the outbreak of the Second World War, but misfiring ruined the attempt.

The extraordinary Peugeot of Boissy during speed trials at Brooklands in 1911. (Photo: Radio Times Hulton Picture Library.)

Originally this lap record could be broken during a race, but later came the ruling that it must be attempted on an empty track, with only the contestant running. Apart from the outer-circuit Brooklands lap record, lap records were recognised for this circuit in the International capacity classes, and for the Mountain and Campbell Brooklands "road" circuits.

The first lap record to be recognised for the Mountain course at Brooklands was that by S. C. H. Davis on 9th June 1930, whose supercharged Riley Nine lapped at 66·86 m.p.h. The final record was made by Raymond Mays (E.R.A.) in a time of 49·96 seconds, 84·31 m.p.h., on 7th September 1936.

The first lap records for the twisting Campbell circuit at Brooklands were recognised on 30th April 1937 when Peter Walker lapped at 72·74 m.p.h. in an E.R.A., and Austin Dobson at 70·11 m.p.h. in the *bimotore* (twin-engined) Alfa Romeo. **The ultimate Campbell circuit lap record** was established by Raymond Mays in a 2-litre E.R.A. on 8th August 1939; his time was 1 minute 44·91 seconds, a speed of 77·79 m.p.h.

The record for the fastest ascent of the Brooklands' Test Hill went from 9·66 seconds (24·86 m.p.h.) by Major G. D. Pearce-Jones's Vauxhall in 1920 to 7·45 seconds (32·44 m.p.h.) by R. G. J. Nash's Frazer Nash in 1932.

The fastest 750 c.c.-Class car round the Brooklands' outer circuit was G. P. Harvey-Noble's M.G., with a speed of 122·40 m.p.h. The best 1,100-c.c. speed was by Major Gardner's M.G. at 124·40 m.p.h.

The 1·5-litre outer circuit lap record was that of Earl Howe who lapped in his eight-cylinder Grand Prix Delage at 127·05 m.p.h., a record made in 1931 and never beaten. In the up-to-2-litre class this record was left at 135·95 m.p.h. by Mrs. Gwenda Stewart's supercharged Derby-Miller, a record she established in 1935. (Note that the use of a supercharger did not alter the classification of cubic capacity.) The 3-litre record over the outer circuit took a big lift in 1938 when C. S. Staniland put it to an unchallenged 141·45 m.p.h. in the Alfa Romeo-based Multi-Union. Only two cars in the up-to-5-litre category ever held this record, Birkin's Bentley with 137·96 m.p.h.—at the time an absolute record—which was bettered in 1934 by Whitney Straight's Duesenberg with 138·15 m.p.h. Oliver Bertram's Barnato-Hassan automatically took the 8-litre Class record with its lap of 142·60 m.p.h. in 1935.

Over the Mountain course the fastest lap speed by a 750-c.c. car was 77·02 m.p.h. put up in 1936 by Charlie Dodson in a blown Austin Seven. The equivalent lap record in the 1,100-c.c. Class was that of R. J. Appleton's Appleton Special with supercharged Riley-based engine, set up in 1936 at 76·10 m.p.h. The 1·5-litre Mountain lap record stands to the credit of Raymond Mays and E.R.A. with the outright speed of 84·31 m.p.h. Mays also held the 2-litre

The versatile Raymond Mays, successful road and track racing-driver—and hillclimb exponent par excellence.

Class record with a lap at 81·28 m.p.h. The 3-litre lap record was put to 82·06 m.p.h. by Whitney Straight's Maserati in 1934—he had broken it on four previous occasions, the only other driver to do so being the establisher, Sir Henry (Tim) Birkin. In the up-to-5-litre category the best Mountain course lap belongs to Sir Malcolm Campbell, whose rebuilt 4-litre V-twelve Sunbeam lapped at 76·41 m.p.h. in 1934. Finally, for this course, the up-to-8-litre record was set for the last time by Austin Dobson's *bimotore* Alfa Romeo, which in 1937 beat the only other holder, Campbell's sports Mercedes, with a speed of 77·84 m.p.h. There was no attempt in the over-8-litre category.

On the Campbell "road" course at Brooklands the class lap records were:

> 750 c.c.: H. L. Hadley (Austin), 69·87 m.p.h.
> 1,100 c.c.: J. H. T. Smith (M.G.), 70·60 m.p.h.
> 1,500 c.c.: A. C. Dobson (E.R.A.), 75·94 m.p.h.
> 2,000 c.c.: R. Mays (E.R.A.), 77·79 m.p.h.
> 3,000 c.c.: K. D. Evans (Alfa Romeo), 73·66 m.p.h.
> 5,000 c.c.: R. M. W. Arbuthnot (Alfa Romeo), 75·57 m.p.h.
> 8,000 c.c.: Austin Dobson (Alfa Romeo), 70·11 m.p.h.
> over 8,000 c.c.: *Not attempted.*

The highest speed recorded officially at Brooklands was 151·97 m.p.h. by John Cobb in the Napier-Railton in October 1935. He was timed to cover a kilometre in 14·72 seconds.

The ladies' outer-circuit lap record at Brooklands was originally recognised in 1928 when Mrs. E. M. Thomas held it at 120·88 m.p.h. in a Bugatti. It was discontinued as being too hazardous for the girls to undertake, in 1935, when Mrs. Gwenda Stewart had lapped at 135·95 m.p.h. in the 1,673-c.c. supercharged Derby-Miller.

The ladies at Brooklands. Mrs. E. M. Wisdom (right) with her co-driver Mrs. Kay Petre at the (1936) 8th B.R.D.C. International 500 Miles Race.

Drivers who lapped Brooklands at over 120 m.p.h. were awarded a special 120-m.p.h. car badge—the ordinary B.A.R.C. badge over-inscribed with the magic speed. The first driver to qualify was K. Lee Guinness who lapped at over the target speed in 1921 in the big V-twelve Sunbeam, although the badge was not instituted until long after this. In all, eighty-four 120-m.p.h. badges were awarded, the last in 1938. They were succeeded by the 130-m.p.h. badge, of which seventeen were awarded, the first for Kaye Don's performance in 1928 and the last to G. P. Harvey-Noble (Bentley-Jackson) in August 1939.

Gold Stars were awarded annually between 1930 and 1939 for track-racing, the holders being Sir Henry Birkin, Kaye Don, S. C. H. Davis, the Hon. Brian Lewis, G. E. T. Eyston, R. T. Horton, E. R. Hall, F. W. Dixon, J. R. Cobb, O. H. J. Bertram, E. W. W. Pacey and I. F. Connell. Cobb and Bertram won the Star twice.

The start of the 1926 Junior Car Club 200-Mile Race. Malcolm Campbell (Bugatti) is leading the field. (Photo: Radio Times Hulton Picture Library.)

The first established series of long-distance races at Brooklands was the Junior Car Club's 200-Mile Race for cars of up to 1,500 c.c., which was instituted in 1921. The winners were Segrave (Talbot-Darracq), Guinness (Talbot-Darracq), Harvey (Alvis), and Guinness (Darracq), for the first four years when this was a purely outer-circuit race. Apart from the J.C.C. 200-Mile Races, the next long-distance race over the outer circuit was the Essex M.C. 100-Mile Race of 1925, won by Purdy's Alvis at 86·77 m.p.h.

The first B.R.D.C. 500-Mile Race was held in 1929. It was continued until 1937, reduced to 500 kilometres for the final year. The winners were Barclay/Clement (Bentley), Davis/March (Austin), Dunfee/Paul (Bentley), Horton/Bartlett (M.G.), Hall (M.G.), Dixon (Riley), Cobb/Rose-Richards (Napier-Railton), Dixon/Martin (Riley), and Cobb/Bertram (Napier-Railton).

Three Chitty-Chitty-Bang-Bang cars ran at Brooklands. Built by Count Louis Zborowski between 1921 and 1924 the first powered by a 23-litre Maybach airship-engine, was the most successful. It lapped the track at 113·45 m.p.h. during a race. The second chain-drive Chitty had an 18·8-litre Benz aero-engine and appeared at only one meeting in the Count's hands. It lapped at 106·42 m.p.h. and was afterwards used for touring in the Sahara. The third Chitty had a shaft-drive Mercedes chassis, Westinghouse air brakes and a 14·8-litre Mercedes aero-engine.

The largest-engined car to race at Brooklands was the 27-litre two-seater Higham Special, also conceived by Count Zborowski. It had a 27-litre Liberty V-twelve aero-engine in a specially built chain-drive chassis. It achieved a lap speed of 125·77 m.p.h. before being used by Parry Thomas to break the Land Speed Record at over 171 m.p.h. Thomas renamed the modified car *Babs*, and he was killed in it at Pendine in 1927.

The smallest car to race at the track was the 350-c.c. single-cylinder motor-cycle-engined Jappic. It appeared in 1924 and the following year H. M. Walters used it to set Class J records at over 71 m.p.h. Another 350-c.c. Brooklands' car was the Gush Special—but this was used only to attack Class records. It took many Class J records in 1934, including the 12-Hours at 42·89 m.p.h., and the Kilometre and Mile Flying-start records in this class at 77·52 m.p.h. (Although stationary after 12 hours, it was also given the 24-Hour Record at 21·44 m.p.h.!)

At Brooklands in 1924 J. G. Parry Thomas used various dodges to try to prolong the life of the tyres on his Leyland-Thomas when going for the World's Hour Record. He tried waiting for a wet day, but the car skidded too much. He hired a fire-engine to flood part of the track from the River Wey, but lost too much speed through wheel-spin which was also bad for the differential. Eventually, he captured the record at 109·09 m.p.h. in spite of having all four wheels changed during the 60-minute run. Thomas's next Hour Record attempt, on Dunlop tyres, was accomplished without a change of wheels. The average speed this time was 110·64 m.p.h., also at Brooklands, in 1925. Competition was such that before the year was out Thomas had had his Hour Record taken from him by Ortmans, whose Panhard-Levassor averaged 116·41 m.p.h. at Montlhéry.

Saloon cars were raced at Brooklands by N. S. Hind (Berliet) in 1914, and by Tommy Hann, whose closed 1911 Lanchester was called *Hoieh-Wayaryeh-Gointoo*, and

Hoieh-Wayaryeh-Gointoo, *the Hann Lanchester, on the Brooklands banking.*

appeared in 1922. Later Myles Rothwell built a closed-cockpit cycle car in which the driver lay prone to reduce wind-drag, but this was not successful. Quaint nicknames for racing cars were much in evidence at Brooklands. There was the 1912 Vauxhall KN (as hot as pepper), the Lanchester called "Winnie Praps Praps" on account of its exhaust note, the Berliet "Whistling Rufus" so named because the wind whistled through its radiator, and Hann's open Lanchester "Softly Catch Monkey" —the naval term for "Proceed with Caution".

The last race to be run at Brooklands was the Third August Outer-Circuit Handicap, on August Bank Holiday 1939. It was won by G. L. Baker's Graham-Paige at 99·46 m.p.h. The last Mountain Handicap Race, on the same day, was won by the band-leader, the late Billy Cotton in an E.R.A. at 77·15 m.p.h.

The last Campbell Circuit Race to be run at Brooklands also took place at the last meeting, over ten laps, the first car home being Raymond Mays's 2-litre E.R.A., which beat Prince Bira's Maserati, averaging 73·91 m.p.h. and doing two laps at 75·29 m.p.h.

A view of the paddock during the Brooklands Whit Monday meeting in 1923 which emphasises the "horse-racing atmosphere" prevailing at the time, with formally dressed spectators clutching race-cards, and bookies' stands in the background. An Austin 20 and 40/50 Rolls-Royce are the subjects of attention.

The notorious Brooklands' silencer regulations of 1925 had six clauses and specified expansion boxes and fish-tails, the latter with dimensions of $\frac{1}{4} \times 6$ inches for engines of up to and including 2 litres, and $\frac{1}{2} \times 12$ inches for engines of over 2 litres.

The use of sports cars to establish 1-hour records of an unofficial nature began when S. C. H. Davis used a 328 B.M.W. at Brooklands to cover 102·22 miles in the hour on 15th April 1937. In 1939, also at Brooklands, Jill Thomas decided the ladies should have a try, and covered 101·22 miles in the hour in a 328 B.M.W., in this newly observed sports-car category. George Eyston used an aerodynamic closed Bentley for an hour run in this Class on 18th July 1939, covering 114·638 miles in a streamlined 4·25-litre car. His fastest lap was at 115·02 m.p.h., and he did eight laps at this speed—his slowest being only 1 second below it.

In pursuit of long-distance International class records at Brooklands many notable events can be recorded. For example, in 1922 Aston Martin and A.C. were rivals in the 1·5-litre field. There was the occasion when A.C. went for the 12-Hour Record and the team were astonished to see the side-valve Aston Martin *Bunny* continuing beyond the first round of the clock. The idea, satisfactorily accomplished, was for *Bunny* to take records in the 12–19-hour category—thereby becoming the first light car to be able to claim World's honours.

Many untoward happenings enlivened racing at Brooklands. Cars have shed their steering track rods and pulled up safely—this happened to Cobb's 10-litre 1911 Fiat after the First World War. A handicap race was once started from the wrong end, the fastest car being despatched first, and it had to be rerun. A foreign driver once turned the wrong way at the first corner in a long-distance contest and removed the tail from Bira's Maserati . . . and an elderly Charron came to rest for reasons inexplicable to the driver until it was noticed that its petrol-tank had fallen off.

The Brooklands Track suffers the depredations of wartime neglect.

MONTLHÉRY

Montlhéry Track was financed by M. Lamblin, proprietor of the journal *L'Aero Sports* and owner of the Lamblin radiator manufacturing company. Work began in May 1924 and the track was opened on 4th October 1924. The area of the estate involved was 12,000 acres, compared to under 400 acres of the Brooklands estate. The work was entrusted to M. Raymond Jamin, a talented civil engineer, and the Manager for the contractors, the Société Français de Construction, was M. Saint Macary. Two thousand workmen laid the concrete banked course at the rate of 35 metres per day. **The first race-meeting** at the new Paris Autodrome took place over the week-end of 4th–5th October, the first race of which being for 500-c.c. cycle cars; this was won by Dhome's Morgan three-wheeler from only two other entries. The 750-c.c. Race was a walk-over for the Austin Sevens from England, finishing in the order Gordon England (who averaged 75·6 m.p.h.), Arthur Waite, Hall and Dingle. Gordon England was a pioneer aviator who persuaded Sir Herbert Austin to let him race Austin Sevens while nursing a leg broken in a gliding accident. He had previously raced A.B.C. cars and is still an active official at B.A.R.C. race-meetings. Waite married Sir Herbert Austin's daughter and was the official Austin Co. racing driver.

A match race on the Sunday of that first meeting at Montlhéry, between J. G. Parry Thomas in the Leyland, Ernest Eldridge in the 300-h.p. aeroplane-engined chain-drive Fiat, and Duray in an eight-cylinder D'Aoust, resulted in a win for the Fiat at 121·04 m.p.h. after the Leyland had developed tyre trouble. During this race Parry Thomas set the **first Montlhéry lap record**, in 42·4 seconds, at a speed of 131·89 m.p.h. At the time his Brooklands lap record stood at 128·36 m.p.h.

The first long-distance race at Montlhéry was held later in October 1924 over 120 laps, or 186·4 miles. It was confined to cars of up to 1·5 litres and the winner was Jack Scales in a Talbot, at 100·3 m.p.h. The second and third places were taken by similar cars driven by Segrave and Bourlier. Segrave made fastest lap at 109·6 m.p.h.

An early race at Montlhéry track on the outskirts of Paris.

The long-distance race at Montlhéry, on 17th May 1925, had a remarkable ending. It was for non-supercharged cars of up to 1·5 litres, and which the Talbots—normally supercharged—nevertheless contrived to dominate. George Duller won, averaging 97·2 m.p.h. for the 312 miles, but Count Conelli, who was behind him driving a Bugatti, skidded and after crossing the finishing-line, overturned and rebounded back on to its wheels. He was allowed second place. Segrave, delayed by tyre trouble, was third.

Record-breaking at Montlhéry started soon after the Paris track was opened in 1924. The first record to fall was the World's 24-Hour Record which was taken by a 2-litre sixteen-valve Bignan, driven by Gros and Martin at 75·86 m.p.h. They covered 1,820 miles—actually 262 miles fewer than John Duff's 3-litre Bentley which held the Brooklands "Double-Twelve" Record, but this had been claimed by Duff only as a Class, not a World, record. The next Montlhéry record attempt was by a 750-c.c. Austin Seven, with three drivers, but the little car broke down—although not before it had taken Class H records of up to 4 hours' duration. The following year (1925), it was laid down that the Montlhéry lap-distance was to be measured almost on the centre-line of the course, and the Bignan's record was amended to 1,801·98 miles. When Segrave tried to break this record, using a 2-litre Grand Prix Sunbeam with riding mechanic, he was unsuccessful. (This attempt was interesting in that Parry Thomas was one of the drivers appointed—the only time he drove for Sunbeam.)

Special badges for record-holders were given by the Montlhéry authorities in 1929; some seventy-four drivers qualified, including three women, Gwenda Stewart, Mrs. Victor Bruce and Violet Cordery. The Hon. Mrs. Victor Bruce set a notable record at Montlhéry early in 1929 when she took the 24-Hour Record, driving a "Double-Twelve" 4·5-litre Bentley without a relief driver. She covered 2,149·68 miles at an average speed of 89·57 m.p.h.; pit-stops to resuscitate the car had to be arranged to coincide with her personal needs while out of the driving seat!

At Montlhéry, after successfully capturing the Class G Record for 1,000 miles at 65·83 m.p.h. with a Riley Nine saloon in 1929, K. V. Thomson, who was co-driving with Ernest Eldridge, fell asleep, and the car rolled on its coming-in lap, luckily without injury to the occupant.

When the indomitable Citroën *La Petite Rosalie* went for records of many *days'* duration (2 days to 133 days) at Montlhéry in 1933, the attempt had to be interrupted while a French Grand Prix took place, after which it came down from the dais on which it had been parked, to resume its run. *La Petite Rosalie* completed its record marathon after it had lapped Montlhéry for a total of 180,000 miles at an average overall speed of 58 m.p.h.

The Citroën La Petite Rosalie *at Montlhéry on the occasion of its marathon duration record in 1933.*

The first car to exceed 100 m.p.h. in the 750-c.c. Class was Captain G. E. T. Eyston's M.G. EX 120 at Montlhéry in 1931. Much earlier, in 1921–22, A.C. had mopped up all the 1·5-litre light car 100-m.p.h. "firsts" over a ½ mile, for a lap of the Brooklands Track and, eventually, for 1 hour.

Montlhéry was the scene of many sports-car 1-hour observed runs and, in 1939, Robert Benoist put in 113 miles in a supercharged 3·3-litre Type 57C Bugatti Galibier saloon, his best lap being at 121 m.p.h. In 1939 the 4·25-litre Bentley streamlined saloon managed 107·42 miles, and a lap at 110·04 m.p.h., driven by William Sleator.

The 1939 4¼-litre Bentley saloon in Paris at the time of its Montlhéry 1-hour record run.

The last record to be established at Montlhéry before the Second World War closed it in 1939 seems to have been Raymond Sommer's lap record of 147·79 m.p.h., never subsequently improved upon. This was, of course, for the banked circuit, but the record was apparently hand-timed so was not truly valid. His car was a 1938 2·9-litre Type 308C Alfa Romeo.

The first resumption of record-breaking at Montlhéry after the war seems to have been the attack on long-distance Class G records by a streamlined Darlmat-Peugeot saloon.

One of the most strenuous record-breaking attempts took place at Montlhéry in 1952 when Stirling Moss, Jack Fairman, Bert Hadley and Leslie Johnson used a Jaguar XK 120 coupé to average more than 100 m.p.h. for 17 days and nights. This was successfully accomplished, the Jaguar covering 16,851·73 miles at 100·31 m.p.h. The fastest lap, by Moss, was at 121·28 m.p.h.

George Eyston, in a Riley, broke records at Montlhéry in darkness while uncompleted track repairs had left a gaping hole near the top of the banking; this was picked out by storm-lanterns which were used to outline the edge of the course at night and which were laid out as dusk fell using an ancient Model T Ford.

Montlhéry was a hazardous place at which to try for records in winter. It iced over very frequently, fog was apt to form, and the short banked circuit induced sleep—as when Freddie Dixon dozed off and crashed the 24-litre Napier-Railton on one of John Cobb's long-distance record bids. As speeds rose above 140 m.p.h., even for 24- and 48-Hour Record bids, the Bonneville

Salt Flats, Utah, were increasingly used, being safer than the Paris track. For such records the Napier-Railton carried its own lighting plant—much as Rapson's Lanchester Forty single-seater of 1924 had been equipped with headlamps.

Gwenda Stewart, who held so many records at Montlhéry in all manner of cars, from Morgan three-wheelers to the 1·9-litre supercharged Miller-Derby, was the daughter of Major-General Sir Frederick Manley Glubb, K.C.M.G., C.B., D.S.O., and her brother was Glubb Pasha of the Arab Legion. She attacked her first record, a "double-twelve", on a 249-c.c. Trump-Jap motorcycle at Brooklands in 1922. Her cars were invariably turned out immaculately.

Gwenda Stewart in the 1·9-litre supercharged Miller-Derby.

INDIANAPOLIS

The Indianapolis Motor Speedway, Indiana, U.S.A. was built in 1909 on 559 acres of ground, seven miles north-west of Indianapolis. It consists of an oval track with four slightly banked corners, the lap distance being 2½ miles. At first a tar/gravel surface was used but this broke up during the first race in August 1909. Brick paving was then put down. This involved the use of 3,200,000 paving bricks (with one gold brick for luck) grouted in cement. The track was the work of four men: Carl G. Fisher, James A. Allison, Arthur C. Newby and Frank H. Wheeler. During the years of the First World War, Indianapolis became an air-base where military aeroplanes were repaired, and 100 acres were farmed. The first 500 Mile Race had been held there in 1911 and the series was resumed in 1919, after abandonment in 1917. The track was bought by Captain Eddie Rickenbacker in 1927, and an 18-hole golf course added. The Second World War caused serious deterioration but the track was saved by

Tony Hulman, jnr., who purchased it from Rickenbacker, at cost, on a no-profit basis, in 1945. The old wooden stands were replaced, and a new asphalt surface covered the last segment of the old brick track. An office/museum building was put up in 1956 and a new, bigger pit-area and control tower in 1957. By 1963 a new ninety-six-unit motel and clubhouse were completed. In 1965 the golfing facilities were extended with an 18-hole Championship course outside the track and a 9-hole course in the in-field. Further improvements followed, including Vista Grandstands on three of the turns, new safety arrangements, a four-lane vehicle tunnel, and hospitality suites.

The Speedway has a permanent staff of more than 100, but on the one race day a year, for the "500", 2,400 safety-patrol men and 1,100 extra staff cater for an influx of some 300,000 spectators, who have 250 doctors and nurses assigned to them, in a field hospital with twelve ambulances and seven first-aid tents. The Indy Museum, which contains the Marmon Wasp that won the first "500", is open daily.

The turns at Indianapolis are banked at 9 degrees 12 minutes and the straights are 50 feet wide, the turns 60 feet wide, the long straights measuring $\frac{5}{8}$ mile, the short straights $\frac{1}{8}$ mile.

The first of the great annual International 500-mile sweepstake races was held at Indianapolis on 30th May (Memorial Day) 1911. The race is traditionally held on this day each year. **The first winner** was Ray Harroun in a yellow Marmon Wasp. Engine size was limited to a maximum of 600 cubic inches, and the winning car, with a 447-cubic inch six-cylinder engine, averaged 74·59 m.p.h. The second 500-Mile Race was won by J. Dawson's National, at 78·72 m.p.h., ahead of a giant Fiat driven by E. Tetzlaff. Thereafter the European cars moved in, Jules Goux's Peugeot winning the 1913 Race at 75·933 m.p.h. from American Mercer and Stutz cars. The 1914 "500" was a victory for a French Delage driven by René Thomas, who averaged 82·47 m.p.h., with another French car, A. Duray's Peugeot second, followed home by another Delage and a second Peugeot.

Winner of the 1911 Indianapolis 500-Mile Race, Ray Harroun's Marmon Wasp.

Ralph de Palma's 1914 Grand Prix Mercedes won the 1915 race, at 89·84 m.p.h., from Dario Resta's Peugeot, chased by a couple of American Stutz racers. Resta won again in 1916 at the wheel of a French Peugeot, and the pattern held in 1919 on Memorial Day—when the 500-Mile Race was revived after the war—although this time an American driver, H. Wilcox, drove a Peugeot to victory at 88·05 m.p.h., compared with Resta's 84·00 m.p.h. average speed in 1916.

Thereafter and for many years the European contingent never managed to break American domination by both drivers and cars, of the special Indianapolis requirements. The 1920s were the years of the straight-eight Frontenac, Duesenberg and Miller cars which lapped the oval very fast—almost without recourse to brakes.

Indianapolis 500-Mile Race rules frequently differed from those of European Grands Prix. For example, between the wars the cars permitted ranged from those with engines of up to 4·9 litres in 1919, 3 litres for 1921–22, 2 litres in 1923–25, 1·5 litres from 1926 to 1929, 6 litres from 1930 to 1937 (with some fuel consumption limits as well in later years), and 4·5 litres unsupercharged or 3 litres supercharged from 1938 to 1956. The 1957 regulations required 4·2 litres unsupercharged or 2·8 litres if supercharged. Thereafter the regulations became more complicated, with rules relating to cars with "stock" cylinder-blocks, Offenhauser and other engines, including turbine-engined cars.

An average speed of over 100 m.p.h. was achieved at "Indy" in 1925 when Peter de Paolo managed 101·13 m.p.h. in a 122-cubic inch Duesenberg Special. Thereafter a 100-m.p.h. race average was not seen again until 1930, when Billy Arnold's Miller-Hartz Special did 100·448 m.p.h. The speed was down again in 1931 but rose to 104·144 m.p.h. in 1932, when the winner was Fred Frame in a 182-cubic inch Miller-Hartz Special. A 120-m.p.h. race average was not to occur until 1949 when the victor was Bill Holland, whose Blue Crown Spark Plug Special took 4 hours 7 minutes 15·97 seconds to cover the 500 miles—a speed of 121·327 m.p.h.

The front-wheel-drive Miller Special, driven by Leon Duray in the 1927 Indianapolis 500-Mile Race; it retired after twenty-six laps.

After 1919 no European car or driver was victorious until 1939 when Wilbur Shaw took the winner's flag driving a car entered as a Boyle Special, which was in fact an 8CTF 3-litre straight-eight Maserati. The same combination scored again in 1940, the average speed this time being 114·277 m.p.h., against Shaw's 115·035 m.p.h. in 1939. Shaw had also won in 1937 at 113·58 m.p.h. with a Gilmore-Offenhauser Special.

The only driver to win "Indy" four times is the remarkable **A. J. Foyt, jnr.** His first victory came in 1961, driving a Bowes Seal Fast Special. He won the 1964 race in a Sheraton-Thompson Special and scored again in 1967 with a Coyote-Ford, equalling Mauri Rose's earlier "triple". Over this period Foyt's average speed had risen from 139·13 m.p.h. to 151·207 m.p.h. Foyt secured his fourth victory in 1977, at 161·331 m.p.h. **Mauri Rose** first won this race in 1941 with a Noc-Out Hose Clamp Special which he shared with F. Davis. Driving the Blue Crown Spark Plug Specials Rose took the 1947 and 1948 Indy races. Even earlier, **Wilbur Shaw** had made the "triple", with victories in 1937, 1939 and 1940. The only other driver to win three times is **Al Unser**, who took the Indy chequered flag in 1970, repeated the winning performance the following year, and did it again in 1978.

In the races after the war, European cars and drivers were again at a distinct disadvantage. A non-works-entered (as a Don Lee Special) Grand Prix Mercedes-Benz fizzled out in 1947, though it lasted for 119 laps. Rudolf Caracciola crashed a Thorne Special during practice for the 1946 Race, and in the 1952 Race Alberto Ascari covered only forty laps in a Ferrari before retiring. However, the new breed of lightweight, rear-engined British Grand Prix-type cars—inspired by Jack Brabham's Cooper-Climax in 1961—rang the changes. In the 1963 race Jim Clark, in a Lotus-Powered-by-Ford, finished second to Parnelli Jones's Agajanian Willard Special, the two cars' race average speeds being 143·137 and 142·752 m.p.h. respectively.

British success at Indianapolis was first achieved in 1965, with Jim Clark's outright win at 150·686 m.p.h. in the Lotus-Powered-by-Ford, the first time this race had been won at over 150 m.p.h. Second place was taken by Parnelli Jones driving an Agajanian Hurst Special. Clarke's victory set the example British drivers needed, spurred on by the enormous "Indy" purses. Graham Hill won the 1966 Race at 144·317 m.p.h. in an American Red Ball Special (a Lola), from Clark's S.T.P. Gas Treatment Special (a Lotus). **The British 2·8-litre turbocharged Cosworth DFX engine** is currently "correct wear" for the would-be leading "Indy 500" contenders.

Wilbur Shaw, winner of the 1939 "Indy 500", at the wheel of his "Boyle Special" (in fact a Maserati). He won the 1940 event in the same car.

Greatest winner of "Indy" purses, A. J. Foyt, with a record four victories.

The first victory for a British engine in a major U.S. track race came in 1976, when Al Unser won the Schaefer "500" at Pocono in a Parnelli powered by a Cosworth DFX. In 1978 the same driver scored the first victory for this engine in the Indianapolis "500", in a Chaparral Lola T500.

Qualifying speeds are naturally faster than the average for the 500 miles of the "Indy" Race. The fastest in 1912 was Bruce Brown's Fiat, at 88·45 m.p.h. A 100-m.p.h. qualifying speed was first exceeded in 1919 when René Thomas's Ballot returned 104·70 m.p.h., and 120 m.p.h. in 1927 when Frank Lockhart made 120·10 m.p.h. in his Miller. It was 1939 before anyone qualified at better than 130 m.p.h.—Lou Meyer doing 130·06 m.p.h. in a Bowes-Winfield. (Incidentally, 130 m.p.h. wasn't cracked again until 1946 when Ralph Hepburn qualified at 133·94 m.p.h.) The 140-m.p.h. barrier was broken in 1954 by Jack McGrath driving a Kurtis-Offenhauser which completed the required lappery at 141·03 m.p.h. It was 1962 when the target exceeded 150 m.p.h., Parnelli Jones making 150·370 m.p.h. in a Watson-Offenhauser. In 1965, the year of Jim Clark's significant victory, A. J. Foyt topped the 160 m.p.h. for the first time when his Lotus-Ford qualified at 161·233 m.p.h. In 1971 Revson qualified the McLaren at 178·90 m.p.h. By 1975 this had risen to 192·98 m.p.h., when Foyt's Coyote-Foyt-Ford gained pole position, as against Bobby Unsen's winning average of 149·21 m.p.h. in the Eagle-Offenhauser.

The race speeds at Indianapolis are very high, but the Brooklands 500-Mile Race was run at higher average speeds in 1935, 1936 and 1937—despite the British race commencing from a standing, as compared with "Indy's" rolling, start:

1935: Indianapolis 500, 106·240 m.p.h. Brooklands 500, 121·28 m.p.h.
1936: Indianapolis 500, 109·069 m.p.h. Brooklands 500, 116·86 m.p.h.
1937: Indianapolis 500, 113·580 m.p.h. Brooklands 500 (kilometres),
127·05 m.p.h.

The size of the "Indy" purse is reflected in the fact that between 1909 and 1975 the Indianapolis Motor Speedway paid out $17,314,173 in prize-money—inclusive of lap or accessory money. Prior to 1946 the top winning "purse" had stood at $96,250 but after Tony Hulman, jnr., had taken over, this rose to an annual prize of more than $1,000,000, from 1970. This compares with $25,000 for the first 500 Mile Race in 1911.

The prize-money which can be won at the 500-Mile Race is prodigious. For example, A. J. Foyt, jnr., netted a total of $375,008·13 up to 1969. This far exceeds the spoils taken by Europeans, of whom Jim Clark, with $205,321·00, was the biggest earner before his death. Graham Hill earned $123,766·67 at this form of racing, and Denny Hulme $54,092·12. Up to 1975 the actual prize money paid out, exclusive of accessory and lap prizes, totalled $13,332,439. The best year was in 1975 when $839,500 was won, but if accessory and lap prizes are included, 1974 just exceeded the 1975 total by $14,365, the total being $1,015,686. In recent times the total prize-moneys to be won at Indianapolis, apart from the pace-car and numerous other awards, have been astronomical. In 1976 they added up to $1,037,775·96, the total for the 1977 race came to $1,116,807·00 and in 1978 to $1,145,225·00.

The "touring" pace car, which conducts the field round its rolling-start lap is traditionally presented to the winner of the 500-Mile Race. In 1916 the pace car was a Premier Six. Since then most of the more illustrious American cars have had their turn. For instance, a Packard V-twelve or "Twin-Six" served in this capacity in 1919; in 1920 it was a Marmon 34, an H.C.S. Six was used in 1921, a National Eight in 1922 and a Duesenberg in 1923. The 1924 Race was started by a Cole V-eight, replaced by a straight-eight Rickenbacker in 1925. A Chrysler took over in 1926, followed by such fine vintage American cars as La Salle, Marmon, Studebaker, and front-wheel-drive Cord. The first post-Second World War "500" was started by a Lincoln Continental, and for 1973 Cadillac built 650 special White-Cotillion Fleetwood Eldorado convertibles for Indianapolis use, and for display, each worth $9,850. Incidentally, in 1976 they had a Buick pace-car, in 1977 an Oldsmobile Delta 88 did the paced start, and for the 1978 race this task was performed by a Chevrolet Corvette.

The four-wheel-drive rear-engined car of Al Miller, seen here at Indianapolis in 1948—the first year in which it failed to qualify.

The late Graham Hill, 1966 "Indy" winner, in the American Red Ball Special.

The first turbine-car entry came in 1962 and this John Zink turbine was followed in 1966 by the Norman Denier turbine car. But 1967 was the year of the turbines and it looked as if Parnelli Jones would win in the S.T.P. four-wheel-drive Lotus turbine car; he led for a total of 171 laps and was in this position on lap 197 when a gearbox bearing failed and he coasted in to sixth place, behind five Ford V-eight-powered cars (Jones's car was the only turbine starter that year; twenty-three of the field had Ford engines, and eight used Offenhauser engines, of which one was Roots-supercharged and the remainder turbosupercharged).

Al Miller's remarkable four-wheel-drive rear-engined six-cylinder supercharged special first appeared at "Indy" in 1938, and it last qualified in 1947.

In his first seven "500s" Parnelli Jones led five of them at some stage of the race, including his "rookie" year. Jim Clark led for the first four races he drove but retired in his fifth without getting into the first ten. Both drivers, however, only won once.

George Bibnotti was Chief Mechanic to twenty-one cars at "Indy" between 1956 and 1967, and during that time he had three winners.

The record entry at "Indy" was ninety cars in 1967, beating the eighty-two cars of 1953 and that of eighty in 1948. **The smallest entry** was twenty-five in 1921. After 1967, the field was limited to thirty-three cars.

The Indianapolis race record was made in 1972 by Mark Donohue at 162·962 m.p.h. By this year the top drivers were doing about 215 m.p.h. along the straights and some 187 m.p.h. round the *slowest* turn—which was quicker than the previous qualifying speed!

The Indianapolis lap record is at 193·924 m.p.h. by Mario Andretti in a Penske-Cosworth established during the 1978 race. The **fastest qualifying speed** to date is 203·620 m.p.h., set up by Tom Sneva in a Penske-Cosworth before the 1978 "500". The Cosworth engine was the first British engine to be used for winning at Indianapolis in that year.

In 1979 Rick Mears, twenty-seven-year-old off-road racer, was the first driver to become a "non-previous" "Indy" winner since 1973.

The rolling start of the 1966 Indianapolis "500"; as is customary the pace car, in this case a Mercury Comet Cyclone GT, becomes the property of the winning driver.

Graham Hill won the race in 1966, but was the second driver to retire in 1967. This "record" was bettered by **Joe Dawson** who won in 1912 but failed to qualify in 1913. **Jimmy Bryan** went from a win in 1958 to last place—only one lap completed—in 1959.

Denny Hulme was the fourth driver to win the "Rookie of the Year" Award, in 1967. **Jim Clark** won it in 1963, **Mario Andretti** in 1965 and **Jackie Stewart** in 1966. The American driver to break this five-year run of "Rookie" wins by foreigners was **Johnny White** of Michigan, the 1964 winner.

Ted Horn never managed to gain an outright victory at Indianapolis, although he was National Champion in America in 1946, 1947 and 1948. He was second in the "500" in 1936, third in 1937, 1941, 1946 and 1947, and fourth in 1938 and 1939, before being killed at the DuQuoin Fairground Track in 1948. He led the Ford-Miller team in 1935 but the cars failed and Ford had to wait until 1965 for an "Indy" win.

Success eluded some drivers at Indianapolis by a narrow margin. Ralph de Palma led for 196 of the 200 laps in 1912; Rex Mays led in nine races—for a total of 266 laps—and Babe Stapp led on 117 laps. Yet none of them won on these occasions.

One of the most controversial Indianapolis 500-Mile Races was that of 1947 when Bill Holland thought he had won but, due to a misunderstanding of pit signals, lost to Mauri Rose (though a similar situation arose between Clark and Hill in 1966). Both were driving Blue Crown Spark Plug Specials, and Holland thought he had a 2-mile lead over Rose at the end of the race; he was mistaken and Rose won at 116·338 m.p.h. (compared with Holland's 116·097 m.p.h.). These two drivers finished the same way in 1948 in the same make of cars, but Holland won in 1949, again in a Blue Crown Spark Plug Special.

The American Society of Professional Automobile Racing was formed in the winter of 1946. It tried to dictate prize-money terms (asking for 40 per cent of the "gate") to the Speedway management, but this was refused almost causing the withdrawal of the leading "Indy" drivers from the 1947 Race. Wilbur Shaw, however, smoothed things out.

Federal Engineering, under the direction of Dan LeVine, put in no fewer than thirty-nine entries at the "brickyard" between 1947 and 1967, of which twenty-four started, but their best showing was a sixth place in 1964.

All manner of racing cars have run at Indianapolis. The so-called "roadster" reigned supreme for many years, often powered by the very long-lived Offenhauser four-cylinder engine. Jack Brabham instituted the later successful rear-engined trend with his Cooper-Climax in 1961. Rear engines were rare—but not unknown—before that at Indianapolis, Lee Oldfield, for example, using this layout in his Marmon-engined Special in 1937. Harry Miller also had a series of rear-engined cars.

Originality did not stop at rear engines. In 1947 Paul Russo used two engines in his four-wheel-drive Fageol Twin Coach Special. Front-wheel-drive was quite frequently used, and turbine engines, even steam propulsion, were featured. In 1935 Miller used Ford V-eight engines in a team of Specials which carried the famous Ford V-eight badge.

Indianapolis 500-Mile Race Winners

1911	Ray Harroun (Marmon)	74·59 m.p.h.
1912	Joe Dawson (National)	78·72 m.p.h.
1913	Jules Goux (Peugeot)	75·933 m.p.h.
1914	René Thomas (Delage)	82·47 m.p.h.
1915	Ralph de Palma (Mercedes)	89·84 m.p.h.
1916	Dario Resta (Peugeot)	84·00 m.p.h.—300 miles ('war-time concession').
1917–18	No races.	
1919	Howard Wilcox (Peugeot)	88·05 m.p.h.
1920	Gaston Chevrolet (Monroe-Frontenac)	88·62 m.p.h.
1921	Tommy Milton (Miller)	89·62 m.p.h.
1922	Jimmy Murphy (Duesenberg-Miller)	94·48 m.p.h.
1923	Tommy Milton (Miller)	90·95 m.p.h.
1924	Joe Boyer and L. Corum (Duesenberg)	98·23 m.p.h.
1925	Peter de Paolo (Duesenberg)	101·13 m.p.h.
1926	Frank Lockhart (Miller)	95·904 m.p.h.—400 miles (rain).
1927	George Souders (Duesenberg)	97·545 m.p.h.
1928	Louis Meyer (Miller)	99·482 m.p.h.
1929	Ray Keech (Miller)	97·585 m.p.h.
1930	Billy Arnold (Miller)	100·448 m.p.h.
1931	Louis Schneider (Miller)	96·629 m.p.h.
1932	Fred Frame (Miller)	104·144 m.p.h.
1933	Louis Meyer (Miller)	104·162 m.p.h.
1934	Bill Cummings (Miller)	104·863 m.p.h.
1935	Kelly Petillo (Miller)	106·240 m.p.h.
1936	Louis Meyer (Miller)	109·069 m.p.h.
1937	Wilbur Shaw (Gilmore-Offenhauser)	113·580 m.p.h.
1938	Floyd Roberts (Miller)	117·200 m.p.h.
1939	Wilbur Shaw (Maserati)	115·035 m.p.h.
1940	Wilbur Shaw (Maserati)	114·277 m.p.h.
1941	Mauri Rose and Floyd Davis (Noc-Out Hose Clamp Special)	115·117 m.p.h.
1942–45	No races.	
1946	George Robson (Thorne)	114·820 m.p.h.
1947	Mauri Rose (Blue Crown Special)	116·338 m.p.h.
1948	Mauri Rose (Blue Crown Special)	119·814 m.p.h.
1949	Bill Holland (Blue Crown Special)	121·327 m.p.h.
1950	Johnnie Parsons (Wynn Friction Proof Special)	124·002 m.p.h.—345 miles (rain).
1951	Lee Wallard (Belanger Special)	126·244 m.p.h.
1952	Troy Ruttman (Agajanian Special)	128·922 m.p.h.

Indianapolis 500-Mile Race Winners—*continued*

1953	Bill Vukovich (Fuel Injection Special)	128·740 m.p.h.
1954	Bill Vukovich (Fuel Injection Special)	130·840 m.p.h.
1955	Bob Sweikert (John Zink Special)	128·209 m.p.h.
1956	Pat Flaherty (John Zink Special)	128·490 m.p.h.
1957	Sam Hanks (Belond Exhaust Special)	135·601 m.p.h.
1958	Jim Bryan (Belond Exhaust Special)	133·791 m.p.h.
1959	Rodger Ward (Leader Card Special)	135·857 m.p.h.
1960	Jim Rathmann (K. Paul Special)	138·767 m.p.h.
1961	A. J. Foyt, jnr. (Bowes Seal Fast Special)	139·130 m.p.h.
1962	Rodger Ward (Leader Card Special)	140·293 m.p.h.
1963	Parnelli Jones (Agajanian Special)	143·137 m.p.h.
1964	A. J. Foyt, jnr. (Sheraton-Offeanhauser)	147·350 m.p.h.
1965	Jim Clark (Lotus-Ford)	150·686 m.p.h.
1966	Graham Hill (Lola-Ford)	144·317 m.p.h.
1967	A. J. Foyt, jnr. (Coyote-Ford)	151·207 m.p.h.
1968	Bobby Unser (Eagle-Offenhauser)	152·882 m.p.h.
1969	Mario Andretti (Hawk-Ford)	156·867 m.p.h.
1970	Al Unser (Colt-Ford)	155·749 m.p.h.
1971	Al Unser (Colt-Turbo-Ford)	157·735 m.p.h.
1972	Mark Donohue (Sunoco-McLaren)	162·962 m.p.h.
1973	Gordon Johncock (Eagle-Offy)	159·036 m.p.h.—332·5 miles (rain).
1974	Johnny Rutherford (McLaren-Offy)	158·589 m.p.h.
1975	Bobby Unser (Eagle-Offy)	149·213 m.p.h.—435 miles (rain).
1976	Johnny Rutherford (McLaren-Offy)	148·725 m.p.h.—255 miles (rain).
1977	A. J. Foyt, jnr. (Coyote-Ford-Foyt)	161·331 m.p.h.
1978	Al Unser (Lola-Cosworth)	161·363 m.p.h.
1979	Rick Mears (Penske-Cosworth)	158·899 m.p.h.

DAYTONA

The first record established at Daytona Beach, Florida, U.S.A., was a kilometre, covered by Winton's Winton Bullet on 26th February 1903 at 68·198 m.p.h. Further records of the fastest-ever type were made there subsequently, including Fred Marriott's famous 127·56 m.p.h. over a mile in his inverted-boat Stanley Steamer in 1906.

The first record at Daytona, officially recognised by the F.I.A., was made in 1927—Henry Segrave's 203·792 m.p.h. for a two-way mile with the 1,000-h.p. twin-engined Sunbeam, now in the Montagu Motor Museum.

The last Land Speed Record to be established at Daytona was Malcolm Campbell's 276·82 m.p.h. for the kilometre with the Rolls-Royce-engined *Bluebird* in 1935.

Perhaps the least successful fastest-ever attempt at Daytona was that by Sartori in 1906. He had Albert Vanderbilt's twin-engined Mercedes Special, but it is said that the engines could not be made to run. As late as 1929, at Daytona, Kaye Don failed to exceed 190 m.p.h. in the twin-engined Sunbeam *Silver Bullet*, and returned home to England without the record.

The 1927 203 m.p.h. "1,000 h.p." Sunbeam, interestingly shown with an early body which was subsequently modified for the actual record attempt (see page 180).

The least-used Land Speed Record car is probably the Irving-Napier *Golden Arrow*, presented to the Montagu Motor Museum by C. C. Wakefield & Co., Ltd., the Castrol Oil people. It was never driven in this country before Segrave took it to Daytona in 1929. He made one practice run, then set the Land Speed Record to 231·36 m.p.h. On 13th March Lee Bible was killed in the Triplex (see below), and Segrave decided to return home. His car had been driven for perhaps 20 miles in all.

The White Triplex, which held the Land Speed Record for a time, had a total of thirty-six cylinders, comprising three Liberty aero-engines with a combined capacity of some 81 litres. Ray Keech took the record at 207·55 m.p.h. in this fearsome monster at Daytona in 1928. It is said that he took a high fee, survived scalding water from a burst hose, exhaust fumes and a fire in the front engine, before he was successful—and said that no money would induce him to drive the car again. Lee Bible was therefore appointed and was killed when he swerved into the sand-dunes.

Many fastest-ever records were recognised by the American authorities at Daytona, but were not homologated in Europe. This was either because they were timed by the A.A.A., or other bodies which the F.I.A. did not then accept, or because they were runs in one direction only—thereby possibly taking unfair advantage of wind or gradient.

In 1919, at Daytona, Ralph de Palma was credited with a mile at 149·875 m.p.h. He drove a Packard powered by a 905-cubic inch V-twelve aero-engine.

Sir Malcolm Campbell on a trial run at Daytona in the Rolls-Royce V-twelve-engined Bluebird *early in 1935. His first record that year was set at 276·82 m.p.h.; later he raised the figure to 301·13 m.p.h. at Bonneville, Utah.*

In 1920 another such record was claimed when Tommy Milton was clocked at 156·046 m.p.h. He drove a specially streamlined Duesenberg with two 300-cubic inch straight-eight engines side-by-side, each driving one back wheel through a separate clutch and propeller-shaft. The story goes that Murphy brought the car out while his boss, Tommy Milton, for whom he was building it, was away on a track-racing assignment in Cuba.

Yet another record made at Daytona, but unrecognised in Europe, was that by Sig Haugdahl who, in 1922, was credited with a speed of 180·27 m.p.h. He drove a car of his own construction powered by a 652-cubic-inch six-cylinder 250-h.p. Wisconsin aero-engine. Even the American Automobile Association ignored this record but it was timed and surveyed by the International Motor Contest Association, and observed by a U.S. Senator and the Mayor of Daytona, and to this day many Americans are certain the speed was authentic and that Haugdahl was the first driver to exceed 180 m.p.h.

The Daytona International Speedway was opened in February 1959 for all kinds of racing over a steeply banked course and a road circuit. Four miles west of Daytona Beach and managed by Bill France, jnr., this speedway provides two circuits for car racing—the 2·5-mile oval and a 3·84-mile road course. The banked track is 40 feet wide in 10-foot lanes and has a 15-foot wide safety apron for its entire length. The east and west turns are banked at 31 degrees, the grandstand turn at 18 degrees, the respective radii of the bankings being 1,000 feet and 1,800 feet. These bankings are connected by a 3,000-foot back straight and by 1,200-foot straights before the grandstands. There is a 5-foot-thick steel-reinforced concrete retaining-wall on the inside of the west turn, with Mr. France's patented guard rail, while the outside of the banked track is protected by a 4-foot-thick retaining wall set at 90 degrees.

Daytona Speedway occupies an area of 455 acres and has ten stands named after such famous drivers as Campbell, Segrave, Keech, Fireball Roberts, Ralph De Palma, and Barney Oldfield. These grandstands can seat up to 75,000 spectators. There is in-field parking for 25,000 automobiles and in all 75,000 cars can be accommodated. Every sort of racing is catered for

Daytona Speedway.

Sedans in close company on the banking of the Daytona Track. The 1980 Daytona 24-Hour Race was won by a twin-turbo Porsche 935, shared by Stommelen, Joest and Merl, by a margin of 33 laps!

from Grand National Stock Cars to Go-karts. Daytona Speedway has five permanent fire-engines (increased to fourteen on race days) and its own two ambulances are supplemented by fourteen more when racing is in progress. Access roads number six, including a two-lane under-track tunnel.

The world's closed-circuit race record was made at Daytona in 1979 by Buddy Baker, who averaged 194·384 m.p.h. in the Busch Clash Race over the banked oval driving an Oldsmobile. **The quickest qualifying lap** over this track is that at 197·845 m.p.h. set up by John Greenwood in a Chevrolet Corvette in 1977. **Fastest qualifying lap over the since-discarded road circuit** is 133·919 m.p.h. by Mark Donohue's Ferrari 512M in 1971, while **the highest average speed** over this course was made in 1970 when the Daytona 24-Hour Race was won at 114·866 m.p.h. by Pedro Rodriguez and Leo Kinnunen in a Porsche 917. Over the 3·84-mile sports-car road course, the best qualifying lap is the 130·276 m.p.h. run of Carlo Facetti's Porsche 935 while, for further comparison with the banked oval, the fastest race to be run over this road circuit was in 1978 when Peter Gregg averaged 117·868 m.p.h. in a Porsche 911S in the 250-mile race.

Alabama International Motor Speedway is the sister track to Daytona. It has a lap distance of 2·66 miles and is banked at 31 degrees in the turns. Mark Donohue lapped it at 221·160 m.p.h. in a Porsche 917 in 1975, the penultimate World's closed-circuit lap record. Lenny Pond's Oldsmobile won the 500-mile Race there at

174·700 m.p.h. in 1978 and in the Stock Car class a qualifying lap at 199·658 m.p.h. and a race lap of 201·104 m.p.h. were made on this track in 1970 by Bobby Isaac driving a Dodge.

Important American Tracks at which 500-mile races are staged include Charlotte Motor Speedway, Darlington International Raceway, Dover Downs International Speedway, Michigan International Speedway, North Carolina Speedway, Ontario Speedway, Ponoco International Speedway, Riverside, and the Texas Speedway.

OTHER TRACKS

Board track-racing was rife throughout America from 1915 until 1930. But the tracks quickly deteriorated and had almost ceased to exist after the 'twenties, dirt-track racing being easier to organise. Two-mile board speedways were built at Chicago and New York, and others followed—of 1½- and 1¼-mile lap distances. The 1½-mile Atlantic City Speedway was the fastest, Frank Lockhart lapping it at 147 m.p.h. in a Miller. Harry Hartz set a record when he won the opening race there over 30 miles at 135 m.p.h., also in a Miller.

The 2-mile Chicago board track opened on 26th June 1915 with a 500-mile race, won by Dario Resta's Peugeot at 97·58 m.p.h. Omaha opened its 1¼-mile board speedway on 5th July that year when Eddie Rickenbacker won a 300-mile race at 91·74 m.p.h. at the wheel of a Maxwell. Then came the Des Moines, Iowa, mile board track which was opened on 7th August 1915 when a 300-miler was won by Ralph Mulford in a Duesenberg at 87 m.p.h. The year 1915 also saw the opening of a 2-mile concrete-banked track at Minneapolis, a 1-mile asphalt course at Rhode Island, and the famous Sheepshead Bay board track where Gil Anderson took the opening 350-mile race at 102·60 m.p.h. in a Stutz.

The Cincinnati 2-mile board track was opened in 1916 and John Aitken's Peugeot won the inaugural 300-mile Race at 97·06 m.p.h. on 4th September 1916, and on 2nd December Uniontown staged its first meeting at which Louis Chevrolet finished first in a 112½-mile event at 90·69 m.p.h., driving a Frontenac.

The First World War then halted proceedings until 1920 when the Beverly Hills 1¼-mile boardway was opened on 28th February and Jimmy Murphy was the star turn in a Duesenberg. The Fresno Speedway opened in October 1920, the Cotati Track at Santa Rosa on 14th August 1921, the Kansas City Track on 17th September 1922, and the well-known Altoona Track on 4th September 1923; at the last-named track Eddie Hearne won a 200-mile curtain-raiser at 111·5 m.p.h. in his Durant Special. As late as 1924 new tracks came into being at Charlotte, North Carolina, and at Culver City, Los Angeles, Tommy Milton's and Bennett Hill's Miller winning the opening races. Laurel followed the fashion with the Baltimore-Washington course on 11th July 1925. During 1926 new tracks also sprang up at Rockingham, New Hampshire, Fulford, Miami Beach and Atlantic City, New Jersey. All were of board construction.

Monza Track, built in a Royal Park in Italy, opened in 1922 as a banked high-speed track with a lap distance of 2·796 miles. It was supplemented by a road circuit which made up a lap distance of 6·214 miles when combined with the banked sections. The high-speed track was not much used and was demolished in 1939 but rebuilt in 1955 for the celebrated American Challenge Race. The new banked course has a lap distance of 2·641 miles and has been used

Fangio at Monza in 1958. Driving the Dean Van Lines Special he qualified for the Monza 500 with the third fastest lap at over 171 m.p.h., but only managed to complete one lap in the race.

in conjunction with the road circuit even for the Italian Grand Prix, the distance being the original 6·214 miles. There have been eleven different Monza circuits, but only two have been banked.

The first banked circuit was used for the 1922 Italian Grand Prix, won by Bordino's 2-litre Fiat at 86·90 m.p.h. It was also the scene as late as 1931 of the *formule libre* Italian Grand Prix, won by the Alfa Romeo driven by Campari and Nuvolari, which averaged 96·79 m.p.h. for 10 hours. The last important race on the pre-war banked course was the 1932 Monza Grand Prix, which Caracciola won at 110·85 m.p.h. in an Alfa Romeo.

The new, more-steeply banked track with sunken non-convex banks was used for the Two Worlds Trophy 500-Mile Race in 1955, which Jim Bryan won at 160·06 m.p.h. driving a Dean Van Lines Special. The following race of 1958 was won by Jim Rathmann in a Zink Leader Card Special at 166·72 m.p.h. This section of the Monza track has now fallen into disuse. As a comparison, today the Daytona banked track has stock-car saloons lapping at close on 200 m.p.h. . . . .

The steeply banked track at Sitges, near Barcelona, was built soon after the First World War, being completed in 1922, but it was used very little. Albert Divo's 2-litre Grand Prix Sunbeam won the opening 248-mile race in 1923 from Count Zborowski's Miller, with an Elizade in third place. The *voiturette* race was won by Dario Resta's Talbot, and the 1,100-c.c. Class by Robert Benoist's Salmson. This Sitges-Terramar circuit exists today, forlorn and overgrown, much as it was in 1922.

Apart from banked tracks built for racing, many manufacturers had such test courses. The 2½-mile banked track belonging to Packard at Utica, Michigan, was lapped by Leon Duray in a 91-cubic inch front-drive Miller at 148·17 m.p.h. in June 1928.

SOME RECORD-BREAKING AND TRACK-RACING PERSONALITIES

Captain George Eyston (1897–1979), perhaps the most prolific record-breaker of them all, was the inventor of the Powerplus supercharger which was used on many of the cars—including the M.G.s—which featured in his long career. He was born on 20th June 1897 in Oxfordshire and was educated at Stonyhurst. During the First World War he was appointed A.D.C. to General Wellesley, winning the M.C., and afterwards went up to Cambridge in 1919, marrying in 1923. His motor-racing career began with Aston Martin and Bugatti cars, and in 1937 he took the World Land Speed Record at 312 m.p.h. with the enormous 7-ton, 73-litre twin-Rolls-Royce aero-engined *Thunderbolt*—again in 1938 at 345·49 m.p.h. and later at 357·50 m.p.h. He was awarded an O.B.E. in 1948. Eyston had made record-breaking in all kinds of car his speciality and he won dozens of awards, including the Brooklands 120 and 130 m.p.h. special badges, the A.I.A.C.R. Gold Medal and the coveted Segrave Trophy. Eyston was a Chevalier of the Légion d'Honneur and a Knight of the Sovereign Order of Malta. He flew in the pioneering days of aviation and took his seaplane pilot's licence on a D.H. Moth float-plane when he was over seventy years of age.

John Godfrey Parry Thomas (1885–1927) was addicted to Fair Isle pullovers and was a lover of Alsatian dogs. He lived on the Byfleet side of Brooklands Track in a bungalow called "The Hermitage". In 1926 he took the Land Speed Record at 171·09 m.p.h. in the aero-engined Higham Special, *Babs*, on Pendine Sands, where he was killed driving the same car in the following year.

Parry Thomas at the wheel of Babs, *shortly before his death in 1927.*

Sir Malcolm Campbell (1885–1949) took his son Donald with him to Brooklands and the U.S.A. on the occasions of his Land Speed Record bids when the latter was only a schoolboy. Sir Malcolm initiated libel insurance for newspapers in the City of London, and was also an agent for several makes of car, including Star and Bugatti. His Land Speed Records were: 146·16 m.p.h. (1924, Pendine); 150·87 m.p.h. (1925, Pendine); 174·88 m.p.h. (1927, Pendine); 206·96 m.p.h. (1928, Daytona); 246·09 m.p.h. (1931, Daytona); 253·97 m.p.h. (1932, Daytona); 272·46 m.p.h. (1933, Daytona); 276·82 m.p.h. (1935, Daytona); 301·13 m.p.h. (1935, Bonneville). He also took the Water Speed Record four times.

A.D.A.C. 1000 Kilometres, 1972, at the Nürburgring: the illuminated lap-scoring board shines through the dusk as the Bell/van Lennep Gulf Mirage M6 leads the Elford/Stommelen Alfa Romeo 33 TT3 into the Sudkerve.

A dramatic night picture taken during the 1969 Le Mans 24-hours race. (Photos: Geoffrey Goddard.)

Jet-propelled record-breaking cars. Art Arfons with the Green Monster, *a combination which established three World Land Speed Records at 434·02, 536·71 and 576·55 m.p.h. respectively at Bonneville in 1964–65.*

The Current World Land Speed Record holder, Gary Gabelich with the Natural Gas Industry's Blue Flame, *on which he returned a speed of 630·38 m.p.h. at Bonneville, Utah, in 1970.*

Malcolm Campbell in the 350 h.p. Sunbeam in 1925.

Donald Campbell, with his father. A picture taken in about 1933.

Donald Campbell, C.B.E. (1921–1967) took the Land Speed Record once, at 403·10 m.p.h., on 17th July 1964 on Lake Eyre, Australia, with the *Proteus Bluebird*. He took the Water Speed Record seven times. He was killed trying to regain this record in his boat on Coniston Lake in England and his body was never recovered.

John Cobb (1899–1952), the ultimate holder of the Brooklands lap record, was a fur-broker by profession. He was a shy, unresponsive giant of a man who specialised in driving big motor cars at the track and later in attacks on the Land Speed Record. These he held in 1938 at 350·20 m.p.h. with his four-wheel-drive Railton, and in 1939 at 369·74 m.p.h. In 1947 he raised this figure to 394·196 with the same car, now called the Railton-Mobil Special. Cobb lost his life in an attempt on the World Water Speed Record on Loch Ness in 1952.

Anthony Joseph Foyt, Jnr. was born in 1935. "A. J." commenced his racing career in midgets and in sprint contests in 1957. He failed to finish at Indianapolis in 1958 but stood in for Trintignant in the Monza U.S.A.C. contest, placing sixth. From then on Foyt showed himself to be the most consistent of competitors in the U.S.A.C. Championships and his first National Championship title came in 1960 when he won four out of five of these 100-mile races on mile-long dirt tracks. Foyt worked on his own machinery and both his second and third "Indy" victories were at record speed. In stock cars, in the longer races over the closed circuits and at Indianapolis, Foyt's strength and endurance have paid off and his trophies have included the Nassau Trophy and Governor's Cup at the 1963 Nassau Speed Week, followed by others too numerous to list—by 1970 "A. J." had won 42 Championship victories, 5 National Championships, 26 sprint car and 19 midget car victories, plus a further 22 in stock cars! In Europe Foyt shared, with Dan Gurney, the winning Ford GT-40 at Le Mans in 1967. (See also pages 208 and 209).

Al Unser comes from a family of racing men, his father, his two uncles and his brother being in the game. Born in 1939, he began racing modified stock cars on his local tracks and finished second in the Pike's Peak Hillclimb of 1960. Unser moved on to big-car championships and was second at Indianapolis on his third appearance in the classic 500-Mile Race. Out of racing for a time due to breaking a leg in a motorcycle accident, Unser was runner-up to Andretti in the U.S.A.C. series of Championship events in 1969 and went on to achieve notable successes with some very impressive qualifying laps at "Indy", where he has won twice in a row, and in stock car and U.S.A.C. National Championship races, he took top honours in 1970 by winning ten firsts out of eighteen starts.

Mauri Rose who was born in 1906 ranks as a veteran driver, and gained his experience on the half-mile dirt and board tracks before graduating to events on the one-mile dirt ovals. Employed as an automobile development engineer by some of the leading American companies, Rose had less time to spend at the tracks in later years than his rivals, but he drove at Indianapolis in 1933. Winning there in 1941 by using an Offenhauser-powered car when his Maserati had developed ignition maladies after being flagged away in pole-starting position, Mauri Rose clinched his triple at Indy by winning two years in succession, in 1947 and 1948, driving a Maserati disguised as a Blue Crown Special. He had won the National Championship the year before gaining these two wins in the Indianapolis 500-Mile Race. He retired following a crash in 1951, when his car overturned while running well up in the "Indy", although, in fact, Rose escaped injury. He may also be remembered as the first American driver to finish in the 1936 Roosevelt Speedway road-race against the cream of European drivers, when he was hampered because his car had lost all gears save top.

Section 5
EVERYDAY MOTORING

Compiled by Michael Sedgwick

Everyday motoring, 1922. The car is an A.C. (Photo: Radio Times Hulton Picture Library.)

THE TRAVELLERS

The first men to circumnavigate Australia by car were Noel Westwood and G. L. Davies, who left Perth on 4th August 1925 and returned to that city on 30th December. Their car was a 5CV Citroën.

The first overland trip from England to Australia by car was accomplished by Francis Birtles on a 14-h.p. Bean. He left London on 19th October 1927, and arrived in Sydney on 15th July 1928.

The first woman to drive round the world was Miss Violet Cordery in 1927. On a 3-litre Invicta she covered 10,266 miles in five continents at an average speed (running time) of 24·6 m.p.h.

The first party to drive from the Cape to Cairo by car was that of Major C. Court Treatt with two 25/30-h.p. R.F.C.-type Crossley tenders. It took them from 23rd September 1924 until 24th December 1926 to do it. The first ordinary private car to make the trip was a Chrysler driven by Gerry Bouwer which left the Cape on 6th February 1928, and arrived in London on 4th June.

Arrival in London of a Trojan car which had travelled 12,000 miles from Singapore on solid tyres in 1926. The journey, which occupied fifteen months, had taken the three occupants through fourteen countries.

The world's longest marathon car run on record was accomplished by François Lecot on an 11CV Citroën in France. Between 23rd July 1935 and 22nd July 1936, he covered 400,000 kilometres (about 250,000 miles), at an average speed of 40 m.p.h. He drove in daily spells of 19 hours, and the venture included participation in the Monte Carlo Rally.

St. John Cousins Nixon (d. 1970) not only took part in the original British Thousand Miles' Trial of 1900 as mechanic on S. F. Edge's Napier, but also re-enacted the Trial on three occasions (1950, 1960 and 1970). In each case his mount was an 1899 3¼-h.p. Wolseley which had taken part in the 1900 event.

The late St. John Nixon in the 1899 Wolseley; left, on the occasion of the 1950 John o'Groat's to Land's End Trial, and below, crossing the Scottish border during the 1960 Trial. The other car is a 1914 Morris Oxford.

THE PRESS

William Frederick Bradley (1876–1971) spent fifty-three years of his life as a motoring journalist in France. Until 1919 he was *The Motor*'s Paris Correspondent; he then served *The Autocar* in a similar capacity until 1956.

The longest record of editorial service on a motoring paper stands to the credit of Charles Faroux, who joined the French *L'Auto* as Technical Editor in 1904 and was still serving in this capacity at the time of his death in 1957.

The British record for continuous editorship of a motoring paper stands to the credit of William Boddy, who took over the editorship of *Motor Sport* on the outbreak of the Second World War and still occupies the editorial chair in 1980.

The first British motor sporting paper was *Motor Sport*, which first appeared (as *The Brooklands Gazette*) in August 1924.

The first independent British motoring magazine devoted to vintage motoring was *The Vintage and Thoroughbred Car*, which first appeared in March 1953. It became *The Veteran and Vintage Magazine* in 1956, and *Collector's Car* in 1979.

The largest circulation of any British motoring journal is recorded by *Car Mechanics* with a sale (January-June 1979) of 123,888 copies per edition.

Harry Ferguson (of tractor and four-wheel-drive fame) was also the first man to fly in Ireland, in an aeroplane of his own construction. This feat was accomplished at Belfast in the winter of 1909–10.

The inventor of the Lockheed hydraulic brake was a Scot named Malcolm *Loughead*, also connected with the American aircraft firm. Both his ventures soon assumed a more phonetic spelling, but the inventor himself did not.

The first woman to manage an automobile factory was Miss Dorothée Pullinger, daughter of T. C. Pullinger. Her factory was Galloway Motors Ltd. of Tongland, Kirkcudbrightshire, in 1921–22.

Sir Charles Kingsford-Smith, the famous Australian aviator, sponsored the Southern Cross car in Sydney in 1934—it was named after his record-breaking Fokker Trimotor. Also named in his honour were the Triumph Southern Cross models of the 1930s; Kingsford Smith was a Triumph-owner.

The father of the modern automobile museum was Count Carlo Biscaretti di Ruffia of Turin. His Museo dell'Automobile was first mooted in 1932, and opened in 1939. Count Biscaretti died in 1959, but a year later a new and magnificent museum supported by Italian industry was opened in Turin's Corso Unita d'Italia.

Two naval officers (Captains Curt Borgenstam and Bertil Lindblad of the Royal Swedish Navy) were responsible for the revival of the Isotta-Fraschini Co. in 1953, after its closure three years earlier. Since the name had been acquired by the Breda group, the new firm had to operate under the name of C.R.M., but it has continued the development of Isotta's marine engines.

Isadora Duncan, the dancer, was accidentally strangled when her scarf was caught in the rear wheel of a friend's Amilcar in which she was riding at Nice on 14th September 1927.

Motor-car bandits were common in the first decade of the twentieth century, but the **first murder case to centre round a car** was that of Alfred Arthur Rouse, who murdered an unknown man and burnt him in his Morris Minor on the night of 5th/6th November 1930, at Hardingstone, Northamptonshire.

The car used in the famous St. Valentine's Day Massacre of 14th February 1929, in Chicago, was a Packard tourer dressed up in imitation of a police car. These were the days when open Lincolns were much favoured by the Law in America.

INSTRUMENTS AND CONTROLS

The conventional "gate" for a three-speed gearbox has reverse and first on the left-hand side, and the two upper ratios on the right, but until 1926 Buick and Dodge favoured a back-to-front layout.

Two gear levers are an archaism associated with the early years of the century, but on French cars with the Cotal electrically selected gearbox (introduced in 1935), a finger-tip column selector was used in conjunction with a floor-mounted forward/reverse lever. Among cars so equipped were Delage, Delahaye, Salmson and Voisin, and one of the peculiarities of this transmission was that it gave four speeds in either direction!

Steering-column gear change (in conjunction with a conventional manual box) was introduced in America in 1938, the first firm to standardise this layout throughout the range being Cadillac. The first British car with column shift was the Triumph 1800 (March 1946); this and the early Standard Vanguard (introduced 1947) were the only right-hand-drive models to have *right-hand* column changes.

One of the odder aspects of American safety legislation is a change in the standard selector positions on automatic-transmission quadrants. These used to be arranged P-N-D-L-R (Park-Neutral-Drive-Low-Reverse), but have now been amended to the safer P-R-N-D-L.

Left-hand drive is almost as old as the industry, having been seen on Benz cars at the turn of the twentieth century. By 1914 the majority of American makes had left-hand drive, and by 1918 only Pierce-Arrow, Stutz and the American-built Fiat (the latter in its last year of production) retained the right-hand layout. Pierce-Arrow, however, defended their conservatism on the ground that it was more convenient for chauffeurs, and did not fall into line with the rest of the industry until 1920. Early Springfield-built Rolls-Royces (1921–23) were also right-hand drive.

Packards of the 1913–17 era had the curious combination of left-hand steering and a left-hand gear change.

Though left-hand steering was general practice on popular continental cars by 1929, the more expensive models retained right-hand drive well into the 1950s. No Bugatti ever had left-hand drive and Lancia's switch in 1956 was dictated only by a growing interest in American exports.

Central accelerator pedals were widely used by European makers until the early 1930s, but though these (like right-hand change) were always considered "U", in Bullnose days Morrises had central accelerators while their M.G. counterparts preferred a right-hand location.

Contrary to general belief, not all Rolls-Royces with manual gearbox had right-hand change. From 1925 to the end in 1931, all cars made in the American factory at Springfield had a central lever, as did the left-hand drive AJS- and AMS-series Phantom IIs made at Derby in the 1930s. Left-hand drive Silver Dawns made between 1950 and 1953 had a column-mounted lever, while three-speed Twenties (1922–25) had central change.

Horstman light cars of the 1913–26 period had mechanical kick-starters in their cockpits, operating on the Archimedes' screw principle. These were retained after the firm went over to electric starting.

The mechanical kick-starter of the 1921 Horstman.

"Indoor" starting-handles were always a feature of the Trojan car, introduced to the market in 1922. They were also found on the 1933 front-wheel drive Stoewers, taking advantage of the engine's back-to-front location.

Box-type arrow direction indicators mounted on each side of the rear number-plate were first seen on the 14–45-h.p. Talbot in 1926.

Morris cars exhibited at the 1932 London Show had three-colour direction signals based on street traffic lights. These were declared illegal, and by early 1933 they had been supplanted by the conventional semaphore type.

The first recorded use of an oil-pressure warning light was on the Fiat 509 of 1925.

An average speed calculator was standard equipment on the Fiat 1900 (1953).

Fully retractable windscreen-wipers were pioneered in 1967 on the American General Motors range.

Mechanical windscreen-wipers were first seen on closed cars in America in 1916. One of the earliest was the Willys-Knight.

Left-hand drive was first offered by a British manufacturer in 1921, when 40-h.p. Lanchesters for export to America were so equipped.

The only firm to fit six-figure odometers instead of the usual five (with or without decimals) is Volvo, this being a gesture of confidence in the car's ability to last well over 100,000 miles.

The foot-operated parking brake is generally believed to be a by-product of automatic transmissions, but the Chevrolet 490 of 1916 had no handbrake; instead a ratchet incorporated in the pedal mechanism could lock it for parking. The modern foot-operated type was standardised by Buick in 1942, six years before the company offered an automatic.

"Umbrella-handle" handbrake levers under the dash were first seen on American cars in 1934; among those adopting this layout was Cadillac.

Automatic overdrive was first offered in 1934 on Chrysler and De Soto cars; but gearboxes with an overdrive top were not uncommon before the First World War, being found on the 40–50-h.p. Rolls-Royce from 1907 to 1909.

"Key starting", now universal, was pioneered in 1949 by Chrysler Corporation. Among the more unusual ignition keys of the 1930s and 1940s was Fiat's plunger, pushed into the lock to give ignition, and rotated to give the various combinations of lights.

A gear-change lever protruding from the dashboard was first seen on the front-wheel-drive Tracta in 1927.

WHEELS AND TYRES

Quick-detachable wheels were almost universal on British and continental cars by 1920, but the fixed wood wheel with demountable rim survived in America on many makes until 1932. It was claimed that these were easier for a woman to cope with in the event of a "flat".

The last recorded use of wood wheels as factory equipment was on the Mercedes-Benz Nürburg in 1939.

Tubeless tyres were used (without much success) on motorcycles and American light cars in the 1890s, but reinvented by the American firm of Goodrich in 1948. Dunlop was the first British firm to follow suit, in 1953.

Balloon tyres were pioneered by Firestone in America in 1923, and first offered later in the year by Cole. The first car to be designed for balloons was the Chrysler 70 of 1924.

Today's "Ro-Style" wheels had their ancestors in the cast-steel spoked type favoured by some American manufacturers, notably Auburn, Marmon and Revere, in 1923–26. They gave the cars a very truck-like aspect and were, of course, used in conjunction with demountable rims.

The first successful radial-ply tyre was Michelin's "X", marketed in 1953.

ELECTRICS AND ILLUMINATIONS

Swivelling headlamps, turning with the wheels, were first seen as regular equipment on the 1967 Citroëns, but the American Tucker Torpedo of 1946 had a swivelling, centrally mounted Cyclops'-eye spotlight. As early as 1928–29, Tilt-Ray swivelling headlamps had been marketed by an American accessory firm, and were frequently found on luxury models in the Cadillac-Lincoln class.

The four-headlamp layout, now general practice on larger cars, was pioneered by Cadillac and Lincoln in 1957, though the last Pierce-Arrows of 1936–38 (and the more expensive 1937 Packards) featured auxiliary headlamps intended for use as pass lights.

The Cyclops'-eye central headlamp, a trademark of the Rover 75 from 1950 to 1952, was anticipated on two American cars, the Garford of 1913 and the Briscoe of 1915.

Headlamp flashers were first used on the Fiat 1500 of 1935.

Headlamps half-faired into the wings were a Pierce-Arrow trademark as early as 1913, though it was possible even in 1930 to specify a conventional mounting. The first British production model with headlamps fully faired into the wings was the Series-E Morris Eight of 1939.

Illuminated radiator emblems were pioneered by Wolseley in 1933, though the American Fageol luxury car of 1917 (which did not go into production) had such a device made of ivory.

Retractable headlamps were first seen on the 1936 Model 810 Cord. Unlike modern systems, these had to be wound in and out manually.

The first car to be offered with a reversing light was the American Wills-Sainte Claire, in 1921.

The Barker double-dipping headlamp system, on which the bodies of the lamps were physically dipped, appeared in 1922. It was standardised on a number of British cars, among them Alvis and Morris, but gave way to **the double-filament bulb,** first seen in America in 1924.

Britain's first foglamp was offered by Desmo of Birmingham in 1928. Previous to this (since 1925) accessory manufacturers had offered "fog-discs" in yellow celluloid which fitted over the headlamps.

THE BODY AND ITS ACCESSORIES

Parallel-opening doors were first seen at the 1935 London Motor Show on a Bentley with drophead coupé bodywork by James Young of Bromley.

The sliding door of the Young-bodied Bentley, seen at the 1935 London Motor Show.

Gull-wing doors were first used on the Mercedes-Benz 300SL, unveiled in 1952 and put into production in 1954.

Doors opening into the roof were pioneered on a custom saloon body built for a Duesenberg Model J chassis in 1930 by Murphy of Pasadena. Their first use on a series production body was on the Riley Falcon saloon introduced for 1933.

Two examples of the classic American Duesenberg of the early 'thirties. Above: A 1930 Murphy-bodied Model J. Below: Weymann-bodied "fishtail" Duesenberg SJ Speedster of 1933. This car has been renovated and is now part of the Harrah Collection at Reno, Nevada.

The first mass-production saloon with fully recessed door-handles was the Fiat 1500 of 1935.

The first power-top convertible to go into production was Peugeot's 1934 *décapotable électrique*. This car's top was of metal, an anticipation of Ford's legendary 1957 retractable, of which 48,394 found buyers in America during a three-season run.

Detachable hardtops, transforming open cars into formal carriages, were common in the early years of the century, e.g. Lanchester (1901), Cadillac (1903). Similar styles of "all-year" bodywork were also listed by a number of American manufacturers during the First World War and immediately after, but the first series-production European style in the modern idiom was the First Series Lancia Lambda (1922). No suggestion was offered as to the best means of storage for this ponderous component when out of use!

First of the modern hardtop convertibles was Buick's original Riviera of 1949. Chrysler had catalogued such a style in their 1946 half-timbered Town and Country line, but made only seven such cars.

The first standard body to conceal its spare wheel in the tail was the Austin Twenty tourer of 1919.

Electric window lifts were first seen in 1946 on the American Cadillac and Lincoln, and the British Daimler DE36 straight-eight.

Seats convertible into a bed were found on the 1921 Pan, an American car.

Skirted front wings were pioneered by Graham on their 1932 Blue Streak models.

Curved windscreens were first used on factory-bodied cars in 1914 by Kissel. The first British use was on 1922 Arrol-Johnston models.

The first curved windscreen without a central divider was found on the most expensive Imperial models (Type CW) of the 1934 Chrysler Airflow range.

Cellulose finish was first standardised on Oakland cars in 1924. The first British manufacturer to offer it was A.C. in 1925.

Electric divisions on limousines were first used by British specialist coachbuilders in 1937. Among the firms fitting them at the 1937 London Motor Show were Hooper, Park Ward and Thrupp and Maberly.

The first car to be marketed with a Weymann fabric body was the French Talbot (Darracq) in 1922.

Tartan loose covers for upholstery are common practice, but at least two manufacturers used tartan fabric for the exterior finish of their bodies: Voisin on a *conduite intérieure écossaise* in 1922 and Willys-Knight on a "Plaidside" roadster in 1930.

ACCESSORIES AND MISCELLANEOUS

Electric fuel-pumps were first used on the 1924 Wills-Sainte Claire. The first British car so equipped was the 2-litre Arab of 1927.

Radiator filler caps are not always what they seem. On A.B.C. light cars of the 1920–28 period the cap on top of the "radiator" was in fact the fuel orifice. The model was air-cooled.

Safety-glass was first fitted as factory equipment on Stutz and Rickenbacker cars in 1926.

The first firms to fit windscreen-washers as factory equipment were Standard and Triumph in 1935. The first American use of these was by Studebaker in 1937.

The first British car to be obtainable with "factory radio" was the Crossley in 1933. Hillman followed in 1934.

During the Model T Ford's nineteen-year currency (1908–27) over 5,000 different accessories were offered for the model. By the 1940s "factory accessories" were an industry in themselves, and by 1942 Pontiac alone were offering over sixty different items.

Thermostatically controlled radiator-shutters were first seen on the 1920 Straker-Squire.

Top left: *Road repairs aren't new; it's just that roads get older. A scene in May 1910 at Piccadilly Circus, London. (Photo: Radio Times Hulton Picture Library.)*

Top right: *Emancipation of the motor vehicle. Steam and motor buses, motor and horse-drawn cabs in Piccadilly Circus, July 1912. (Photo: Radio Times Hulton Picture Library.)*

Bottom left: *The leisurely pace of Marble Arch, London, 1912. A view looking down Oxford Street. (Photo: Radio Times Hulton Picture Library.)*

Bottom right: *Post-war traffic congestion. Looking down the Mall after a Buckingham Palace Garden Party in 1919. (Photo: Radio Times Hulton Picture Library.)*

The largest tool-kit supplied with a car in current production (1979) is the twenty-two-piece set on the Russian Moskvitch and Lada.

Air-conditioning was first offered in 1940 by Packard. Nash's much-publicised 1938 system was merely one of controlled heating and ventilation.

Bug deflectors on bonnets were first seen as regular accessories in 1952.

The first recorded instance of a radio receiver on a private car was in August 1921, when the Cardiff and South Wales Wireless Society installed a set. In September 1922, a Burndept set was fitted to a Cadillac coupé for a lady customer in London. American manufacturers started to offer radio as an option on cars in 1929–30, among the pioneers being Chrysler and Marmon.

A radio-telephone service for cars was first offered in Great Britain in the summer of 1959.

Record-players were first offered as a factory option by Chrysler in 1956.

Smith's Jackall permanent four-wheel jacks were introduced in 1929, and first fitted as factory equipment to Star cars in 1931.

An ingenious solution to the parking problem was the Parkmobile of 1928, a species of four-wheeled "retractable undercarriage" which could be lowered to give lateral movement. It was standard on an obscure American car of the period, the New York Six.

Heaters are almost as old as the industry, "motor hot-water bottles" (upholstered to match the interior trim) being recognised accessories in the first decade of the twentieth century. The hot-water type fed off the car's cooling system made its appearance in America in 1926, though a foot-warmer so operated was found on Cannstatt Daimlers of the 1897–1900 period. Defrosters were recognised accessories by the middle 1930s. One of the oddest arrangements of all was found on the 1954 air-cooled Dyna 54 Panhard. This had a catalytic-type petrol heater mounted on the engine bulkhead and fed from the main tank. It was asserted that this device worked at a temperature low enough to eliminate any fire risk, but it was soon discarded in favour of a more conventional installation drawing hot air off the cylinders of the engine.

MOTORING IN GENERAL

The first Earls Court Motor Show was held in October 1937: previous shows had been staged at Olympia in West Kensington, the venue since 1905. From 1920 to 1922 the London Motor Show was divided between two venues: Olympia and the White City. They were linked by a coach service.

The largest number of different makes of car to be exhibited at a London Motor Show since 1919 was 179, in 1920. The biggest special coachwork exhibit was in 1927, with sixty-one stands. By contrast the 1970 figures were seventy-seven and nine respectively.

The record attendance figure for a London Motor Show was in 1965, when 660,257 people passed through the turnstiles. The pre-1939 record was 275,000 in 1927. After 1976 Shows were held biennially at the National Exhibition Centre in Birmingham.

Before the Second World War the Glasgow Motor Show was an annual event, but since the war it has become biennial, resuming in 1949. Unlike its London counterpart, it is a traders' rather than a manufacturers' exhibition.

British motor-vehicle registrations first topped the million mark in 1923. The first "million year" for private cars was 1930, and the 5 million mark was reached in 1949. Great Britain had 14,388,800 private cars in 1977.

In the 1975–78 period the best-selling car in Great Britain was the Ford Cortina, with cylinder capacities falling within the 1·3–2·3-litre bracket. This confirms previous national preferences for cars of 1,300–1,600 c.c.

The first Flying Squad cars were supplied to London's Metropolitan Police in 1920: they were R.F.C.-type Crossley tenders. The first high-performance cars to be used by Scotland Yard were 1·5-litre Lea-Francis delivered in 1927.

Britain's first self-service petrol-pump went into operation at Southwark Bridge, London, in November 1961. There was an isolated experiment with "shilling-in-the slot" petrol, at Patcham, Sussex, in the early 1930s, but this was abandoned because the machine was too easily bilked.

RULES AND REGULATIONS

Great Britain's overall speed limit of 20 m.p.h.—set in 1903—was not finally abolished until the end of 1930.

The 30-m.p.h. speed limit in built-up areas came into force during March 1935.

The "blanket" speed limit of 70 m.p.h. in Great Britain came into force on 1st January 1967: this was the first time that such legislation had been applied since 1930, if one excepts the 20-m.p.h. limit imposed in blackout hours during the Second World War. During the energy crisis of 1974 further restrictions were imposed. Graduated limits called for a maximum of 70 m.p.h. on motorways, 60 on dual carriageways and 50 on all other nominally derestricted roads.

The British "breathalyser law" came into force on 9th October 1967. From that date it became an offence to drive a motor vehicle with more than 80 milligrammes of alcohol per 100 millilitres of blood in the bloodstream.

Third-party insurance cover has been compulsory for motorists in Great Britain since 1930.

The minimum age at which a Briton may hold a car driving licence is seventeen, except in the case of a three-wheeler without reverse gear, in which case the motorcycle limit of sixteen applies.

The Ministry of Transport (now Department of the Environment) Driving Test has been in force since May 1935: the L-plates which the holder of a Provisional (i.e. learner's) Licence has to wear on his car are, however, peculiar to Britain.

The Ministry of Transport's (now Department of the Environment's) Roadworthiness Tests for cars came into force on 12th September 1960, being initially applicable to vehicles ten or more years old. Their application has since been extended and, as from April 1967, three-year-olds must be tested annually.

The British Motor Trade Association's Covenant Scheme to restrict racketeering in the resale of new cars was imposed in July 1946, and was originally valid for a period of six months. The "covenant" period was extended to one year in March 1948, and to two years in September 1950. From 1952 onwards the more expensive models were progressively released, but popular cars were not finally freed until well into 1953.

Registration books were first introduced in Great Britain in February 1921. They do not constitute a legal title to the car.

The horsepower tax in Great Britain, based on a formula taking into consideration only the number of the cylinders and their bore in millimetres, was first imposed in 1921. After 1946 it ceased to be applicable to new cars, but older models were still taxed on this formula until 1952. The lowest rate charged during the years of the horsepower tax was 15 shillings ($£0.75$) per unit of taxable horsepower, from 1935 to 1938.

The phrase "Road Fund Licence" has had no meaning in Great Britain since 1925, when Winston Churchill, the then Chancellor of the Exchequer, first authorised the diversion of moneys received in car tax to other purposes.

British Purchase Tax was first applied to motor cars in October 1940, when the rate was $33\frac{1}{3}$ per cent. The highest standard rate ever charged was $66\frac{2}{3}$ per cent (1951–53). From April, 1973, this levy was superseded by a Value Added Tax as used in other countries of the European Economic Community.

The Ministry of Transport was not set up until September 1919: **the first Minister** was the Rt. Hon. Sir Eric Geddes, G.C.B., G.B.E., P.C. (1875–1937).

Safety-glass windscreens were made compulsory by law in Great Britain from 1st January 1937.

Seat-belts for both front seats were compulsory on all new cars registered in Great Britain from 1st April 1967.

Drama in a London street, February 1936, with characteristic audience. No one suffered in this accident, and less than one year later legislation made safety-glass in windscreens compulsory.

ROADS

The first modern motorway to be opened to the public was a 21-kilometre stretch of *autostrada* between Milan and Varese (Italy). Work was started on this in June 1923, and it was first opened to traffic in September 1924.

Britain's first motorway—the Preston By-pass—was opened in December 1958.

The first stretch of German *Autobahn*, from Frankfurt to Darmstadt, was opened in May 1935.

A motorway scheme to link London with Liverpool was put forward by John, Lord Montagu of Beaulieu in 1924, and got as far as a Private Member's Bill in Parliament before being dropped.

The first American twin-track toll road was the Pennsylvania Turnpike, opened in October 1940. It followed the line of a disused railway.

Traffic lights of the three-colour type were first used in Britain at Wolverhampton in 1928.

The world's first traffic light was installed in Detroit, U.S.A., in 1919.

Green on a traffic light does not mean "go". It means "proceed if the way is clear".

The world's first parking-meter was installed in Oklahoma City, U.S.A., in July 1935. Britain's first meters did not appear until 1958.

Zebra-crossings for pedestrians were first seen in Britain in October 1951.

Britain's first roadside petrol-pump was set up at Shrewsbury in 1913. These were not in general use until 1921, although America had had them since 1906.

The world's earliest parking meter, Oklahoma City, U.S.A., 1935.

Characteristic of the Motor Age in the United States are the traffic complexes, especially in towns and cities. The Harbor Freeway, Los Angeles, California, was during the 1960s the world's busiest highway.

The first underground car park in the United Kingdom was opened at Hastings in December 1931.

A multi-level interchange on a motorway requires at least 60 acres of ground.

The country with the world's biggest road mileage is the U.S.A.: the figure is 3,838,000 miles.

White lines as road dividers were first used in Great Britain in 1927.

The first flyover junctions in Great Britain were on the Winchester By-pass, at the junctions with the Alton and Alresford roads, and with the old A33 road at Compton. The By-pass was opened in 1939.

The steepest average gradient on an A-class road in Great Britain is on the A169, between Sleights and Guisborough, Yorkshire. The gradient is 1 in 6.

Tramcars are not extinct in Great Britain, being in full operation in Blackpool. London's last trams ran in July 1952, and Glasgow's in September 1962.

The two longest traffic jams recorded in the history of British motoring both measured 35 miles in length: the first of these was between Torquay and Yarcombe (25th July 1964), and the second between Egham and Micheldever (23rd May 1970).

The worst pile-up in the history of British motoring took place at Thelwell near the Lymm interchange on the M6 Motorway on 13th September 1971. Two hundred vehicles were involved, and casualties amounted to 11 dead and 60 injured.

Multiple pile-ups were relatively rare until the "Age of the Motorway". This one, at Finchley in 1924, was more spectacular than serious, as it is unlikely that any of the drivers were travelling at more than 25 m.p.h.

The first conviction for speeding based on a radar trap in Great Britain was recorded in Lancashire on 19th August 1959. The alleged offender was fined £3.

Britain's first motel, the Royal Oak, was opened at Hythe, Kent, in 1953.

The first airline to offer a car ferry service was Silver City Airways, who inaugurated their Lympne–Le Touquet run at Easter 1949. In October 1946, however, a new Morris was flown to a Guernsey dealer from Reading Airport, probably the first delivery of a car by air in the United Kingdom.

WORLD MOTORING MISCELLANY

The worst year for road deaths in Great Britain was 1941, with 9,169 people killed.

The worst year for road deaths in the U.S.A. was 1969, with 54,895 people killed.

The country with the worst record for road deaths per head of population is Japan. Some 16,285 people were killed on her roads in 1969.

In the U.S.S.R. it is an offence to use a dirty car on the roads.

As late as 1923 Sunday motoring was still banned in some parts of Switzerland, exceptions to this rule being doctors and veterinary surgeons.

Private cars are banned by law from the Island of Sark. They were also banned in Bermuda from 1908 to 1946.

Only Japan, Britain and Commonwealth (or former Commonwealth) countries now apply the left-hand rule of the road. Sweden, the last holdout in continental Europe, changed to the right in September 1967.

The highest number of motor-vehicle registrations in the world are those of the United States—137,285,000 in 1976.

The biggest producer of crude petroleum in the world is the United States, with an annual output of 516,000,000 metric tons. Second is the U.S.S.R. with 328,800,000 metric tons.

The lowest official price charged for petrol in the United Kingdom was 1s. 0½d. (a little over 5p) per gallon in April 1928, but some garages were in fact selling R.O.P. (Russian Oil Products) fuel that year for as little as 9d.–10d. (4p approx.) per gallon.

Petrol rationing came into force in the United Kingdom on 16th September 1939, and was not freed again until 26th May 1950. It was rationed again during the Suez Crisis (December 1956–May 1957).

Since 1946 France has had a discriminatory horsepower tax with a sharp rise in the rate payable on cars of over 15 *chevaux-vapeur* (about 2·8 litres). Such a car is charged the equivalent of £23 ($55.00) a year, but bigger models are charged about £77 ($180.00).

The largest density of cars per head of population is recorded in the Island of Jersey, where there is 1 to every 2·1 inhabitants. By contrast the ratio is 1 to 2·4 in the U.S.A. and 1 to 5 in the United Kingdom.

Between Pearl Harbor and the end of the Second World War the American automobile industry turned out 4,121,000 engines, 5,047,000 guns, 2,812,000 military vehicles, and 27,000 complete aircraft, this last figure representing 10 per cent of the national total for the period.

From 1921 to 1925 the term "cyclecar" had a legal status in France. Cylinder capacity might not exceed 1,100 c.c., and not more than two persons might be carried. The maximum permitted weight with bodywork and all accessories was 350 kilogrammes, and few so-called "cyclecars" could get within these limits—hence "stripped" specifications and, sometimes, two invoices for the purchaser. The term *voiturette* never had any legal significance.

In the United States it is estimated that motor cars disseminate annually:
60 million tons of carbon monoxide;
1 million tons of sulphur oxide;
6 million tons of nitrous oxide;
12 million tons of hydrocarbons;
1 million tons of "smoke".

The first full-length comedy play based on the motor car was *Six-Cylinder Love*, presented at the Sam H. Harris Theater, New York, on 25th August 1921. There was a silent film version in 1923, and a talkie in 1931.

The first drive-in cinema was opened at Camden, New Jersey, in 1934, and **the first drive-in bank** at Los Angeles, California, in 1937.

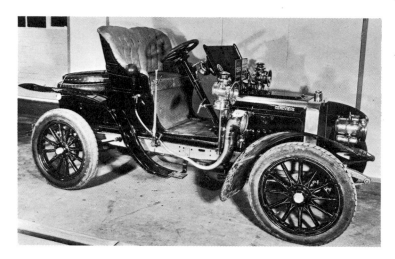

Genevieve, *the 1905 12-h.p. Darracq made famous by the 1953 film.*

The two cars which starred in the film "Genevieve" (1953), a story of the R.A.C.'s London–Brighton Commemoration Run, were a twin-cylinder Darracq and a four-cylinder Spyker. Both were subsequently redated as 1905 by the Veteran Car Club of Great Britain and became ineligible for the Run. Both have since been exported: the Darracq to Australia and the Spyker to the Netherlands.

One in every six businesses in the U.S.A. is connected, directly or indirectly, with the automobile.

Synthetic rubber (buna) was first manufactured in Germany in 1936.

The first American State to introduce compulsory car inspections was Maryland in 1932.

Closed cars outsold open-bodied ones for the first time in America in 1925.

NUMBER-PLATES AND ALLIED SUBJECTS

Great Britain is one of the very few countries where number-plates are permanent: i.e. they are worn by a vehicle from the day of its first registration until it is scrapped. In other countries a car is "registered" only when tax is paid on it, and a car's registration number can change if it moves from one Province or State to another.

Contrary to general belief the number-plate "MG" (Middlesex) current in the 1930s was not reserved for M.G. cars. It was reserved for vehicles sold by University Motors Ltd., the M.G. distributors for the London area, and was also seen on other makes of car sold by this firm, notably Delage and Dodge.

The first British three-letter registration to be issued was "ARF" (Staffordshire) which appeared in July 1932.

The first reversed letters/numbers combination to be issued in Great Britain was "H" (Middlesex)—in June 1953.

The first of the new combinations (three letters, three numbers, and a suffix letter denoting the year of first registration) were issued by Middlesex in February 1963. The suffix letter "A" denoted 1963, but from 1967 onwards the suffixes have been changed, not in January, but in August when new models traditionally start to appear.

The first trade number-plates issued under the current system in Great Britain appeared in 1921. "Limited" plates have red lettering on a white background, and "general" plates have white letters on a red background. In both cases letters and numbers are reversed. The system in force up to 1920 was different: there were usually three letters (one or two for the registration authority and two for the "owner" of the plates) followed by two or three digits. Thus plates issued to Wolseley Motors of Birmingham had the prefixes "O" (for Birmingham) and "WY" (for Wolseley).

A narrow yellow border round a British number-plate signifies that Special Car Tax (formerly Purchase Tax) has not been paid on the car which carries it. The treatment is given to vehicles purchased new in Britain and used there temporarily by foreign residents.

Number-plates issued by American State authorities are produced in prisons.

The international circulation mark "D", for "Deutschland", is worn by tourist cars from both the Federal German Republic and the German Democratic Republic.

Japan is not a signatory to the appropriate international convention, and thus has no official International Circulation Mark.

The City of Rome issued her millionth car registration under the current system on 15th November 1966. The car registration 1-ROMA was issued on 15th March 1927, and the half-millionth mark was reached on 4th January 1962.

In South Australia between 1916 and 1930 a car had to be registered and was charged an annual tax *whether it was in use or not*, so long as it was complete. This accounts for the large number of Veteran cars unearthed in dismantled condition in the State.

VETERAN AND VINTAGE

The London–Brighton Commemoration Run for Veteran Cars was first staged in 1927 under the sponsorship of the *Daily Sketch*. The 1928 and 1929 runs were sponsored by *The Autocar*, but since 1930 the Royal Automobile Club has been responsible for the series. This makes the "Brighton" the only annual event for early cars organised by a *national* automobile club. Only cars made up to 31st December 1904 are eligible for the Run.

Since 1961 the terms "Veteran" and "Vintage" have been internationally recognised, with meanings agreed on by the governing body of Veteran and Vintage motor sport, the F.I.V.A. (Fédération Internationale des Voitures Anciennes). All cars made up to the end of 1918 are "Veteran", and "Vintage" vehicles are those made in the years 1919–30 inclusive.

The term "Edwardian" is often loosely applied to post-1904 Veterans ineligible for the London–Brighton Run. It has no significance and is, in addition, meaningless as many of the greatest so-called "Edwardians" (the Prince Henry Vauxhall, for instance) were made during the reign of King George V!

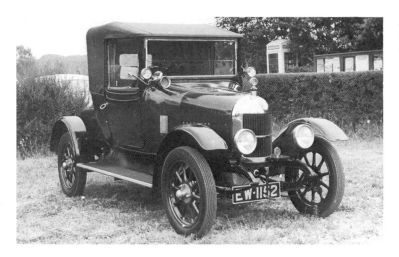

A 1921 Morris Oxford ("bullnose"), 11·9-h.p. doctor's drophead coupé.

The terms "post-Vintage Thoroughbred" and "Classic" have no international significance. The former is a strictly British classification drawn up after the Second World War by the Vintage Sports Car Club, to embrace cars of the 1931–42 era which the Club felt were "made in the Vintage tradition". Classics are cars of roughly parallel merit covering the years 1925–49 inclusive, and approved by the Classic Car Club of America.

The world's first old-car club was the Veteran Car Club of Great Britain. It was founded in November 1930, at the end of that year's London–Brighton Run, at a meeting at the Ship Hotel, Brighton. The three "founding fathers" were S. C. H. Davis, J. A. Masters and J. A. Wylie.

The Vintage Sports Car Club was founded during 1934 to promote the use of sports cars made up to the end of 1930. It is currently Britain's biggest old-car club with a paid-up membership of approximately 5,500.

The world's largest antique-car club is the Antique Automobile Club of America, with 40,000 members. There are 245 regions (including six in Canada). It is also **the oldest antique-car club in the United States,** having been founded in November 1935. Of the two other big American clubs, the Horseless Carriage Club of America (initially California-based) made its appearance in November 1937, and the Veteran Motor Car Club of America in January 1939.

Great Britain alone had (in 1979) 112 one-make clubs catering for 68 different makes of car, by no means all of them British. The oldest one-make car club in existence is the Southern Jowett Car Club, which can trace its origins back to 1923. It started as an offshoot of the Jowett Light Car Club formed in the marque's native city of Bradford in 1922.

The world's first Veteran and Vintage car auction was staged at the Montagu Motor Museum, Beaulieu, in July 1960 by Southern Counties Car Auctions. On this occasion an original *open* 1923 20-h.p. Rolls-Royce made only £170 ($470).

The record price paid for a Veteran and Vintage car at auction was $400,000 (approximately £200,000) at Los Angeles, California, in February 1979, for a 1936 Mercedes-Benz 500K Special Roadster from the collection of the late M. L. Cohn.

The record price paid for a Veteran or Vintage car in a public auction in the United Kingdom was £40,000 for a 1921 Rolls-Royce Silver Ghost at Sotheby's Kenilworth sale in August 1978.

The longest event for Veteran and Vintage cars staged annually is the American Glidden Tour, organised by the Antique Automobile Club and the Veteran Motor Car Club. An average distance would be 500 miles, and its duration one week.

The first international match event between two antique-car clubs was staged in August–September 1954, when a team from the V.M.C.C.A. of five Veterans and five Vintage cars took on a parallel team of cars nominated by the British Vintage Sports Car Club, over a road rally course ranging from Liverpool to Chichester. The American club won a return match played in the Eastern United States in April 1957.

The world's largest automobile museum is Harrah's Automobile Collection in Reno, Nevada, U.S.A. In February 1976 it contained 1,434 cars.

The oldest firms with continuous records of car manufacture are Daimler-Benz of Germany, a fusion of two concerns with roots going back to 1885, and Peugeot (1889). The oldest surviving British firm Daimler (1896), and the oldest in the U.S.A. is Oldsmobile (1896).

The world's three largest producers of private cars (1977 statistics) are (1) The United States of America, (2) Japan, and (3) Federal Germany.

The world's highest percentage of exports in relation to car production is scored by Japan, which exported 3,042,000 out of a total production of 5,976,000 units delivered. France managed just over 50 per cent, and Federal Germany just under this figure.

The longest production run ever achieved by a basic private-car design stands to the credit of the flat-twin Jowett (1911–53). After 1945 private-car production of the model was limited to station-wagon versions of the Bradford light van. Jowett made flat-fours from 1936 onwards as well.

The Jowett flat-four engine seen here in the 1951 Le Mans sports car. The cylinder-heads may be seen inboard of the front wheels.

The longest production run of the post-Second World War era was scored by the long-stroke (78 × 100 mm.) 11CV four-cylinder Citroën engine first fitted to *traction-avant* models at the end of 1934. It was dropped from the firm's private-car range at the end of 1966, but was still being fitted to light commercials in 1975. Another French private-car engine with a long history was the 12/13CV four-cylinder Hotchkiss (1933–54 in cars, and 1936–64 in trucks).

The beginning of the 11CV Citroën line—a 1934/5 front-wheel-drive roadster.

The largest-capacity private-car engine to be marketed since 1918 was Bugatti's Type 41 Royale of 1927. This 12,760 c.c. straight-eight unit developed 300 b.h.p. but was fitted to only six cars.

The largest-capacity private car offered since 1945 is the American Mohs Ostentatienne Opera Sedan with 8,990 c.c. V-eight engine, a special-order item.

The largest-capacity models in series production in 1979 were the American V-eight Cadillac and Russian ZIL, of 6,962 c.c., though Panther of Great Britain were still offering their special-order six-wheeler with the superseded 8,194 c.c. Cadillac unit as fitted by that make in the 1970–76 period.

The largest-capacity six-cylinder private car made since 1918 was the 11,160 c.c. Stoewer D7 of 1919. It used what was basically a First World War aero-engine.

The largest-capacity engine fitted to a rear-engined car in series production since 1918 was the 3·4-litre air-cooled V-eight Tatra of 1937. Only one of the British Burneys (1930–33) had the bigger Lycoming straight-eight and the American Stout Scarab and Tucker Torpedo were never made on a commercial scale.

The largest air-cooled engine fitted to a production car after 1918 was the 6·4-litre twelve-cylinder Franklin of 1932.

The Checker Aerobus Limousine, widely used by American hotels on runs to and from airports.

The longest private car in production in 1979 is the Checker Aerobus Limousine, a twelve-seater with a wheelbase of 189 inches and an overall length of 270 inches. By contrast a Cadillac limousine is 244 inches long, and the 600 Mercedes-Benz Pullman 246 inches.

The heaviest private car in current production is the Russian ZIL-117 limousine with a dry weight of 7,001 lb.

The world's largest three-wheeler to be marketed since 1918 was the American Davis (1947–49), powered by a 2·6-litre four-cylinder Continental engine.

The smallest four-wheeled petrol car in current production in 1979 is the Italian Lawil minicar (Willam in France), 81½ inches long and 50 inches wide (Fiat's 126 is 120¼ inches long and 54¼ inches wide, and another Italian lightweight, the Zagato-built Zele electric city car, only 77 inches long). The Lawil was also the four-wheeler with the smallest-capacity engine, a 246-c.c. twin-cylinder two-stroke.

The most expensive car listed "complete" in the United Kingdom between the two world wars was the 12·8-litre Bugatti Royale saloon exhibited at Olympia in 1932. The quoted price was £6,500.

The most expensive car catalogued in Britain in 1980 was the Panther De Ville Convertible at £72,215, followed by the Rolls-Royce Camargue at £71,137. Price of the latter company's Phantom VI limousine was now quoted "on application". An average big Rolls-Royce limousine would have cost £7,300 in 1952, and only £2,900 in 1939.

The first four-wheeler to sell for under £100 in Great Britain after the 1918 Armistice was the Grahame-White Buckboard, price 95 guineas (£99·75) in December 1919.

The first four-cylinder car to be catalogued at £100 in England was the 8-h.p. Gillett of 1926. This was not produced commercially: **the first such vehicle to reach the market** was the side-valve 847 c.c. Morris Minor in January 1931. Great Britain's first £100 saloon was the 8-h.p. Model Y Ford in October 1935.

The 1930 Thomson & Taylor lowered chassis for the Daimler Double-Six 50. The 7,136-c.c. engine developed 150 b.h.p. at 2,480 r.p.m.

The first catalogued private car with a five-cylinder in-line engine was the Mercedes-Benz 240D 3-litre diesel saloon announced in 1974. Audi offered a five-cylinder petrol engine from 1977, though diesel power units of this configuration have been in regular use in commercial vehicles since the early 1930s.

The cheapest full-size American car of the inter-war period was the Model T Ford—$290 (just under £60) for a roadster in 1925. The cheapest full-size American car of the 1930s was neither Ford not Chevrolet, but the 1933 Continental Beacon roadster at $335.

The fastest touring car catalogued in 1979 was the Panther Six six-wheeler for which over 200 m.p.h. were claimed. Second fastest was the Italian Lamborghini Countach S (196 m.p.h.).

The most expensive Mini on record was a Mini-Cooper S supplied in the summer of 1970 to G. B. King, chairman of Radford, Freestone and Webb, the coachbuilder. The quoted price for this customised version with electric windows, estate-car tail panel and eight-dial instrument board was £5,300. It took 2,300 man-hours to make the conversion, and beat the previous record of £3,640 (exclusive of British Purchase Tax) for the Mini-Cooper S supplied by the same Company to Mike Nesmith, of the Monkees Pop Group, in 1967.

The greatest number of forward-gear ratios offered on a private car for normal road use was eight, on Maybachs with their own *doppelschnellgang* (dual overdrive box) as fitted in 1931–39. Four reverses went with this package, which was

The Rover T4 Turbocar of 1962.

available as an option in Britain on 1932 models of the 3-litre Lagonda. This was equalled by Mitsubishi of Japan on their Mirage series, offering a four-speed dual-range transmission, though only one reverse.

The world's first gas-turbine-powered private car was the prototype Rover two-seater (JET 1) first demonstrated at the M.I.R.A., Lindley, in March 1950.

The first gas-turbine private car to be made in series was the Chrysler Turbo Dart (1964). Fifty of these were loaned to selective customers for appraisal, and subsequently recalled.

The world's first five-wheeled car was the Smith Flyer (1917), an American buckboard on which the fifth wheel incorporated a small air-cooled engine and took the drive. Very similar was a later "car" made by Briggs and Stratton in 1920.

The greatest financial flop recorded by a make of car was Ford of America's Edsel—the loss in three seasons (1958–60) was $250 million.

The largest four-cylinder private car listed after 1918 was the Belgian Pipe of 1921. It had a bore and stroke of 120 × 200 mm., giving a capacity of just over 9 litres. There was no series production, but at least one was exported.

The British record for the highest percentage of export sales on a long production run does not, curiously enough, stand to the credit of the Jaguar XK120; home sales for its first five seasons (1949–53) amounted to 8 per cent. The British Motor Corporation's MG-A (1955–62) sold 101,000 units, ran for a year longer than the Jaguar, and during this period home sales were only about 6,000 cars—just over 5 per cent.

Export bestseller: MG-A.

Runner up: the great Jaguar XK120 of the 1949–53 era.

TECHNICAL—FIRSTS AND LASTS

Only three sixteen-cylinder private cars have ever been marketed, and of these Bugatti's Type 47 of 1930 was never made in series. The other two were both American, by Cadillac in 1930–40 and Marmon in 1931–33. The 1931–32 prototypes by Bucciali and Peerless came to nothing; also stillborn was a plan to develop a super-sports coupé out of the original 1934 Grand Prix Auto Union.

The 1933 V-sixteen Cadillac coupé.

In 1932 American buyers had the choice of six different makes using twelve-cylinder motors: Auburn, Cadillac, Franklin, Lincoln, Packard and Pierce-Arrow. In the same year **France** offered two twelves (Hispano-Suiza, Voisin) as did **Germany** (Horch, Maybach) and **Czechoslovakia** (Tatra, Walter). **Britain,** however, offered only one (Daimler) and **Italy** none at all, though in 1979 she is responsible for two of the world's five sole catalogued twelves (Ferrari, Lamborghini).

The world's last production straight-eight was the Russian Z.I.S. (1959) which outlived its American prototype, the Packard, by four years.

The first diesel-engined private car to be marketed was the Mercedes-Benz 260D of 1936. The first British diesel-engined private car was a version of the Phase II Standard Vanguard of 1954.

The first touring car to be made in series with a twin overhead-camshaft engine was the D Type Salmson of 1922. The Ballot 2LS, introduced during 1921, was a super-sports car made in very small numbers.

The 1932 V-sixteen Cadillac engine.

The Chevrolet Corvette.

Overhead-camshaft drive by cogged belt was first seen on the German Glas S1004 of 1962.

The first petrol-engined touring car with fuel injection as standard equipment was the Mercedes-Benz 300SL of 1954. The first American car on which fuel injection was offered was the Chevrolet Corvette of 1957, and Britain's first example was the Triumph TR5 of October 1967.

The first catalogued cars with superchargers were the 6/25/40 PS and 10/40/65 PS Mercedes exhibited at the 1921 Berlin Motor Show. The first British car to be catalogued with a blower was the 12/80-h.p. Alvis of 1926, but the first one to be made in series was the S Type Lea-Francis of October 1927.

Sealed-for-life cooling systems were pioneered in 1961 on Renault's 750- and 850-c.c. R4 model.

The world's first series-production straight-eight was the Type 8 Isotta Fraschini of 1919, which was reaching customers by the end of 1920. A contemporary in America was the Kenworthy Line-O-Eight of 1920 but it is doubtful if any of these cars were sold commercially.

The world's first series-production twelve-cylinder car was the Packard Twin-Six, introduced for 1916 and made until 1923.

1931 Type 8A Isotta-Fraschini straight-eight with landaulette body by Castagna of Milan.

The world's first production six-cylinder engine with a capacity of less than 1·5 litres was the PS Type Mathis, marketed in 1922. Capacity was 1,140 c.c.

The first British "six" of less than 1,500 c.c. to go into production was the 12/30-h.p. Talbot of 1923. A 1,500-c.c. version of the 2-litre A.C. Six was announced in 1919, but did not become commercially available until 1927.

The first inexpensive light car with an overhead-camshaft engine was the 10·5-h.p. Wolseley of 1919.

The first cars to be offered with synchromesh gearbox were the 1929 Cadillac and La Salle. The first British makers to adopt synchromesh were Vauxhall and Rolls-Royce in 1932.

The first all-synchromesh gearbox was announced by the German ZF component firm in 1931, but the first car to fit such a gearbox as standard was the British Alvis Speed Twenty in October 1933. The first German production car so equipped was the 3-litre Adler Diplomat of 1935.

The first of the modern generation of automatic transmissions was General Motors' Hydra-matic, first offered as an option on the Oldsmobile (*not* the Cadillac) during the 1940 season. Between 1934 and 1936 a handful of 18-h.p. Austins were fitted with the American-designed Hayes infinitely variable gear, but the first British "automatic" to be standardised was the Brock-house Turbo-Transmitter as used on the Invicta Black Prince of 1946–50.

Alternating current (as a replacement for direct current) was first seen on the Plymouth Valiant of 1960.

The last steam private car to be catalogued was the American Doble of 1932. It was a four-cylinder machine with "flash" generator weighing over 2 tons and costing about $12,000 (£2,400). Top speed was in the region of 90 m.p.h., and the burners were ignited electrically. The last Dobles of all used the chassis, bodies and running gear of ordinary petrol cars, usually Buick or Cadillac.

The combination of front-wheel-drive and a transversely mounted engine is usually credited to Sir Alec Issigonis with his B.M.C. Mini of 1959, but these features were found on twin-cylinder D.K.W.s as early as 1931.

The first production car with front-wheel-drive and all-independent suspension was not, as is often claimed, the 1934 *traction-avant* Citroën, which in any case did not have true i.r.s. Both features were, however, present on the 12/75 Alvis sports-car introduced in 1928.

Not all that it might seem. Abner Doble's own E24 steam car. (Photo: Montagu Motor Museum.)

Russian four-wheel-drive sedan, 1941.

Two-speed rear axles supplementary to the main gearbox were first seen on the British Cooper two-stroke car of 1909. They also featured on an American car called the Austin (1913) and on 1914 Cadillacs. They were rediscovered by Voisin in 1928, and reintroduced to America by Auburn in 1932.

The first hypoid bevel back axles were found on 1927 Packards. Their first European application was by Mathis in 1928.

The first four-wheel-drive sedan (saloon) for civilian purposes to be made in series was the Russian $3\frac{1}{2}$-litre six-cylinder GAZ-61 of 1941. Four-wheel-drive passenger cars had, however, been marketed in a modest way by Twyford (U.S.A.) in 1902, the Dutch Spyker firm in 1904–05, and by another American company, Badger (forerunner of the F.W.D. truck) in 1909.

The first production car with swing-axle rear suspension was the rear-engined Rumpler of 1921.

The first American production car with all-round independent suspension was the Chevrolet Corvair of 1960.

The first mass-produced British car with all-round independent suspension was the Triumph Herald of 1959.

Full unitary construction was first offered in Britain in October 1937, on the 10-h.p. Vauxhall. This was not, however, General Motors' first such design, as the Opel Olympia from their German branch was unveiled at the 1935 Berlin Motor Show.

The first car to be marketed with a unitary fibreglass structure was the Lotus Elite of 1958.

The first car to go into series production with a fibreglass body was the Chevrolet Corvette of 1953.

Piccadilly Circus, June 1922, and the horse has almost disappeared. At the moment this picture was snapped a cab rammed another (see upper left), yet scarcely a head is turned.

The West End goes home at the end of the day; Lower Regent Street, June 1922. And still the buses run on solid tyres.

Traffic scene at Blackfriars, London, on the first morning of the May 1926 General Strike. But, as usual, the police were there to keep things moving.

The original caption to this photo, taken in November 1928, read: "London's worst traffic point; the Director-General of Roads gave as his opinion that more traffic passed Hyde Park Corner in twenty-four hours than any other place in the world." It is unlikely that a similar sighted picture taken during a weekday today would disclose fewer than twenty times as many vehicles! (All photos: Radio Times Hulton Picture Library.)

Above: *The Ferrari BB512 Berlinetta Boxer by Pininfarina is the fastest road-tested car with its 5-litre flat-12-cylinder engine, at 163 m.p.h. However, test conditions were such that it seems likely that the car's maximum speed is nearer the manufacturer's claimed figure of 188 m.p.h. (Photo: Neill Bruce.) Below: The Panther De Ville convertible is the most expensive catalogued car in Britain at £72,215. (Photo: Geoffrey Goddard.)*

Ford Cosworth V-8 (1967).

Matra V-12 (1968).

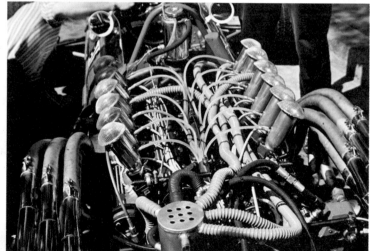

The Ferrari flat-12 engine with gearbox removed, Belgian Grand Prix, 1975. (Photos: Geoffrey Goddard.)

The first station wagon to be offered as a private car rather than as a commercial vehicle was a version of the Model A Ford announced in 1929. The first factory-bodied British station wagon was the 10-h.p. Commer of 1937, based on the contemporary Hillman Minx.

The last private car to be offered with solid tyres was the Type XL Trojan of 1929.

The world's first servo-assisted four-wheel brakes were fitted to the Type H6 Hispano-Suiza in 1919.

The last private car to be marketed with a double-sleeve-valve engine was the six-cylinder Panhard of 1939. The last models to be marketed with single-sleeve-valve engines were the Scottish Argyll and Arrol-Aster, discontinued in 1931. Slide-valve engines were used by Imperia of Belgium until 1934.

The first car to go into series production with a Wankel rotary-type engine was the N.S.U. Wankel Spyder, displayed at the Frankfurt Motor Show in September 1963. Deliveries started a year later.

All-wooden unitary construction was used in prototype cars by Frederick and George Lanchester in 1922–23, and by Marks-Moir in Australia in 1923. The first production application of this system was on the original Marcos GT coupé of 1960.

Disc brakes of modern type were first raced by Jaguar (in the 1952 Mille Miglia), but they had been used on touring cars long before that. Early attempts by Lanchester in 1903 and A.C. in 1919 had no sequel, but the most expensive 1949 Chrysler models had hydraulic discs on all four wheels. In the same year they were also tried briefly on another American make, the 722 c.c. Crosley minicar.

Pre-selective gears are not an invention of the 1920s, much less of the 1930s, though they were one of the fads of that decade. Lanchester had them in 1900, and three-speed De Dion-Boutons of 1902 also had a primitive system of pre-selection. The Wilson box (best known of the pre-selective systems) was tried experimentally by Vauxhall in 1927 and first catalogued as an option in the 1929 Armstrong Siddeley range. It was, however, anticipated by the German ZF-Soden box, fitted to several makes of car (Fadag, Lindcar, Szawe) in 1923.

Hydraulic four-wheel brakes were pioneered by Duesenberg on their Model A straight-eight in 1921. The first mass-produced car to fit them was the Chrysler 70 of 1924. First British use was on 1925 models of Horstman and Triumph.

Chain final drive on four-wheelers was effectively dead by the 1930s, except on a few cycle cars and the Frazer Nash. Its last use was, however, on the Honda sports car, made in various engine sizes from 1962 to 1969.

Full power steering was first offered by Chrysler on their 1951 Imperial models.

Self-levelling interlinked front and rear suspension was pioneered on the Citroën 2CV tested before the Second World War and announced at the 1948 Paris Salon. Hydro-pneumatic suspension (on the rear wheels only) was first seen as an option on the same firm's 1954 six-cylinder 15CV, and was applied to all four wheels on the 1956 Model DS19. An electrically controlled form of self-levelling suspension was used on 1955 Packards.

Cruciform-braced frames were first seen on the 1921 6·6-litre six-cylinder Hotchkiss, a prototype which did not go into production.

PRODUCTION RECORDS

Ford of America's first "million year" was 1922, with 1,216,792 delivered. This was also the first "million year" for any automobile manufacturer in any country.

Chevrolet's first "million year" was 1929, with deliveries of 1,328,605. Chevrolet first beat Ford in 1927, but the comparison is hardly fair, since at the time Ford was converting from Model T to Model A. Their first outright win was in 1931, and in the remaining pre-Pearl Harbor years they were always ahead, with but one exception—1935.

The first European manufacturer to produce a million private cars in a single year was Volkswagen, in 1962.

The first British manufacturer to produce over a million units in a single year was the British Leyland Motor Corporation, in 1968. Of 1,001,105 vehicles delivered, 807,067 were private cars. The best-selling model was the front-wheel-drive Austin/Morris 1100/1300 range, with 229,703.

The first European manufacturer to produce over a million units of a single basic model was Volkswagen, whose millionth "Beetle" was delivered during August 1955.

The first British model to sell over a million units was the Issigonis-designed Morris Minor, between October 1948 and January 1961. During this period three different engines were used—a 918-c.c. side-valve (1948–52), an 803-c.c. overhead-valve (1953–56), and the 948-c.c. "1000" overhead-valve (from 1956).

The one millionth British-built Ford on display at the London Dorchester Hotel in August 1946. Right: The one millionth Morris Minor, a Minor 1000 of 1961, passing through final inspection at the factory.

The millionth Morris car was delivered in June 1939, thirty-six years and three months after the despatch of the firm's first Oxford. Austin took rather longer to achieve their first million, from April 1906 to June 1946.

The European record for the "quickest first million" of an individual model stands to Volkswagen with their Golf—in 31 months exactly (1974–6).

The first maker to produce 2 million cars in a year was Ford of America, in 1923.

The 2 millionth Mini was delivered on 19th June 1969. Over 1¼ million of the cars delivered since 1959 were standard Austin and Morris types. Vans were the next most popular variant with 339,985, and the various Cooper models amounted to nearly 115,000 units.

Only one manufacturer produced over 2 million cars in 1977—Chevrolet (2,293,927). Second place did not, however, go to Ford, but to Toyota of Japan with 1,823,927 units.

Two manufacturers produced over 2 million private cars apiece in 1968—Ford of America (2,159,817) and Chevrolet (2,144,622).

The record year for private-car production in Great Britain was 1972, when 1,921,311 were delivered.

General Motors delivered their 100 millionth car on 21st April 1967. Their 25 millionth was produced during January 1940, and their 50 millionth on 23rd November 1954. All three "landmark cars" were Chevrolets.

Britain's largest independent maker of cars (and her second largest which is entirely British-owned) is Reliant of Tamworth. Production runs at 20,000 a year, though most of these are three-wheelers.

The most instantly successful all-new model from any manufacturer was the American Ford Mustang introduced in April 1964. Sales in the first three years amounted to 1½ million units.

The record for the first season's sales of a new make stands to the credit of the Plymouth—58,031 in the second half of 1928, the year in which it was introduced, and 102,347 in 1929, its first full year.

NAMES AND THEIR ORIGINS

The Volkswagen was originally publicised in 1938 as the KdF (*Kraft durch Freude*, or "Strength Through Joy")—this being the slogan of the National Socialist Labour Front.

Overall height: forty inches! The Ford GT40 of Dan Gurney and A. J. Foyt won the 1967 Le Mans 24-Hour Race. Note the bump in the roof to accommodate the helmet of the lanky Gurney.

The Volvo derives its name from the Latin verb, meaning "I roll".

The term "gran turismo" was first applied to a long-chassis version of the supercharged 1,750 c.c. six-cylinder Alfa-Romeo in 1931.

The fastest version of the 38/250-h.p. supercharged Mercedes-Benz of 1928 is always known as the "SSK", but the "K" does not stand for *kompressor* ("supercharger"): it stands for *kurz* ("short").

Daimler's 2·5-litre Conquest saloon (1953–58) was so called because its original basic price before the addition of British Purchase Tax was £1,066.

The Ford GT40 sports car of 1964 was so designated because the design specification called for an overall height of 40 inches from the ground.

Simca stands for "Société Industrielle de Mécanique et de Construction Automobile", the firm's original title. Before 1951 the firm built Fiats under licence.

The Jaguar first appeared on the market for the 1932 season as the S.S. These initials never *officially* stood for anything, though they fitted such apposite names as "Standard Special", "Standard Swallow", and "Swallow Sports". The first cars to bear the name of Jaguar were the 1·5-litre and 2·5-litre models introduced for 1936, but the SS name was not officially discarded until March 1945, when the hexagonal SS emblem gave way to a monogrammed "J" on the cars' rear bumpers.

Fiat, of course, stands for "Fabbrica Italiana Automobili Torino". When the famous Italian firm opened an aircraft department in 1916 they perpetrated an ingenious pun by translating the Latin of their own name (which means "let it be") into Italian, as "Sia". This also, conveniently, stands for "Societa Italiana Aeronautica".

Contrary to general belief, **the initials "D.K.W."** have not always stood for *das kleine wunder* (the little wonder), though this was the name given to the firm's first two-stroke motorcycle in 1919. They originally stood for *dampf kraft wagen* (steam car) after an experimental effort by D.K.W.'s founder, Jorgen Skäfte Rasmussen, in 1916.

The initials "M.G." stand for "Morris Garages", W. R. Morris's original retail and repair business in Oxford. The first M.G. cars were put together from standard Morris chassis by Cecil Kimber, the Garages' Manager, in 1924.

Exports can render nomenclature complicated. From 1933 to 1939 Plymouths and from 1932 to 1937 De Sotos became "Chryslers" when sold in England, and though from 1920 onwards Darracqs were "Talbots" (pronounced *à la Française*) in their native France, they remained "Darracqs" in Britain to avoid confusion with the Talbots made in London. William C. Durant's cheap car of the 1923–28 period was a Star, but not in either Britain (where it was a Durant) or in the British Empire (where it was a Rugby), thanks to the presence of an all-British Star made in Wolverhampton. Such complications have survived into modern times. From 1958 to 1965 B.M.C. made a popular compact 1·5-litre saloon as the Wolseley 1500 or Riley One-Point-Five: but when made in Australia it was always either an Austin Lancer or a Morris Major!

The Amilcar was so named, not because of anyone's enthusiasm for ancient Carthage, nor, as has often been stated, after its designers. These were André Morel and Edmond Moyet, both formerly of Le Zèbre. "Amilcar" is a contraction from the names of Joseph **Lam**y and Emi**le Akar**, who financed the venture.

Full frontal: Hispano-Suiza V-12, 11·3-litre Type 68 Bis, 1934. Note stork mascot and radiator badge.

BADGES AND EMBLEMS

The "cigogne volante" ("flying stork") mascot found on Hispano-Suiza cars after 1918 was the wartime badge of Georges Guynemer's fighting-scout *escadrille*. His pilots flew S.P.A.D. aircraft powered by V-eight Hispano-Suiza motors.

The four rings on the Auto Union badge commemorate the four German firms which amalgamated to form the Auto Union group in 1932—Audi, D.K.W., Horch and Wanderer.

The double chevron on the Citroën emblem commemorates the silent bevel gears which André Citroën manufactured before turning to complete cars in 1919.

The entwined "Rs" on the Rolls-Royce emblem changed from red to black during 1933, but this had no connection with the death of Sir Henry Royce that April. It was decided by the Board that black was better suited to the firm's image.

Jaguar's famous "big cat" mascot was designed by Frederick Gordon-Crosby, The *Autocar*'s artist, in 1936. Originally an optional extra, it disappeared for good in 1970, a victim of safety regulations.

The octagonal M.G. badge has not always been used on the cars, making its début on 1928 Mark IV models of the 14/40-h.p. car. Previous M.G.s used the round Morris badge with the Oxford ox and the words "M.G. Super Sports". The octagon was, however, in use as an advertising trademark as early as 1924, and on some parts of M.G. cars in 1925.

The Packard car never wore a radiator badge except between 1929 and 1931: the name normally appeared only on the hub-caps.

Salmson cars of the 1921–29 period carried the Cross of St. Andrew, Scotland's Patron Saint, on their radiators. This commemorates André Lombard, the original sponsor of the Salmsons designed by Emile Petit, and later responsible for a sports car bearing his own name. The "AL"-type prefix used on touring Salmsons of the period also commemorates the Lombard connection.

Sleeve-valve Panhard cars of the 1910–39 period carried a twin-S monogram on their radiators, standing for *sans soupapes* ("no valves"). After the First World War, their former great rivals, Mors, standardised on Knight engines, and sought to go one better with a triple-S (the third consonant stood for *silencieuse*). It did no good: Mors were on their last legs by 1924, and dead by 1927.

NATIONAL FACTS AND FEATS

More than one make of car changed nationality after the Armistice of 1918. When Alsace and Lorraine were returned to France Bugatti and Mathis (both formerly German) became French. The new State of Czechoslovakia acquired three ready-made makes from the defunct Austro-Hungarian Empire—Nesselsdorf (Tatra), Praga, and Laurin-Klement (later Skoda).

After the Second World War there were no changed nationalities, though the B.M.W. (Bayerische Motorenwerke) concern was split in two by the partition of Germany. The Eisenach factory, now in the Soviet Zone, continued the production of B.M.W.'s pre-war six-cylinder models under the name of "Awtowelo" (later "E.M.W."). Appositely, the colour of the quartering on the radiator badge was changed from blue to red, but not until 1951.

There were 105 makes of British private car on the market in 1920, and 42 in 1930—but only 34 in 1960, 27 in 1976, and 33 in 1979.

Only one make of three-wheeler was produced in Britain in 1979, the Reliant. In 1934 there were five three-wheeler makes, and as many as seven in 1924.

In 1919 41 per cent of all motor vehicles (with the exception of motorcycles) **registered in the United Kingdom were Fords.** This is almost certainly a record for a "foreign" make in any country, though many of these vehicles were, of course, assembled in the Ford Motor Co.'s factory at Trafford Park, Manchester.

The last private cars to be designed and built in Scotland were the Arrol-Aster and the Argyll, both discontinued during 1931. The next private car to be made north of the Border was the Hillman Imp, which went into production at the Rootes factory at Linwood, Glasgow, early in 1963.

The Marmon Roosevelt of 1929; with an eight-cylinder 3,310-c.c. side-valve engine, this car sold for under £200.

The last private car to be designed and built in Ireland was the Shamrock, a 1·5-litre B.M.C.-engined convertible made at Tralee, Eire, in 1959.

Wales has produced only two makes of private car since 1918: the short-lived Gwalia from Cardiff in 1922, and the Gilbern, which was made at Pontypridd from 1960 to 1974.

Before the Great Depression of 1929 the United States had forty-eight makes of private car on the market. By 1932 there were only thirty-five, and the figure had dropped to twenty-one by 1941. There are still twenty-seven in 1979, though some of these (e.g. Clenet and Excalibur) are made in only tiny numbers.

The first eight-cylinder car to sell under $1,000 (£200) in the United States was Marmon's Roosevelt of 1929. The first "eight" for less than $500 was the first Ford V-eight of 1932.

State-controlled automobile factories exist outside the Communist bloc. Alfa Romeo of Italy have been State owned since 1933, and the French Renault concern was nationalised in 1945. In addition Rolls-Royce (since 1971) and British Leyland (since 1975) have been the subject of State-aided rescue operations.

The first Egyptian private car was the Ramses, a twin-cylinder 600-c.c. model based on the N.S.U. It appeared in 1958.

The first Egyptian private car, the Ramses, seen here in 1962 cabriolet form.

*Israeli cars, left, the 1963
Sabra Carmel and, below,
the Sabra Sussita.*

The first Israeli private car was the Sabra (1961), a design to suit local conditions by Reliant of Great Britain. Ilin of Haifa were, however, assembling American Kaisers as early as 1951.

The first private car to be designed and built in the U.S.S.R. was the NAMI-1, a small twin-cylinder tourer of which a small batch was turned out in 1926.

The first Russian private car imported into Great Britain was a Z.I.S. eight-cylinder limousine sent to London for the use of M. Ivan Maisky, the then Soviet Ambassador to the Court of St. James's, in 1938.

The first Australian car to be exported commercially was the Holden, of which the first overseas shipments went to New Zealand in 1954. The first exports by the Australian industry to Great Britain were in 1967, when the Rootes Group marketed the Adelaide-built Plymouth Valiant as a replacement for the recently discontinued big Humber models.

The first private car made in China was a prototype produced by the Mao Tse-tung Government in 1951. It was referred to simply as "the People's Car".

The first Turkish private car was the Ford-engined Otosan Anadol of 1966, designed by Reliant of Tamworth for Turkish manufacture.

The first Indian-built private car was the Hindusthan Ten of 1946. This was identical to the Series M 10-h.p. Morris, and was the first of a series of Morris models built by Hindusthan Motors.

Japan's first private-car exports were three Ohtomos shipped to Shanghai in 1925. Datsuns were not exported until 1935. By contrast in 1978 Japanese industry exported 3,042,237 private cars, 1,528,045 trucks, 30,453 buses, and 3,749,415 motorcycles.

INDIVIDUAL MAKES AND UNUSUAL FACTS

The S.T.D. combine, formed by the fusion of Sunbeam (Wolverhampton), Talbot (London) and Darracq (Paris) in 1920, collapsed in 1935. Nevertheless, all three partners are now reunited under the Chrysler banner. Chrysler acquired Simca in 1961, and with this came Darracq (by now renamed "Talbot"). In 1964 they bought Rootes, and thus also became owners of the Sunbeam and English Talbot names. When Chrysler sold their European operation to Peugeot in 1978, it was decided to revive the Talbot name for the passenger-car products, hitherto either Chryslers or Simcas.

Some aircraft firms moved on to car manufacture, rather than the other way round. Notable examples are Voisin and Salmson (1919), Bristol (1946) and Saab of Sweden (1949). The Swedish firm's badge depicts a twin-engined bomber of the type produced during the latter part of the Second World War.

Three hundred thousand Austin Sevens were made between January 1923 and March 1939. The model was also made under licence in France as the Rosengart, in Germany by Dixi (B.M.W.) and in the United States by the American Austin Co. of Butler, Pennsylvania. The Baby Austin engine had a far longer run than the car itself, being used in 1953 models of the Rosengart, while the Reliant Engineering Co. Ltd. took over the manufacturing rights after Austins abandoned manufacture, and fitted their version of the Seven to three-wheelers until 1962.

In over forty years of manufacture, Ettore Bugatti never made a six-cylinder car. Other long-standing firms with similar records include Bianchi, Cadillac and Isotta Fraschini.

Production of the Baby Austin at Longbridge during the 1930s. (Photo: Radio Times Hulton Picture Library.)

The first public appearance of a Ferrari sports car (the T815 of 1940 was not a true Ferrari) was in the Circuit of Piacenza Race in May 1947, when two 1·5-litre twelve-cylinder Type 125s were entered by Giuseppe Farina and Franco Cortese. Only the former actually competed. The first Ferrari touring model was the 2-litre Type 166 Sport of 1948.

"You can have it in any colour so long as it is black", is a saying traditionally applied to Henry Ford, but it applied also to the French-built 11CV and 15CV Citroëns of the 1945–52 period, on which the only relief was furnished by cream wheels. Early 2CVs were, by contrast, always grey.

Lancia did not market a private car with an in-line engine between 1923 and 1972. This rivals Cadillac's record, for though V-eights have been in continuous production since 1915, the firm offered a straight-eight under the La Salle name between 1934 and 1936.

Maserati are famous for sports, racing, and GT cars, but their other products include or have included trucks, motorcycles, air-horns and sparking-plugs.

Toyo Kogyo, manufacturers of the Japanese Mazda car, were founded in 1920 to make "cork products".

The first Mercury, introduced in November 1938, for 1939, was a 3·9-litre development of the American Ford V-eight made by Ford's Lincoln Division. First year's sales were over 60,000, and it was the sixth make of car to bear this name. Of its predecessors, three had been American and two British.

Traditionally, M.G. chassis serials for each new type used to start at 0251. It was for the factory's telephone number (251).

The MG-B is not the first M.G. to bear this type number, which was originally assigned to the 18/100-h.p. Mark III Tigress of 1930.

In nearly seventy years of car manufacture (1911–79) Morgan have never sold a car with a beam front axle. The form of "sliding-pillar" independent front suspension adopted on the first three-wheeler is still used.

The first Morris-Cowley of 1915 was essentially an American car. Engines (by Continental), gearboxes, drive units and axles were all imported. All-British examples did not reach the public until 1920.

The American Peerless factory in Cleveland, Ohio, became a brewery after car production ceased in 1932. The British Peerless GT (1957) was built by a firm which started its career (in the 1920s) reconditioning war-surplus American Peerless lorries.

From 1907 to 1939 Rolls-Royce cars were made at Derby, but between 1920 and 1931 they were also built in America at Springfield, Massachusetts. Only two models—the Silver Ghost and the Phantom I—were turned out.

The first private car to bear the name of Skoda was a licence-built version of the 6·6-litre Hispano-Suiza introduced in 1925. In Czechoslovakia this car (the H6 in France or T41 in Spain) went under the designation 25/100 KS.

Studebaker were still making horsedrawn wagons alongside their cars and trucks as late as 1919.

Triumph cars and Triumph motorcycles, now members of two entirely separate combines, were made in the same factory under the same management from 1923 until 1936.

Perhaps the most unusual warranties ever issued by the motor industry were bore guarantees given by two British makers in the 1930s. British Salmson cars of the 1934–39 period had their cylinder bores guaranteed for 40,000 miles, and a 25,000-mile guarantee on similar lines was offered for 1939 Singers.

The first exchange-engine service to be offered by a British manufacturer was announced by Ford of Dagenham in July 1934. Prices were £9 10s. for an 8-h.p. unit, and £11 10s. for the 14·9-h.p. and 24-h.p. types, both figures were inclusive of labour charges.

The first batch of 4 × 4 scout cars (later known as "Jeeps") were built for U.S. Army trials in 1940–41 by Bantam, makers of the American Austin Seven. These did not have the Austin engine, but were powered by four-cylinder Continental units. Their first major testing programme was in manœuvres staged in Louisiana under the direction of Colonel (later General) Dwight D. Eisenhower.

THE ODDBALLS

Motorised perambulators were marketed in 1922 and 1923 by Dunkleys of Birmingham. Power was provided by small two-stroke engines and there was a platform at the rear for the nursemaid. Unfortunately, English Law did not permit such vehicles to run on the pavement.

A "diamond" wheel formation was tried on prototypes by Voisin in 1935, Vannod in 1958 and Pininfarina in 1960. The two latter were exhibited at international motor shows.

Front-wheel-drive and rear-wheel steering were featured on a prototype light car by a Belgian, M. Demati, in 1937.

The Bucciali Double-Huit exhibited at the 1931 Paris Salon, but never marketed, had a sixteen-cylinder power unit made up of two straight-eights mounted side by side and driving the front wheels. Twin radiators were used.

Six-wheeled private cars are usually adaptations of commercial or military vehicles, but at the 1930 London Motor Show Crossley exhibited a six-wheel limousine with a 3·8-litre six-cylinder engine. It did not go into production. In the same period Morris Commercial Cars of Birmingham made a small number of 6 × 4 executive limousines with six-cylinder engines. In 1977 the Panther firm announced a sporting open six-wheeler with Cadillac engine.

The Le Dauphin tandem-seated cycle car made in France during the German Occupation in 1941 could be fitted with petrol or electric motors, but was normally pedal-propelled.

A few prototype straight-twelve-engined cars of 6 litres' capacity were made by Voisin in 1936. The two rear cylinders intruded into the cockpit.

Wooden chassis were standard on all Franklin cars up to the end of the 1927 season, and were found on certain 1928 models as well.

A 1928/29 Crossley six-wheel cross-country shooting-brake with Hooper coachwork, used by H.M. King George V.

A central driving position and three-abreast seating were found on the original Type 77 Tatra of 1934 and also on 1937 Panhards. By contrast, on the 1921 Rumpler and 1922 Stoneleigh the driver sat centrally, with his passengers behind.

Airscrew-propelled motor cars were offered in the 1920s by two small French firms: Leyat in 1920–21 and La Traction Aérienne in 1921–26.

A fully roadable aeroplane was tested in 1947 by the Consolidated Vultee Aircraft Corporation in America. The basis of this was a conventionally driven small saloon car which served as fuselage and undercarriage. To turn it into an aircraft a powered wing and tail unit were attached. It did not go into production.

Aero-engined private cars were almost invariably "one-offs" for racing, but several water-cooled car engines found their way into light aeroplanes in the 1930s. These included Model A and V-eight Fords, Studebakers, Plymouths, and Sir John Carden's version of the 1,172-c.c. British Ford Ten, popular with "Flying Flea" builders. A 1,750-c.c. six-cylinder Alfa Romeo engine was successfully flown in a Caproni biplane in 1931.

The only amphibious car produced in quantity to civilian account was the German Amphicar of 1961–68, a small Triumph-engined convertible which attained 68 m.p.h. on the road, and 6½ knots on water. Over 3,000 were sold.

Mail-order cars are traditionally associated with the motor buggies offered by the American firm of Sears Roebuck from 1908 to 1912, but other transatlantic concerns tried their hand at this game. Sears Roebuck's great rivals, Montgomery Ward, offered the Modoc car in 1909, between 1916 and 1924 two Chicago makes (Birch and Bush) were sold exclusively through the mails, and Sears Roebuck themselves had a second try in 1952 with their Allstate, a special version of the small Kaiser model. It lasted only two seasons.

There are currently (1979) only two cars on the market designed specifically for taxicab use— the British Austin, the American Checker. The Reliant-based "rickshaw", the Italindo Helicak from Indonesia, also bit the dust quite recently though active specimens may be observed in Jakarta. Other taxicabs (e.g. Dodge, Mercedes-Benz, Nissan, Peugeot) are standard private-car designs. By contrast, no fewer than twenty-two firms were offering special taxi models on the British market alone in 1908.

Italindo Helicak from Jakarta.

VERY IMPORTANT PERSONAGES

The only person in the United Kingdom permitted to use a motor car without number-plates is the Reigning Sovereign.

Certain leading personages in Britain are allocated "zero" number-plates for their official cars. Notable among these are the Lord Provosts of Glasgow "G O" and Edinburgh "S O" and the Lord Mayor of London "L M O".

The Duke of Edinburgh's first car was a 1934 Standard Nine acquired in Ceylon in 1940.

No Bugatti Royales were ever sold to any Crowned Heads of Europe, though the names of Carol of Romania and Alfonso XIII of Spain have frequently been linked with the model.

Pius XII was the first Pope to use a motor car regularly. Pius X was presented with an Itala as early as 1909, but refused to ride in it.

H.R.H. Prince Philip's first car, a 1934 Standard Nine.

The Royal Daimlers. Above: *One of the British Sovereign's cars, February 1925.*

Above right: *A Hooper-bodied 1936/37 4½-litre straight-eight limousine.*

The first reigning sovereign of Great Britain to drive a motor car regularly was Edward VIII. Edward VII was taught to drive (by the second Lord Montagu of Beaulieu) but was never an active motorist.

The first member of the British Royal Family to be actively engaged in the motor industry was the Hon. Gerald Lascelles, younger son of the Princess Royal. He worked for the Ford Motor Co. from 1950 to 1951, and later with Aston Martin Lagonda Ltd. from 1952 to 1954.

The first Government official appointed to control motor sport (and motoring clubs generally) was Fritz Hühnlein, named as Korpsführer of the Nazi N.S.K.K. in 1934.

A similar car, with Hooper landaulette body, used by H.M. King George VI.

MANUFACTURERS AND DESIGNERS

George Brough, famous for "The Rolls-Royce of Motor Cycles", also built a Brough Superior car between 1935 and 1939.

A successful one-man car factory was operated by Mike Cannon of Tonbridge, Kent. Between 1953 and 1966 he built or partly built 120 Trials Specials using 10-h.p. Ford mechanical elements. All this work was undertaken without any assistance.

Sketch of the beautiful 1937 3½-litre Brough Superior.

A. G. Booth, who designed the original Clyno light car of 1922, could not drive at the time and did not learn until later on. He was later largely responsible for the first Hillman Minx and for the Singer Nine.

Archibald Frazer-Nash, of G.N. and later Frazer Nash fame, hyphenated his name: the cars, however, never did.

Herbert Austin's Buckinghamshire origins (he was born at Great Missenden in 1866) were emphasised by his preference for Chiltern and Thames Valley place-names for the body styles in his range of cars. In the 1930s there were the "Iver", the "Eton", the "Windsor", the "Wycombe", the "Burnham" and the "Beaconsfield", among others.

Sir Herbert Austin was Unionist Member of Parliament for the King's Norton Division of Birmingham from 1918 to 1924.

Sir William Lyons of Jaguar fame began his career in industry in 1921, making aluminium-bodied sports sidecars in a small factory in Blackpool.

Sir William Lyons, FRSA, RDI, D Tech, with Jaguars. He retired in 1972 when he was 70 years of age.

Richard and Allan Jensen in their earliest project—a modified Austin Seven chassis with their own body design, 1928.

The Jensen brothers (Richard and Allan) made their reputation by designing the first Avon bodies for Standard chassis from 1929 to 1932. They founded their own coachbuilding firm at West Bromwich in 1934, and progressed to car manufacture at the end of 1936.

W. O. Bentley's first successful design was not the 3-litre sports car of 1919, but a rotary aero-engine for the Admiralty in 1916. Its successor, the BR2, was one of the most powerful Allied rotary engines of the First World War.

"W.O." in the prototype 3-litre.

Lord Nuffield gave away over £30 million to charity between 1926 and his death in 1963, inclusive of the disposition of his will.

Lord Nuffield (centre) hands over the 100,000th Morris Eight at Cowley, July 1936.

The first member of the British motor industry to be raised to the Peerage was **Sir Charles Cheers Wakefield** (Castrol) who became Baron Wakefield of Hythe in 1930. The first motor manufacturer to be so honoured was **William Richard Morris, who became Baron Nuffield** in 1934.

The first foreign car owned by a reigning British Monarch was not the "famous black Buick" (CUL 421) which **King Edward VIII** bought in 1936. His grandfather **Edward VII** purchased a 14/20-h.p. Renault landaulette in 1906, and this was retained by his widow, **Queen Alexandra,** until her death in 1925. In 1908 the King bought a 45-h.p. Mercedes. In 1901, incidentally, **Queen Alexandra** took delivery of a "City and Suburban Electric Phaeton" which she used to drive about the grounds of Sandringham House. For all its English-sounding name, this was a Columbia made in Hartford, Connecticut.

William and Reginald Rootes did not become manufacturers, as the Rootes Group, until 1932. Before this they were distributors and world exporters for the Humber concern, which merged with Commer in 1926 and with Hillman in 1928. After its formation the Group acquired Karrier in 1934, Sunbeam and Talbot in 1935, and Singer in 1956.

Several American automobile-company executives have attained political distinction. **John North Willys** served as U.S. Ambassador to Poland from 1929 to 1931. **Paul Hoffman,** President of Studebaker from 1935 to 1948, went on to head E.C.A.; and **George Romney,** President of American Motors from 1954 to 1962, become Governor of the State of Michigan.

William Crapo Durant, founder of General Motors, died a relatively poor man in 1947. After the collapse of his last automobile empire (comprising Durant, Star, Loco-mobile, Flint) in 1932 he went into the supermarket business.

The first automobile manufacturer to make use of sophisticated advertising techniques was **Edward S. Jordan,** whose first advertisement for the famous "Playboy" speedster appeared in the May 1919 edition of *Vanity Fair.* The classic "Somewhere West of Laramie" advertisement did not, however, make its appearance (in the *Saturday Evening Post*) until 25th June 1923.

Two of the greatest inter-war names in the American automobile industry—**Walter P. Chrysler** and **Charles W. Nash**—were former senior executives of General Motors. Nash was President from 1912 to 1915, and Chrysler Vice-President in 1919.

W. C. Durant

Walter P. Chrysler.

Charles W. Nash.

The three **Graham Brothers—Joseph, Robert and Ray**—are commemorated by the three heads on the radiator badge of 1928–31 Graham-Paige and Graham cars.

Fred S. Duesenberg, who made some of America's finest luxury, sporting and racing cars before his death in 1932, was in fact born in Lippe, Germany, in 1876. The family emigrated to the U.S.A. before he was ten years old.

The last man to attempt a full-scale invasion of the American automobile industry was **Henry J. Kaiser,** the millionaire shipbuilder, who bought Ford's Second World War bomber factory at Willow Run, Michigan and introduced two makes of car (the Kaiser and the Frazer) in 1947. The venture lasted only eight years, despite a merger with Willys.

The first man to be appointed officially as a stylist to the motor industry was Harley J. Earl, who joined General Motors in 1926. His first creation was the Model 303 La Salle of 1927.

Ferdinand Porsche designed automobiles for nearly half a century, working for Löhner, Austro-Daimler, Daimler-Benz, Steyr, Auto Union and, of course, Volkswagen, but the only car to bear his name appeared a mere two years before his death.

The 1927 La Salle.

In 1932 it was possible to buy three entirely different cars of different makes from the drawing-board of **Dr. Fritz Fiedler** in Germany: straight-eights by Stoewer and Horch, and the small four-cylinder B.M.W.

Many German designers moved round from factory to factory, but few could match the record of **Paul Henze,** who worked for Cudell in 1903, Imperia in 1907, R.A.F. in 1910, Steiger in 1920, Simson in 1922 and N.A.G. in 1929: unlike Porsche he did not run a design bureau. For his last employers, N.A.G., he produced Germany's first V-eight, introduced in 1931.

Fred S. Duesenberg.

Harley J. Earl.

Ferdinand Porsche.

The record for continuous management of a single automobile factory is held by Charles Weiffenbach, with fifty-five years (1898–1953) at Delahaye.

The French firm of Hotchkiss was managed by an Englishman, **H. M. Ainsworth,** from 1923 to 1940.

The world's most prolific creator of makes of car is almost certainly the Frenchman **Marcel Violet.** Twelve different breeds from his drawing-board have been offered to the public, most of them small two-stroke cycle cars. The score embraces the La Violette (1909), Violet-Bogey (1912), Major (1919), S.I.C.A.M., Mourre and Weler (all in 1921), Buc (1923), Sima-Violet (1924), Deguingand (1927), Galba (1929), Huascar (1930), and 4CV Donnet (1931). To these may be added a scooter (1923), an engine for ultra-light aircraft (1935), a military motorcycle (1938), a light military 4×4 (1939) and a Formula 3 racing car (1948).

Two of the world's greatest automobile designers, Marc Birkigt and **Georges Roesch,** were Swiss, but neither produced an automobile in their native land though some of Birkigt's early designs were made under licence there. Birkigt's work for the Hispano-Suiza firm took him to Spain and France, while Roesch made his name with the English Talbots of 1926–37.

Marc Birkigt.   *Georges Roesch.*

Fiat has been under the continuous ownership and management of the **Agnelli family** since its foundation in 1899.

Ferruccio Lamborghini's first product was a tractor built up of war-surplus Morris, Ford and G.M. bits and pieces, made in 1948.

The present-day Peugeot business stems from the cold-rolling steel-mill set up by **Jean-Pierre Peugeot** at Sous-Cretet, Doubs, in 1810. His sons, Jules and Emile, made clock and watch springs and coffee-mills, corset stays and umbrella ribs.

Heinrich Nordhoff (1899–1968) is remembered as the man who "made" Volkswagen, but in the 1930s he was an American-trained director of General Motors' German subsidiary, Opel. He was appointed to the Managing Directorship of Volkswagen on 1st January 1948, by the *British* Military administration.

Henry Ford remained "absolute monarch" of his company until 1945, when he resigned the Presidency in favour of his grandson **Henry Ford II**. Ford stock was not offered to the public until the beginning of 1956.

Index

The numerals in *italics* refer to the page numbers of illustrations.